Industrial Town

Frontispiece:
Shop at Eccleston Lane Ends.

Charles Forman

Industrial Town

Self Portrait of
St Helens in the 1920s

Cameron & Tayleur
in association with
David & Charles

Published by Cameron & Tayleur (Books) Limited,
25 Lloyd Baker Street, London WC1X 9AT
in association with David & Charles (Publishers)
Limited, Brunel House, Newton Abbot, Devon.
Distributed by David & Charles (Publishers) Limited.

First published 1978.
Printed and bound in Great Britain.
ISBN 0 7153 7633 0

House editor: Elisabeth Cameron.

Setting by Richard Clay (The Chaucer Press) Limited,
Bungay, Suffolk
Printing by T. J. Press Limited, Trecerus
Industrial Estate, Padstow, Cornwall.
Binding by Leighton-Straker Bookbinding Company
Limited, Standard Road, London NW10.

Illustrations are reproduced by permission of
St Helens, Leigh, Atherton and Wigan Public
Libraries, the National Coal Board, Pilkington
Bros Ltd, the Trustees of the British Museum and
the author.

Contents

Preface

This project wouldn't have come to fruition without the active support of the people I met in St Helens. It is based on the time and effort which the 70 contributors to the book put into it – it is their book.

But many other people, too young to make their own contributions to the book, gave it their assistance. In particular, thanks are due to Jimmy Forsyth (Trades Council) W. McDermott (Branch Securetary, NUM, Bold Colliery) Ray Jackson (Branch Secretary, NUM, Sutton Manor Colliery) Mr Anderson (Manager at Quaker House Colliery Billinge) Andrew Davies (Researcher, GMWU) Gordon Leyland and Len Williams (Labour Party) Don Benson (EEPTU) the staff of the old people's homes at Moss Bank, Ashton's Green and Nutgrove, Mr Caistor (ex-librarian St Helens library) Bill Dooley (Branch Secretary, Cowley Hill GMWU) Norman Tatlock and Jack Roberts from the same branch; George Crosby (NUM, Sutton Manor) Dr Merrick; Sister Ashmore; Horace Foster and Steve Lee of Pilkingtons' research department; Harry Hull (Trades Council); Sister Duffy (Providence Hospital), the Glover family of Parr for James Glover's diary; Alan Wild for information from his thesis on unionization at Pilkingtons.

Many other people helped me chase things up and find things out, especially Roger Hart and the staff of local history sections at St Helens, Leigh and Atherton libraries and of the NUM offices in Bolton. All the libraries have fascinating collections of local information easily accessible.

Thanks also to all the people in doctors' waiting rooms, Town Hall departments, insurance brokers' offices and so on, who had useful advice to give.

Finally, I much appreciated the support I got from friends, especially Chris Fagg, Frances Heasman and not least my mother.

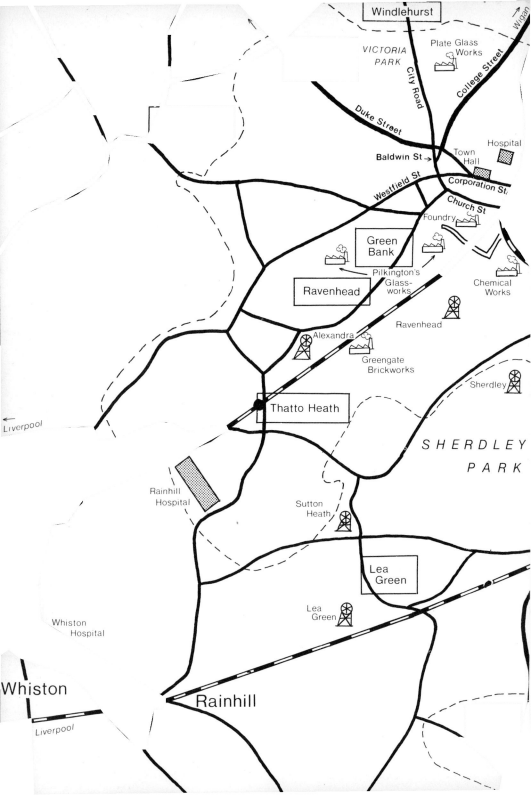

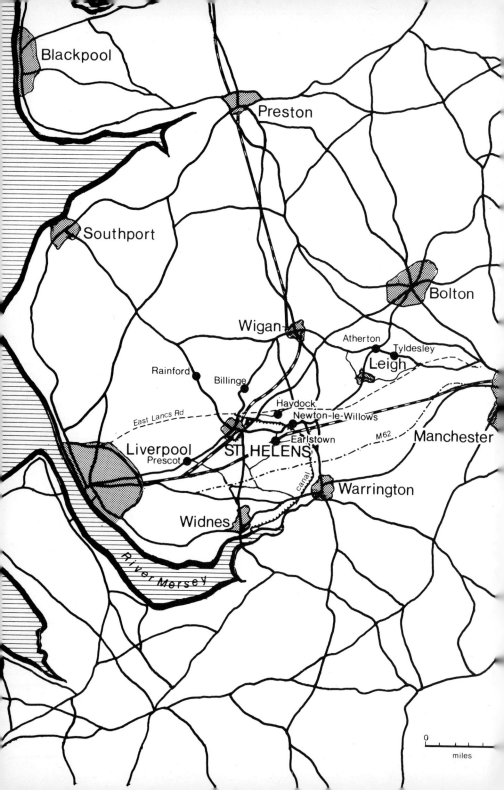

Introduction

You don't have to go to St Helens. If you look at a modern Ordnance Survey map, you'll still be able to pick out the villages from which it grew. Fifty years ago, the town was like an overgrown teenager, its main roads, like gangly arms, only just connecting up with the outlying centres of Sutton, Parr, Thatto Heath, Eccleston and Windle. From Sutton Manor and Clock Face in the south-east to Denton's Green in the north-west is a good four miles.

Even today, people identify with the smaller unit: 'He comes from Sutton,' or 'They were a Parr family'. Some of the villages are older than the coal industry, but others grew up round the mines. The mine shaft at Clock Face was not sunk until the beginning of the century, and the coal company responsible built houses for the miners who were to work there. Older villages like Parr were densely packed along the sides of the main road in rows of red-brick terraces, some back-to-back. Interspersed with these centres of population were the industrial railway lines, piles of industrial waste, mine shafts, some of the fields from the farms and, in one or two places, a bit further out, the old country estates like Sherdley and Knowsley. Most of the big factories, such as Pilkingtons, the foundries and Beechams, were right in the heart of the town.

People in the South know St Helens mainly for its rugby team and have very little idea of where the town is. In fact, it is separated from the suburbs of Liverpool only by Knowsley Park – the town centres are eleven miles apart. But it is a bit misleading to think of St Helens in that way, because it probably has more in common with Wigan, Leigh, Haydock and Newton-Le-Willows in the other direction, as they all lie on the same coalfield, and some of them must have grown up in the same way as St Helens. Perhaps people are ignorant about the town's position as it's not on the way anywhere. Nowadays it is completely enclosed by the M6 motorway to the east, M57 to the west, M62 to the south and the East Lancs Road to the north, but none of them goes near the town centre. Even the Manchester–Liverpool Railway bypasses the centre. The town's first industrial freightline, the Sankey canal, which joined it with the River Mersey six miles to the south, is now intermittently filled in and no longer reaches St Helens.

The town is built literally and metaphorically on coal. The South Lancashire coalfield stretches right under its centre. To the north, there are large sand deposits and, to the south, the Cheshire salt fields. Given these raw materials, the industries which developed in St Helens are not surprising. In some form, coal has been mined there for centuries, and supplied fuel for the glass furnaces. The basic materials used in glass production are sand, which has to be melted, and soda which combines with it to reduce its melting point by nearly half. The salt fields fed the chemical industry, the source of the soda.

The Sankey canal, completed in 1757, was the first operational canal in the country and linked the town with the Mersey, Liverpool and the sea. With the canal, industry developed. Coal was transported by barge, and industrial sites were valued on their proximity to the canal. Greenalls, the brewers, made an appearance in the eighteenth century, and so did glassmaking.

By the mid-nineteenth century, there were 15 glassworks (5 owned by Pilkingtons), 11 chemical works and no less than 35 collieries, which by 1845 were raising a million tons of coal a year. These collieries, scattered over the town in a totally unplanned way, were worked until they became unprofitable and then abandoned, so that the town became increasingly pockmarked with the burrowings of entrepreneurs who had sunk shafts, extracted the maximum profit in the minimum time and gone.

Obviously, this industrial growth did not develop out of nothing. It was guided, from the second quarter of the nineteenth century, by a clique of capitalists who were remarkably closely knit. They were mostly self-made men, rather than established landowners. In the first generation or two of success, they might not have passed off too well as gentlemen; but their collaboration and intermarriage was not only an immediate success, it was a primary factor in establishing the present industrial set-up in St Helens. Certainly the families who were intermarrying in the 1830s – the Pilkingtons, the Greenalls, the Gambles, the Daglishes – were still in the saddle at the end of the century. Most of them spread their influence over a lot of the different industries in the town. For instance, the Pilkingtons did not simply own the glassworks, they owned the mines which provided the coal for them, the chemical works which provided their soda and the railways which took their products away.

These new families stabilized industrial development in the town. Between 1845 and 1870, only two new collieries were started, both of them failures. By 1870, Pilkingtons was one of the three companies producing 70% of British glass. Engineering and the foundries grew naturally with the other industries, as a great deal of plant was needed to supply the mines and glass factories, but there was very little new industry. Between 1870 and 1890, a period that corresponded with prolonged national depression, nothing much changed the situation until United Alkali stepped in and bought up all the chemical works in 1890, although the firms were still known by their old names.

As in many working-class towns before the rise of the Labour Party, the same employers had a pretty free rein in local politics. The Beechams, Pilkingtons and Gambles were all mayors at some time, while others became MPs. The Pilkingtons continued their activity in local politics even after the Labour Party became dominant at the Town Hall.

There was nothing like the same coherence among the working class of St Helens that there was among the employers. One division was geographical. If people still have a sense of identity with a particular part of the town today, it must have been paramount when all the mining villages were separated. Even among old people alive today, there are few who switched from glassmaking to mining or vice versa. Another was religion. St Helens has always been a Roman Catholic area, and there may have been Protestant–Catholic feeling. Certainly, 50 years ago, Catholic families lived in clearly defined areas.

There were also the Irish who came over to escape the famines. A kind of folklore claims that they ended up in St Helens because it was as far as they could walk from Liverpool docks without dropping from exhaustion. But they arrived at a time of industrial expansion when new hands could be accommodated. It is noticeable that since World War I, and particularly since immigration started from the Commonwealth, no one has come to St Helens – there aren't the jobs. The Irish in St Helens are not longer a race apart, but even now there are old people born in the town who speak with an Irish accent – they must still have been part of a self-enclosed group when they were growing up.

In the accounts that follow, a strong Trades & Labour Council is taken for granted. It is worth remembering that 75 years of sporadic struggles and fleeting organizations passed before anything as permanent as the Trades & Labour Council was set up. The only continuity in the nineteenth century was the operation of the Friendly Societies which might provide a place for a drink, and insurance against illness. It's interesting that the Glass-Makers' Society had rules which excluded pitmen and colliers.

Industrial disputes could be long and vicious – the miners' strike of 1844 was systematically broken by the bringing in of 'knobsticks' – but the experience of a particular struggle did not seem to lead to any more permanent organization. One of the earliest examples where this was not the case was with the miners' strike of 1881, where one of the demands was the disbanding of the Lancashire & Cheshire Permanent Relief Society – a management inspired Friendly Society. Out of this struggle, in which wage increases were gained, came the Lancashire & Cheshire Miners' Federation, but even this had difficulty in getting all the areas in Lancashire to affiliate, and went through some very thin patches before it had an assured future.

After two failures, a Trades Council was set up in September 1890 with 17 unions involved. Tom Glover, who did much to achieve this, later went on to become the first Labour MP for St Helens in the election of 1906. This is significant because it was only six years after the Labour Representation Committee had been set up as the way of getting the voice of the Labour movement into parliament. At that election, only 29 LRC MPs were returned. Thus St Helens, earlier than most places, had established links between the Labour Party and the working class.

This brings us to the St Helens which is described in this book. The bare outline of it is given in the 1921 census, when the population stood at nearly 103,000, which was still increasing very slowly. That made it the seventh town of Lancashire – after Manchester, Bolton, Oldham, Blackburn, Preston and Burnley.

One immediate indicator of the standard of living was the appalling housing situation. With Haydock, St Helens had the largest average family size in Lancashire, and there were only four rooms for every five people living in the town. Nowhere else in Lancashire was as overcrowded, and the situation was getting worse. There were 21,000 people sharing at least two to a room (ten years before there had been 16,000). This amounted to 21% of the population, while in Lancashire as a whole, hardly famed for its good housing, the figure was 'only' 8%. It is in part explained by the fact that nearly half of all families had at least four children.

This overcrowding wasn't spread evenly. In the more middle-class area around Denton's Green, there was one room per person, but out in Parr there were only two rooms for every three people. On the other hand,

Parr was still surrounded by fields – there were only nine people living to the acre. In the middle of the town, either side of Duke Street and up the City Road, people were living 120 to the acre. This was the only really continuous housing, with terrace streets stretching out in all directions for half a mile or more. Most of them have now been demolished – some of the houses were just one up and one down.

Another factor contributing to bad conditions generally was the average age of the population, which was 27 (43% of the inhabitants being under 20 years old). This meant a high proportion of dependents to people working, a problem exacerbated by the very poor employment prospects for women – only 24% had jobs in 1921. The textile industry, which was such a large employer of women in Lancashire, did not operate at all from St Helens. Altogether, then, only 42% of the population were in work – leaving the other 58% as dependents.

Of the 9,000 women who did work, a quarter were in personal service. But this source of employment was drying up, as the Victorian ideal that every middle-class family should have its maid faded under the economic pressures of the inter-war years. 16% were in what was called 'commerce' in the census – they were mostly shop assistants, barmaids etc. There were a few things that women could do at home, like taking in washing or dressmaking, but openings for them were in general very restricted. The labour market was male dominated. This is a total break-down of the figures from the 1921 census:

Employment	No. of Men	%	No. of Women	% of women at work
Agriculture	265	0·7	44	0·5
Mining	10,594	27·2	264	2·3
Brickmaking	362	0·9	192	2·9
Glassmaking	5,293	13.6	805	8·4
Chemicals	547	1·4	52	0·6
Metal	2,617	6·7	58	0·7
Electrical	526	1·3	152	1·8
Textiles	32	0·1	114	0·3
Cloth/sheet makers	410	1·1	670	7·6
Food and drink	246	0·6	149	1·7
Woodworkers	1,045	2·6	46	0·5
Printers	97	0·2	72	0·8
Builders	1,041	2·6	10	
Decorators	298	0·8	1	

_ View from the clock tower at
the town centre, 1925.

s factory, looking north across ___

Employment	No. of Men	%	No. of Women	% of women at work
Mixed workers	68	0·2	8	
Gas, Water	128	0·4	1	
Railways and other transport	1,998	5·0	166	1·9
Commerce	1,661	4·3	1,420	16·1
Public Administration	490	1·3	85	1·0
Professional	568	1·5	888	10·0
Entertainment	102	0·3	57	0·6
Personal Service	445	1·1	2,185	24.7
Clerks	1,027	2·6	709	8·0
Warehousemen	495	1·3	396	4·5
Stationary Engine Drivers	848	2·2		
Labourers	3,380	8·7	332	3·7
Retired	861	2·1	194	2·2
Unemployed	3,470	9·2		
TOTAL	38,914		8,170	

This leaves 28,000 women unaccounted for, as they had no job recognized by the census.

With male employment, the heavy industries of coal, glass, metal work and chemicals take up exactly half of the working population, while the rest is very evenly spread. The other significant figure is for the labourers and unemployed – a total of 6,850 men. A lot of the labourers would be on casual work, liable to lay-off whenever a job was over, or when work was slacker in winter.

The rest of this book concentrates on St Helens in the eight years just after World War I, from 1918 to 1926. What was going on there must be put in some political and economic context.

The economic situation was quite complex. During the war, the economy had been under an unprecedented amount of Government control. To pay for the war, living standards had had to be cut. Income tax had been doubled, and in the first three years of the war real incomes had been cut by up to 40%. The government requisitioned the railways, ran the mines, established rent controls, sent directives to farmers to change cropping, took over jute and sack production and many other things.

Above all, however, it rigidly controlled the labour force. In 1915, it got 35 of the 36 major unions to end restrictive practices (so that semi-skilled people could take on skilled jobs), to guarantee there would be no strikes, and to control the mobility of labour so that no one could get a job without a certificate proving permission to leave the last one. Although the government promised to control profits, and pay any excessive ones amassed because of union agreement into a state fund, this was never done. The war was extremely profitable for many capitalists, as there was no more control on prices than there was on profits.

1919 saw the start of a trade boom in the replacement of consumer goods and the processing of raw materials which had been stockpiled in other countries. It seemed that the good times for business were going to continue. At the same time, the standard of living for working-class people had been re-established at pre-war levels. Indeed, some sections like the engineers actually made gains. But the boom was artificial.

The engineering and shipbuilding industries had had to expand during the war, but it was an expansion which couldn't be sustained. The mines had exhausted a lot of the easily accessible stocks, and now had to start working on more difficult seams. But, more important, the volume of world trade rapidly diminished – and while the war had been going on America and Japan had secured a larger part of it. Good international trade depended on financial stability. But Britain wasn't in a position to be chief international banker by reverting to the gold standard. As well as borrowing a lot for the war in short-term loans, it had also lent allies £1,800 million out of permanent resources.

It was a period of economic nationalism, and British exports were hard hit, especially in the old industries of coal, cotton, steel and shipbuilding. Britain sold 70% of its exports to distant agricultural markets which had often found other sources of supply during the war. Latin America could be supplied by the United States. The cotton which had gone to India was either produced over there or taken from Japan. Coal was hit by low prices on the continent and also by improved technology which reduced fuel consumption.

The boom reached its peak in 1920 and suddenly collapsed. In September 1920, there were a quarter of a million unemployed in Britain – nine months later the figure stood at two million, mostly from these four industries. There was a gradual recovery until 1924. But unemployment in these peaks of activity between the wars was at a level that had previously been known only in the most disastrous depressions. Though things were bad in Britain, the pattern was repeated across the industrial world.

This was the economic background to the biggest surge of activity the Labour movement in Britain had ever experienced. In 1914 the total membership of the Trade Union movement stood at just over four million. By 1919, it had topped eight million. A lot had happened during the war. The three biggest unions, with two million members between them, the miners, railwaymen and transport workers, emerged with a Triple Alliance, which was an agreement to get all their wage deals to start and end at once. Obviously, this meant that in the event of their not achieving what they asked for, they could act in unison to fight for their claims. For the first time, too, there was a strong shop stewards' movement, particularly on Clydeside and in Sheffield. This had developed as a reaction to the Trade Union leadership, whose hands had been tied by the agreement they had made with the Government.

The shop stewards' greatest trial of strength was on the Clyde at the very beginning of 1919. Workers from different industries, including engineers and shipbuilders, were demanding a forty-hour week. No official union support was forthcoming – and the Amalgamated Society of Engineers actually expelled its district officials. The demands were not met, and after this point the shop stewards' movement went into a decline, although a lot of those who were active in it became founder members of the Communist Party when it was established a year later.

1919 saw a tremendous surge of industrial unrest as men came out of the army. In the artificial boom created by the making good of supplies lost through the war, workers were pressing hard for shorter hours and higher wages in circumstances of full employment. Two of the unions in the Triple Alliance put in major wage demands. In addition, the miners asked for shorter hours and nationalization of the industry, the railwaymen for an eight-hour day. The Lloyd George government set up the Sankey Commission to look into the miners' demands. The benefit of a sympathetic chairman gave the miners a majority of one on the commission, which consequently endorsed their view.

The railwaymen failed to get their rise, and came out on strike in August. J. H. Thomas, the railwaymen's leader, made a point of asking other unions not to come out in support. However, they won their basic demands within a fortnight. The miners weren't so lucky. The government refused to implement the recommendations of the commission. The miners asked the Trades Union Congress to come out in a general strike to force the issue, but their request was turned down by a majority of

18

four to one. The Triple Alliance, which had not been set up with any constitution or formal standing, took no part in the year's events.

Nevertheless, the issue of calling a general strike remained a live one in the Labour movement. The right wing felt that it undermined the whole force of the Labour Party, which was to work through electoral procedure to achieve a majority in parliament. *Then* it would be able to legislate on any matter of concern. The left considered that a parliamentary majority was too far off to provide any answer to immediate problems. In particular, they felt that in giving tacit support to the forces fighting against Russia, parliament was not working constitutionally, anyway. The issue finally came to a head in August 1920, when the government threatened direct military intervention in support of Poland against Russia. The Labour Party mobilized, asking all local branches and Trades Councils to organize demonstrations and set up Councils of Action. They were preparing to call a national conference to vote on the question of an all-out strike to prevent war. There was no need to go any further. Lloyd George categorically stated that troops would not be sent to Poland.

In the next nine months, the economic situation deteriorated. Many capitalists believed that the economy would return to pre-war prosperity if Britain returned to the gold standard. That would make it necessary to revalue the pound – making exports more expensive – and the easiest way to lower the cost of exports was to cut the price of labour. The short, sharp disputes of 1919 were replaced by longer lasting wrangles. There were many lockouts.

Central in this wage cutting was the mining industry. Germany was making part of its reparation for the war in coal, and the export price of British coal slumped. At this sticky point, Lloyd George decided to hand the mines back to their owners after the period of state control which had lasted since the war. The owners' solution to looming unprofitability was to enforce wage cuts. The miners resisted. It was a clear case in which the full strength of the Triple Alliance was needed.

A date was fixed for the other unions to come out. On the night before it, Frank Hodge, secretary of the miners' union, suggested in parliament (without his union's authority) that the miners would be prepared to accept district settlements for wages – which would have entailed cuts for many. That was something that the miners had always resisted. So it wasn't just the fact that Hodge's statement was untrue which was important – it should have been clear to the TUC leadership that he had no authority to say what he did. Nevertheless, on the word of this one man, the other unions called off their support of the miners. On 15th April 1921, Black Friday, there was no strike, and it was then revealed that the miners had not accepted any deal. They were locked out for almost three months before accepting wage cuts.

The failure of the Triple Alliance revealed a contradiction facing the union leadership. For most leaders, their unions were there to protect their members' interests and no more. They insisted that they were not political organizations – after all, what had they got the Labour Party for? That was their political voice. But in the desperate economic climate of the early 1920s, when living standards were constantly under attack and unemployment weakened any attempt at industrial action, workers could only hold their own in a situation like the Triple Alliance. So the means to their limited aim of maintaining living standards – an inter-union or general strike – had unlimited, even revolutionary implications. When the General Strike did come, the TUC insisted that it was a national sympathy strike. But they knew it wasn't – in 1921 and 1926 the organized working class of the country was prepared to take on the government. The only way of preventing wage cuts in the mining industry would have been to nationalize it. A strike which was asking this of a Tory government had very wide implications.

The next three years saw a continued war of attrition with more lock-outs and a further decline in the standard of living. More unions joined together – the Transport & General Workers' Union was formed in 1921, the General & Municipal in 1924. The Labour Party's policy of gaining strength through the electorate seemed to be paying off. From the 400,000 votes in the last election before the war, they reached 2·2 million in 1918 and 4·3 million in the election of 1923, which gave them 190 seats. The Tories had more seats but decided for tactical reasons to let the Labour Party form an impotent minority government. Through the Labour government, miners' wages were increased at a time when coal production on the continent had temporarily stopped.

The Labour government chose not to take an aggressively socialist stance. If they had done so, they would not have brought anything through parliament, but they would have been able to call a General Election in which socialist policies were the issue at stake. Instead, when they were forced into calling an election, it was on Tory terms. Despite their conspicuous moderation, their links with Russia and Bolshevik influence were the main issues, fuelled by the 'Zinoviev letter', which the

Daily Mail claimed to have discovered in the Foreign Office. It was a document which 'proved conclusively' the Labour Party's links with Bolshevism. All trade unionists and possibly most Tories believed it to be a forgery. Instead of discrediting the Labour Party, it polarized opinion. The Liberal Party was the main loser. The Labour Party's vote increased by a million and the Tories' by two million. The Tories emerged with an overall majority, and Stanley Baldwin became Prime Minister.

This was the set-up in 1925 when, with the return to the gold standard making exports even dearer and the reappearance of foreign competition in the mining industry forcing coal prices down, the mine owners faced another crisis. Predictably, their solution was further wage cuts. Another confrontation developed, where the major unions committed themselves to coming out in support of the miners. At the last moment, Baldwin stepped in with a government subsidy to maintain wages at the same level for nine months. This – Red Friday – was heralded as a great working-class victory.

Everyone quotes Stanley Baldwin's statement in his biography that the government were not ready, which was the reason for the nine-month subsidy. It's true – the government had not made preparations to counter a general strike in 1925. Nine months later, when the subsidy ran out, they had. Their baby was born right on time. A lot of right-wing voluntary bodies had been taken over, and with troops in reserve they had a strategy which could systematically blackleg, and therefore break, a general strike.

Meanwhile, yet another Commission had been set up to look into the mines, this time led by Herbert (later Lord) Samuel and without miners' representatives. The report, issued in March 1926, stated broadly that in the short term miners would have to accept cuts, while in the long term the industry would have to be rationalized, but not nationalized. Throughout these nine months, there was no firm commitment by the TUC Industrial Committee or General Council to support the miners if the subsidy wasn't continued. There were endless discussions between the TUC, the miners' union, the government and the mine owners. No one compromised.

It was out of this stalemate that the General Strike took place. Its failure now seems a turning-point for the Labour movement between the wars. Its betrayal extinguished the last glimmer of promise that 1918 had held, and the bitter deprivation of the ensuing Miners' Lockout looks towards the black and hopeless years of the 1930s. The last section of this book goes into the events of 1926 in detail.

Most history is written from the viewpoint of the class of people in control – employers, leading politicians, landowners. Part of their control extends over the making and keeping of almost all written records. This class is good at recording itself – it has the confidence in its own importance to do so. The working class are the object of records, not the subject. Their school attendances, their apprenticeships, their national insurance contributions, their marriages, their crimes, their divorces and deaths are not recorded for their own benefit or understanding. The figures seek to define, explain and control them.

In contrast, this book attempts to be a working-class history of a town, not because it is describing the conditions in St Helens just after World War I, but because it has a working-class point of view. The conditions at home and at work in the town in the 1920s were often appalling – but that's not the point. What is central is an understanding of how working-class people survived these conditions and organized and struggled to impose their own.

This is the significance of these few years. The Labour movement was just growing to maturity – the local Trades & Labour Council had been firmly established only 25 years before, incorporating for the first time the idea that Unions from different trades had a political unity which outweighed their individual interests. Support for socialism came, not from some vision of Utopia, but from the reactions to conditions like the ones described in this book. Many industries experienced full unionization for the first time while the Labour Party took power in the town halls. It was the point at which the great hopes invested in the Labour movement had their first opportunity of being put into practice. Those hopes weren't realized, but they left structures of local government and trade unions which have often been left without serious challenge since.

The contributions to this book appear anonymously for two reasons. The first is simply that many people asked that their contributions should remain anonymous. But, secondly, people often didn't feel it important that they were identified individually, as a lot of what they had to say was of experiences shared with many others. The best way of showing this is by quoting the case of the diary kept by a Parr miner in the 1920s. It had no information about his own life in it. It kept records of when pubs changed hands, when people were hurt in the pit, when old people died, the results of rugby matches and so on. It was actually kept in the pub and used to settle disputes about when this or that happened. Now it's so thumbed and dog-eared that it's sometimes difficult to read. So from the collective experiences recalled by the contributors here, an overall impression of the working-class community is developed.

Nearly 100 people contributed their information and opinions, mostly at first hand. But drawing the material together to give an expression to a whole community has dangers in it. To begin with, it would be a mistake to judge it as an oral history. It is a written 'translation' from verbatim notes of what people said. This is because the way that people easily listen to spoken information is very different from the way they easily read written information. Written information is much more concise and deals with topics one at a time.

In *Working Lives: a People's Autobiography of Hackney*, such 'translation' was done only with the close co-operation of the people concerned. It hasn't been possible to do that here because the information and opinions have had to be split up to suit the way the community is presented and some of the individual flavour is inevitably lost. The question is: to what extent does this combination of individual histories represent the community as a whole?

Although a lot of people contributed, there are many sections of the community left out. By definition, there was nobody to talk from experience about what it was like being old in the 1920s, when there were virtually no provisions for pensioners. There is very little about the Irish immigrant community, which two generations later has largely lost its identity. But at that time there were still many of the original migrants alive. There is nobody who talks about living off crime. Women are very under-represented. This is partly because in following up contacts you were passed on by men to other men, and when husband and wife were talking together the husband usually, but not always, dominated the conversation. Above all, the section on industries gives the misleading picture that everyone had one trade which he stuck to. Although this was true of the miners, and to some extent the glassmakers (you rarely find people who worked in both industries), many people of course drifted from one period of unemployment to another with odd jobs in between. And as many more lived without any definite jobs at all – the bookies' runners, greyhound racers and such like. It is a record which could be endlessly extended: there is no reason to feel that this book is 'finished'.

There is also the problem of what kinds of event are most accurately portrayed by people thinking back 50 or 60 years. Certainly, the daily routine comes to mind far more readily than individual occurrences. The process of a workshop job or the work of bringing up a household of children was repeated endlessly. With a particular meeting or a particular disaster, things become confused in time and place. Maybe, to an outsider, this or that event seemed to be important in explaining what followed. But although these people were present, the event never had a clear historic significance at the time, and they never marked it. This is one reason why the last section, which is dealing with particular events through 1926, relies more than it should on other sources.

Another difficulty lies in trying to record faithfully people's attitudes and opinions. Political opinions change – traditionally drifting to the right with age, although this isn't always so. But any political analysis made now of events during the 1920s will be from people's present viewpoint, and may have little bearing on their attitude at the time. This is the area in which first-hand accounts of past events are at their weakest.

There are other allowances which should be made. Although most of the material refers to the years 1918 to 1926, obviously many of the people's attitudes were formed by events which took place before this; descriptions which show this have been included. Some of the material refers to neighbouring towns, but many of the people who lived in St Helens travelled as far as Prescot and Wigan to work. Miners often crossed the 'border' into the Wigan coalfield for jobs. Occasionally accounts contradict each other; where this isn't a matter of opinion, it can be explained by the accounts referring to the same thing at different dates. At other times, speakers suggest impossible proportions or figures – they are sometimes presented like that for effect. In the last section quotations from speeches have often been abridged.

Finally, the employers come into this account only insofar as their employees perceived them. Their policies and lives are well documented in other books which they had the money to commission privately. In fact, very few of them lived in St Helens – the mine owners had managers to run things for them. The exception which proves the rule was the Pilkingtons, and even then one of the women in the family lamented: 'I've had an unhappy life, and the unhappiest part of it has been living in St Helens.' This book puts their political influence to one side, even though there were still a lot of working-class Tories, because I have chosen to centre the accounts round the political alternatives that were being presented in order to provide an understanding of where some of the roots of those alternatives lay inside the community.

Part I

Work

Coming Home

MINER FROM PARR, BORN 1893
When the war ended, the guards just left the prison camp, and we were alone with nothing more than what we stood up in. We were left to find our own way back to England. We walked to Hamburg and went down to the docks – there were lots of others like us, looking for a ship. There was a naval vessel in – they were reluctant to take us as they said it was full, but we got aboard in the end, and that's how we came home.

RELIEVING OFFICER
World War I changed everything. It seemed to be a new concept of life – they came back with new ideas. I remember I was bristling to go, but I was called up just two months before the end of the war, so I never got out there. When my brothers came back on leave, they told me, 'Just you keep away from this, it's dreadful.' People saw a bit of the world, though. Who'd been to Egypt before that? Only Prime Ministers. If you went to the Isle of Man, it was quite a journey – 70 miles. I remember when the first family went there on holiday they put flags out in the street. After the war, there was a song, 'How're you going to keep them down on the farm, after they've seen Paree?' They came back thinking 'This is the life,' but it wasn't to be. Unemployment bit in a dreadful way in the 1920s.

1 The Mines

St Helens was never just a mining town, but in the 1920s coal was the main industry, still employing over 10,000 people, 27% of the adult male population. There were 24 towns in the South Lancashire coalfield where the proportion of workers who were miners was greater, including Leigh, Wigan and Atherton. Indeed there were nine towns where over half the men worked down the pits. One of them was Haydock, which even then was almost a suburb of St Helens.

But St Helens was the biggest of the mining towns. In spite of having a relatively small proportion of men down the pits, it had the biggest single voice in the coalfield. The whole field employed 100,000 miners, so one in ten came from St Helens. Production in the field was fairly stagnant; over the years it had taken more and more men to raise the same amount of coal. The difficulty in increasing production was largely the result of lack of investment in new machinery. This wasn't the formula for a successful coalfield, and is the main reason why the Lancashire miners' union was always committed to a national level of wages. In district settlements, their wages were lower than most because of the expense in getting the coal.

As background to the account of the mines at the time of the' 1926 lockout, it's useful to have an idea of what proportion of the workers were doing which job. These are the figures from the 1921 census:

	Men	Women
Owners, Managers	38	
Supervisory	480	2
Hewers	3,986	
Drawers	2,496	
Road repairers	440	
Others below ground	2,204	
Surface workers	905	197
	10,549	199

The figures don't include a lot of men whose work was partly or wholly dependent on the mines – blacksmiths, electricians, mechanics, carpenters, bricklayers who built the shafts, railway workers, clerks and so on.

In fact, the job divisions were very complex, as is revealed later. What this account attempts is to give a view of different aspects of the mine and show the interdependence of the enormous range of jobs, rather than dwelling on each job in proportion to the number of workers involved.

The wages structure was also complex. There were all kinds of allowance and deduction varying from pit to pit, but the broad outlines are explained.

At the time we're considering, the 1920s, there were twelve collieries still going:

Lea Green	Alexandra
Sutton Heath	Ravenhead
Sherdley	Havanagh
Sutton Manor	Southport
Clock Face	Ashton's Green
Bold	Collins Green

These 12, some of them near closing, were far fewer than the 36 pits that had flourished 70 years previously; only about half of them lasted till World War II, and only Bold and Sutton Manor are going today. Each colliery had two or three shafts, and it was said that you could tell which ones were working by the different noises the pit winding gear made.

Not every colliery was individually owned. Richard Evans, who owned some of the pits in Parr, had his centre of operations in Haydock. Wigan Coal & Iron, which set up Clock Face, was based in Wigan as its name implies.

What follows is a compilation of about 20 miners' talks, which have been put together round the different aspects of mine work.

At the Coal Face

COAL CUTTER AT RAVENHEAD, BORN 1892

The cutter was the first person on the seam. He was cutting *underneath* the coal. There was one seam I used to cut at Blundells colliery [in the Wigan coalfield]; it was 5 ft and there was dirt in the middle. You used to cut that out as well. All that dirt had to be cleared away and put in what they call packs. To hold the weight of the coal face, they used to put in square wood chocks about 2 ft in length and 6 in. square at the end. They shoved these sprags about every 2 yards under the coal where the dirt had been cut out. There was a man whose job it was to come up with the coal cutter and put them in on his own – he was called a daywage-man. Then the packers would come down and pack the dirt up. After that, a chap came round to drill holes all the way down the coal face. The shotlighter fired shots of explosive in these holes to break the coal up. They took the sprags out then, and the coal dropped down to the floor in pieces.

It was the collier who put the coal in boxes. Sometimes he'd have to break it up, but nine times out of ten the shotfiring used to do that. There were about 20 colliers on one coal face, each with seven or eight yards of the coal face to clear. The collier cleared his own piece off and did his own timbering.

MECHANIC, BORN 1896

There was a rota. In the day turn, they filled – they got the coal cleared away. In the afternoon turn, starting at three o'clock, they'd go and do all the drilling and cutting under and shotfiring. You couldn't do the shot-firing till you'd cut out the 6 in. of dirt – they called it the scuftings – underneath the coal. In the night turn, all the belts had to be moved forward the 4 ft., say, which had been cut in the last turn. Each 24 hours they cut, drilled and filled.

THE COAL CUTTER AT RAVENHEAD, BORN 1892

They used to have very low seams. I worked in one of 2 ft 6 in. – only 2 ft of coal, but it had 6 in. of dirt underneath it. That seam was at Ravenhead colliery, where there was another one of about a yard. I worked on my knees, and my coal cutting machine was only about 18 in. high. The coal cutting face would be about 135 yards long. I used to have to cut that before I came home, if it took me two turns. When the machine broke down, you'd have to wait for someone to repair it. As you cut the dirt away from under the coal, you had someone behind you putting in the wood to take the weight off the cutter. If the coal fell on your jib you'd have to drag it out. With a bar machine, if the weight came down on it, it would stop, and the rope you were working with would break. I cut that coal face every night to a depth of 4 ft 6 in.

Once I went to a colliery over at Brynn [in the Wigan coalfield] where they said 'Start on Sunday night.' I had nothing on – only a pair of slips. It was red hot. I'd been going a good way and about half past one in the morning, I said to the chap with me: 'How far off the coal face are we?' He said 'Oh, we're nearly there.' It took two hours walking – and I kept stopping for a rest. You used to walk with a stick to save you stumbling. When I got there, I found the cutting machine – but there were no tools. The fireman found them and said: 'If you cut 25 yards, nobody'll be bothered.' I cut 35 yards and started off back. The fireman said: 'Make a report at the surface.'

'I'm not going to bother,' I said.

'Why not?'

'Because I'm not coming down here no more.'

Sometimes you're on your knees at the coal face, but I've seen men work on their belly. There was one place at Ravenhead where it was raining harder than you've ever seen on top, and never stopped – the colliers were up to their knees in water. At Lea Green it was better – they used to make a din about everything – and you were paid a shilling a day for being wet.

Half-way through the turn you'd stop. For a break you'd go out and sit down where the roof was blown about 5 ft 6 in. high. The food didn't get dirty or nowt like that – we had a Tommy tin for it. Bobby Williams used to eat everybody's food – if someone felt ill and had to go up he'd say: 'Leave your food here. I'll eat it.'

When you were cutting, you couldn't talk to each other. If the day-wageman wanted to say anything, he'd wave the lamp. I'd stop the machine to see what he wanted.

Sometimes the roof would break off the coal and sink down a bit. Sometimes I've seen it fall, then you'd get squashed. I've seen one or two buried with falling roofs and get very injured. I've never been buried, but I've been trapped in. I've gone to the corner of the face with my cutter and I've had to wait for the others to clear it up before I could get out.

THE MECHANIC, BORN 1896

I've always been in engineering, but the first machine I remember is the bar machine cutter. It had a drum on with a rope around it and they fastened the rope to a prop and it pulled itself along. It was compressed-air driven – we had no electricity. It was a four-cylinder job – the bar had little picks in. The face was 300 yards long, and they used to cut that in a shift.

Mavours & Coulson were the biggest firm of mining engineers there were. They made one of the first cutters. It didn't work both up and

30

down the seam – when it had cut right down the face, they had to drag it back again to the top.

The relations between the men and the managers weren't bad. In many cases the manager was working to orders – you didn't blame him. I used to have a row or two, get threatened to be sacked, because I wouldn't do certain things as a shotlighter. That's what I'm blaming for my chest now, to a big extent – I did about seven years' shotlighting. You were driving tunnels and firing shots in the coal; instead of waiting for the gases induced by the explosion to dissipate, you were going in and getting ready to fire another one. Especially in a tunnel where there was only one way in and one way out, the ventilation was bad. You'd try all sorts – we'd use compressed air, if we had it, to try and blow the gas out – but the men who were working the face would be on piece, so there was the urge for you to get in there and fire the shots as quickly as you could.

DEPUTY, BORN 1890
MINER FROM PARR, BORN 1893
All the timbering was included in the 1s 5½d paid for a ton of coal. That included putting up timber, bringing timber in from wherever it was kept, setting it, clearing any dirt. You wouldn't do it badly for your own sake. You wouldn't be a collier if you did it badly. The main roads were timbered properly. They were whitewashed, and at Bold they were big enough for a man to stand up in all the way down.

DEPUTY, BORN 1890
Every mine has different rules. In one mine, the timber must be set not more than 4 ft apart and nearer if required; with another it can be not further than five; in another, three, according to what the nature of the roof is in that district. Sometimes, if it's a good roof, they'll set the timber 4 in. further apart. That makes less work for a collier – he's not got so much timber to set. The inspector comes round. He knows; you can't tell him his job. He finds the distance between these two bars is 4 ft 4 in. instead of 4 ft, which is 4 in. over the limit. What that means is that the deputy in charge has to face the manager. 'How is it that the timbering is 4 ft 4 in. apart?' he'll be asked. He gets a good dressing down off the manager.

THE COAL CUTTER AT RAVENHEAD, BORN 1892
In those days, they had a drawer to each collier. The drawer's job was to take the full boxes of coal out from the coal face to the main roadway

where the haulage would take them to the pit shaft. The collier paid the drawer – he used to give him about eight shillings a day.

THE MINER FROM PARR, BORN 1893

I went as a drawer to Bold No. 3 shaft. This was a rise in wages because on No. 3 at Bold the collier and the drawer were joined – you shared equally in the product that you mined and sent to the surface. The rate of pay at that time for a ton of coal got by the miner, brought by the drawer to the haulage, a distance of up to several hundred yards, and pushed in several cases along fairly bold inclinations was 1s 5½d per ton. That meant that to secure 15s a day – that was a very good wage in those days – you'd have 60 tubs, 10 tons of coal, to fill and bring to the mechanical haulage during the 8-hour shift.

Men ran to work because more often than not there were empty boxes very near the place of work. Being on piecework, they were paid by the number of boxes filled, or the weight filled.

They used, once they got down the pits, to throw everything off. You stripped yourself at pit bottom to just a pair of short drawers. You had a light on. You ran down because you were in a hurry to beat the next man. There were eight or ten of you in one shunt [one passage taken off the main road] working a section of the coal. You ran in, took empty tubs, and it wasn't just a question of pushing them on a level down that mine, we had to go up a fairly steep inclination with them, then along a level – like I'm saying, it could be a 100 yards or more – fill it at the other end and come out with it. Down the incline it was so steep that a full tub would have run away with you, so you used a locker on the wheel. That took you down to the level. You went in to where the empties and fulls stood side by side; you left the full one, picked up an empty one and went back in.

MINER FROM NEWTON ROAD, BORN c. 1900

There were 13 drawers in our district at Bold, and the roadways were so narrow that we used to have to turn our box over while we leant against the wall to let others pass. My back was a scab all over. All that on a bottle of water and a couple of jam butties a day – I did ten years on that. We were on piecework and I used to like the money. The man at the face would get a penny a ton more for his coal for every inch of dirt he had to clear away from under it.

MINER FROM FLEET LANE, BORN *c.* 1905

At Wood Pit, there was a seam about 2 ft 8 in., but in places it was lower. You'd get nothing extra for that. Pigeon House, Sherdley was only 2 ft, and water ran down the face. You had to crawl with your spade on your behind and your lamp round your neck. They had flat spades in those mines. You could sit cross-legged sometimes. If you knocked your light out, you'd had it; you couldn't light it again. The men would be 8 yards apart all the way down the face.

THE MINER FROM PARR, BORN 1893

Here, they used to check you by your lamp. When you drew your lamp, that lamp had gone. They'd know if the lamp wasn't handed in at night you hadn't come out, if anyone was in charge at the lamprooms, you see.

If you put shots in, you had to pay for the powder you used, and you paid for the oil in your lamp, in them days, a penny. You bought all your own tools, and paid for their sharpening. There was nothing provided by the employer.

PIT BROW LASS FROM THATTO HEATH

At Sutton Manor, I used to clean the lamps. You had to put them on a machine to brush them clean, and then you had to put in the glass and fill the lamps with oil. If you filled it in the wrong part, it'd squirt over you. I've been sick with that job a few times – it was dirty work. There was a little hole, and if you didn't get the oil in that hole you'd get drowned. The lamps are all electric now.

Contractors

Unlike the tunnels to the face, which were timbered as part of a collier's job and allowed to collapse when the seam was exhausted, the main passages were repaired and maintained by labourers employed for the purpose.

THE MINER FROM PARR, BORN 1893

Not only were there very large families, but many of the people had lodgers, mainly young Irishmen – single men who'd come over for seasonal work, and stayed. Many of these men are now assimilated in the area. They're married, and they're all Lancashire people in effect. The young Irishmen were generally working in the mine on the afternoon or night shift. They didn't work on the coal, but for a man known as a contractor in the mine, who engaged them and was paid by the number of men he had taken on for each particular job.

In the main, they were men who were enlarging the roadways after coal had been extracted – the main roadways, which would last for some time. They had to be kept open for the passage of tubs or wagons down the road. These men were mainly on that sort of work. They were fairly safe, because the man in charge would be very experienced. They wouldn't all be coming in as one gang. They'd be people who'd work for a year or two while others were coming in. They'd not had experience in mines at all. They were mainly agricultural workers and they gradually settled into this type of work. They were moving the rubble after it had been drilled, fired and brought down. There could be a tremendous heap at times – tons upon tons of it – and in general it had to be moved before the pit started the following morning. There'd be haulage hands so the work of getting the coal could go on. This debris was of course used to pack the roadway. It was thrown off the roadway into the space that was left vacant when the coal was extracted. This was quite skilled work when men got used to it. They had to build dry stone walls around the loose material they had, and this was built up from the floor to the roof and formed the main support of the roadway itself. It was one of the big factors – good packs put on meant a higher degree of safety for the men working on the coal.

THE MINER FROM FLEET LANE, BORN *c.* 1905
By the time the mine closed [*c.* 1930], there were only Irishmen there and they went off somewhere else. No one else could get the jobs, because the contractors were Irish. They'd come on a Monday, and on Tuesday morning they'd be working. There was a scissors-to-grind man who sat at the side of Fleet Lane, and the Irishmen would come up and say 'Which is Mr Dock's Pit?'

Pony driving
SUTTON MINER, BORN 1890
Where we lived there were just two trades – the railways and the mines. It was a question of getting a job as quickly as you possibly could after leaving school. There wasn't much of a choice. Boys who went down the pit would generally go to the same colliery as the one where their mates

34

were. They were determined to be members of the union, simply and solely because their fathers were members. Wages were shockingly low.

I had no mother or sister, so I had to do what my father said. All he said was 'Go down the pit,' and I had to go. I went down Havanagh No. 1 as a pony drawer. Ponies brought the tubs from the coal face to a main level. They were drawn out then by bigger ponies and horses to the endless rope haulage. You had to start on haulage, then from haulage you graduated. The men had you drawing for them – I went drawing for my father. The old men in those times were using and exploiting the youth. They'd make you run all day long – you'd come home fagged out. They were getting £10 per week, the two colliers filling the boxes, and you were getting less than £1 of it. Then, at 18 or 19, you had to use your own judgement. As I got older, I went contracting at Clock Face. Then you're in charge of a gang, you put them to work and the management give you extra money. I got that when I'd learnt more about pit work.

THE MINER FROM PARR, BORN 1893
Not many horses were used in this locality – the mines were fairly steep. Far more horses were used in the Midland coalfield, where the mines were flatter and more undulating. Much movement of coal in the tubs was by boys and young men – wagoners was the local name for the boys who did this. Where they did have horses, it was always said that if there was an accident the owners would ask for the horses up before the men; they were more valuable.

THE MINER FROM NEWTON ROAD, BORN c. 1900
The ponies down the pit, they had as much sense as us. They knew when there was danger. There were some clever ones – I've seen them chewing tobacco. I used to take carrots there, and bits of turnip. They definitely knew. They were bloody cruel to them, the colliers. If they thought they weren't making enough money – any old stager will tell you – they used to hit them with pick shafts. I've seen a few ponies killed down the pit. I used to be a pony driver and I could lift one up, it was that small.

Mechanics
ENGINEER FROM CLOCK FACE, BORN 1910
I was born in Clock Face, and when I was young I could tell you the name of every family between here and Clock Face Inn. I started work at

Clock Face Colliery. Of course, times were very bad then with the '21 and '26 strikes. I lived in the colliery yard as a boy – that's how I knew so much about the colliery. We had access and we could go anywhere. When I left school, my father said 'What do you want to do?' and I said, 'Work in the engine house.' My father was an overseer; he got on well with the manager. He just had a word with him and I got in.

I got to be in charge of the fan house. Ventilation down the mine meant keeping the fan running all weekend because of the firemen on inspection work. Whatever happened, you had to keep it running – the men's lives depended on it. If it stopped, you had a limited amount of time to get the men up. If that happened, you got a message down the shaft for all the men to leave the coal face, go back into the tunnels and then back to the pit bottom where there was some air. It was the coal face that the poisonous gas came from. If there was no sign of repair, then the men would have to come out. There is only a certain amount of time. We had an emergency generator on the main fan shaft, but I never saw it used. All we had to do was continually watch it. Every hour we had to record the gauges, the steam pressure, the vacuum, the speed and the speed counter – that counted how many revolutions the fan made every hour.

THE MECHANIC, BORN 1896, WORKING OUTSIDE ST HELENS AT PEMBERTON
I learnt a lot by knocking about. I've no degree of any sort, just these two hands. I've only had practical experience. There were two fitters, two blacksmiths and two joiners at Pemberton who were paid a bit more [out of a total of 33 fitters and 21 blacksmiths]. They relied on me being around. As a fitter, I was paid 0·16 of a penny per ton during the First World War. So work out for yourself how much I was making when you consider we were raising 15,000 tons a week. I paid one lad and one labourer – I paid the lad sixpence and the labourer a shilling above their wages.

Our hours in those days were six to five, but I used to be out four nights a week to breakdowns. My own lads never saw me for weeks at a time – I came in after they were in bed and was out before they got up. One of the longest spells we did was from Monday morning to Wednesday night without going home. I was young then and in good fettle. I walked a lot – I'd think nothing of a 15-mile walk over Parbold Hill and into Parbold Village after tea on Sunday in my spare time. We'd get back as it was getting dark.

Then I did my own work in my spare time. I went to Upholland Laundry to put in a new engine there. I went to Billinge quarries where they had engines and conveyors that needed maintaining. At the bake-house I did a lot in my spare time.

At the pit, we'd winding engines, fan engines; we'd 30 Lancashire boilers, 9 locomotives. We had a by-product plant, but they closed it during the war because it created a lot of light and they couldn't black it out. We had some gas engines which drove generators – the gas was made out of coal – we had all sorts of coal cutters, and tipplers for tipping the coal. We had creeper engines for taking empties up an incline so that they would run up where we wanted them. We had Parson's compressors for making compressed air. On the winding engines, there had to be some-thing to stop the winding if the winder had a fit or something – the finest overwinder was made at Mellins foundry. So you see there was a lot to keep an eye on.

You had to have a paper from the manager to ride on the cage top or work in the shaft. Once every 24 hours, you were let down very slowly on the top of the cage with lights. They let you examine everything. There are spouts to catch the water. The air and water works would need repairing, the brickwork attending to. There were three sets of pitmen – a carpenter, joiner and bricksetter. For everything that wanted a fitter, they took me with them. There were pipes that had to be let off – this is in places where they had a lot of coal they intended gathering. We put some bore holes in and then put a sort of pipe to the top of the pit. The pumps were put in to drain the water away. The drips from this went into a pipe. All we had to do was to open a valve and the water would siphon itself away to the big pump at Wigan Nine Feet. To do this we had a plank which we put over the edge of the cage to the wall of the shaft. Two of us stood on one end and the other walked out on the plank. I've thought since how stupid it was; we would have done it more safely if we'd taken more time, but we just didn't bother. People were killed falling down the shaft, especially building it. You laid the bricks for the shaft from the top downwards. The men laying the bricks would be on a platform, and below that would just be a hole down to the bottom of where they'd dug to. If you fell off the platform to the bottom, you'd be killed. I've known men picked up and brought up in a bag.

There were several styles of haulage. One was 'mane and tail' with a load of 30 tubs – the mane rope was attached to the first tub and the tail rope to the last. When they got to the pit eye, there'd be 30 empties waiting. They took the ropes off the full tubs once they were in the cage and coupled them to the empties – so what had been the tail rope for the full tubs was now the mane one, pulling the empties in for loading.

37

In another type, motion or endless rope haulage, the rope has no end. It is wound four times round a wheel on the engine and runs all the way to the end of the main road. In this case, they run the tubs in sets of six down the pit and fasten them to the rope by means of a linking chain. That motion goes at about two miles per hour; as full tubs are going to the eye directly under the pit head, the empties are going in – there's a pulley at the end. In some places on the main road, we had clutch wheels so that we could take a district out of gear. As the clutch went out, the brakes came on, otherwise the tubs could run down any incline. Each district had a separate rope connected through the clutch to the rope on the main roadway – so we could stop first south if there was trouble there, and let second south and the main roadway go on.

When one cage was at the top, the other had to be exactly at the bottom, or the tubs wouldn't be able to run straight in. The ropes stretched when they were new, and if they were a bit long we had to mend the gear temporarily until we got a chance at the weekend to take some links out of the chain at the top. The life of a winding rope was three years by law; it hadn't to go a day over, or you were breaking the law. If it was due on a Wednesday, we used to do it the Sunday before so we were three days to the good and not to the bad.

The cappings had to be changed every six months. They used to cut 6 ft off the end of the rope, so that the same piece of rope wasn't on the pulley in the same position. We had what we used to call an inquest on the 6 ft cut off. The blacksmith took every strand and wiped it with petrol to see if there was any flaw, or a broken strand. That came under the Coal Mine Regulations Act. I've not seen any ropes broken, but I've seen rods break. The rods are what the corners of the cage run on to stop it swaying about. There's a fixture at the top end and at the bottom, and we had to add cheese weights at the bottom – so much weight on the rods for every 50 yards (I forget the formula now). They were sunk into a big girder at the bottom so they couldn't swing about.

There are various types of fan. Walkers of Wigan are well known for fans. Our ventilation was done with one that was 48 ft in diameter. It was direct drive on a crankshaft and only did 39 revolutions a minute.

For ventilation, you need to have an upcast and a downcast – in any pit, you must have two shafts. The upcast is fenced off, and it has the fan at the top sucking the impure air out. Cold, fresh air comes in the downcast. It's the same down the pit, one air flow for the fresh air and another for the impure air. There are two roads. When you're crossing from one to the other, you have two or three sets of doors – you open one set and go

Above: Clock Face colliery in the 1930s. *Below:* The colliery buildings at Lea Green.

Above: Miners queueing for their pay in the colliery yard at Leigh, 1921. *Below:* Pit brow lasses cleaning coal on a belt at Atherton, 1911.

through, then you shut it and go through the other. If you open both at once, there'd be a short circuit. You'd have a great wind blowing up all the dust, and a lot of bad language from the men working.

Work on the Pit Brow

THREE PIT BROW LASSES FROM THATTO HEATH, BORN IN THE LATE 1890s
We started on the belts at Sutton Manor and Lea Green as soon as we left school at 14 – it was either that or going into service. You had about five of you standing at intervals on either side of the belts, and the coal used to come down a chute to be split and cleaned of dirt. As you picked the dirt off with your fingers, you got a big pile at your feet. We had hands full of blisters. At half past two, or an hour before we stopped work, the belts stopped sending down coal and you had to shovel the dirt on the belts to go down to the wagon.

If the lumps of coal were too big, you had to split them with a hammer. The person at the end of the belt was responsible for seeing that no coal went into the wagons with dirt on it, and if there was too much coming she'd have to pull a lever behind her to stop the belt and ring a little bell to tell the people at the top of the chute to stop sending any more coal down. When you'd cleared it all out, they started the belt again. There were five belts at Lea Green – one from King pit and one from Queen pit (that was the best coal), one from old pit, one they called normal, and one for the slack that had been sieved out.

The belts were like venetian blinds and undulated up and down; as they lifted up you could pull your finger out. When the plates got worn, they could be as sharp as razors. You got your nails pulled off and you used to get septic in your fingers, but there was no first aid – you'd to wait till you got home. They wouldn't let us wear gloves nor rings. When you were climbing over to the other side of the belt, you could get the iron of your clog caught and it would go out into the wagons down the chute. The fellow that was on the chute used to have to go down into the wagons for the clogs. One woman caught her arm fast in the belt. It cut her arm clean off, there was only a little stump left. She got nothing for it, and she couldn't work, only having one arm. She was only young.

We had to walk to Sutton Manor from here in Thatto Heath over the fields – there were no buses or anything. All we wore for the weather were shawls and black clogs. It'd take half an hour each way, and if you were wet when you got there, you had to work in damp clothes.

Where we were, inside on the belts, the wind used to come through. We used to get snowed on and everything. There was no heating at all. You had a man's jacket on to protect you from the cold, and put one foot on the other leg to keep warm. Though your hands used to be like puddings, chapped and cut, you had to work like lightning. Sometimes, it was so cold that you couldn't tell what was your hands and what was the pick. There were no showers for us, so we had to have baths when we got home, and we put strips of cloth under our caps at work to stop the dirt from getting in our hair.

You were placed at equal distances down the belt and daren't move, even if there was a drip straight down on your head. If you kept moving, they'd put a box round your legs. You daren't talk to one another, or you'd be sent home. There was a glass ceiling over the belts. The boss used to lie on the glass on his stomach, looking through a hole to see what you were doing. Oh God! He was awful, Joe Naylor. He'd shout through the hole, 'Off wi'ee 'om'.' That's the way he spoke. Then there was no pay, so we used to get thumped when we got home; our parents used to give us a good hiding.

It was 8s 4d a week when you were 14. You had to be in by six, and you worked till half past three. We got 3d a week back off our parents, then 6d, then 9d, up to the highest, 1s 9d. You were sent home if you were five minutes over your time, so you hadn't to have diarrhoea. They let you go down to the toilet twice a day, and you were only allowed 20 minutes for dinner. You took sandwiches and a can of tea – sometimes it used to be stone cold. Once, I was waiting to go on, and there was someone else there. When the boss saw me, he just said 'Go home.' He wouldn't let me explain to him. Another time, I was coming out after break finishing my pie. 'Haven't you had your breakfast?' he asked. I shook my head. 'Off with you.' And you'd get no pay – that was your punishment. I have a picture fixed in my mind of Nellie Sims – she's dead now. She came in a few minutes late, absolutely dripping – her clothes were soaked. She'd only just set one foot through the door. 'Home!'

Any complaint, and they sacked you and took someone else on. You were frightened of that, because you couldn't get another job, but no one would take today what we put up with. You only got a rise on your birthday – and you'd to take your birth certificate with you, though it was only a few coppers, anyway. During the war, I had to pay the union, but they didn't bother about us women. A lot of women were working there until the war was over. I went on until I got married. In the war, I used to empty three wagons of coal a day into the boilers. When I put it down the chute, the boilerman would be ready to put it in the boilers for the winding wheel. A reporter came to our house one evening then, and our picture appeared in the paper with the caption, 'A family a credit to the king and country,' under it. All of us were at the pit except the lad, and they said he was keeping the home fires burning.

Weighing

THE MINER FROM PARR, BORN 1893

Coal was weighed on the surface. The proprietors of the mine had a weighman who weighed the coal. To check him and see the miners got their just weight was a man known as a checkweighman who was employed by the miners. He checked every tub that went over the scale – the weight slid up and down.

Occasionally your tub was tipped up on the pit top and examined for dirt. It had to be coal in those days that you filled. If the dirt was over a percentage, you'd be called out of the mine – I've been called out. You'd have to come out, with no pay for it. That was the punishment, and that amount of dirt could be deducted from whatever you filled in the other boxes. The tare was the empty weight of the box, which they knew to some degree, and they could tell when a box weighed too heavy. You only had an ordinary oil lamp in those days, so it was hard to tell what was dirt, but your eyes got accustomed to the light, and you could tell by the weight as well. For all you were careful, there was always loose dirt about, both on the roof (it might be thin, running in layers) and on the floor (that had to be moved, otherwise you filled it in with the coal, which you couldn't afford to do). So you had a lot to do.

They knew whose box was whose when it got to the surface because everyone had a number – a tally. Every box had a tally hole in it, not more than half an inch in diameter. A tally was a rectangular piece of metal with a loop and your number on it. You put one through the hole, put bits of string through it and pulled it tight. In the Midlands, they used to chalk a lump of flat coal on the top or paint it on with whitewash. Everybody had a number – it was your number for everything.

Deputies

THE DEPUTY, BORN 1890, DIED 1976, WHO WORKED IN THE WIGAN COALFIELD
When you got to the pit bottom, the coal face could be two miles away.
I'll tell you how they worked it. They cut different roads different ways –
they call them districts, first south, second south, first west and so on.
There's a deputy in charge of each district. My 94 men included daywage –
men, maintenance men, pony drivers, as well as men at the face. When
you were in charge of a district, apart from keeping things in order, you
had to make the district pay.

Each district stood on its own feet. You had to send coal out in the ten-
hundredweight tubs fast enough to make it pay. When the tubs got to the
surface, they were all weighed and put down in the book. At the end of the
week, all the accounts were checked up – how many tons had come from
such a district. We'll say 400 tons, just as a figure of speech. You'd divide
that 400 by as many men as were working in the district and then you
got the amount of tons a day for each man. There was a certain limit, and
if you were under that limit it was a cold morning – it wasn't paying.
Well, they started making enquiries: there's only so much coal up. Why?
How? What are we going to do about it? They sent overmen down to
investigate, to see if they could see any loopholes. They might solve the
problem that way. The second was the condition of the mine – was the
coal very hard, had they a bad roof, had they water in the place? The
third, but not least, was the question: were the men working?

I'll try and put it to you as plain as I can. A deputy was once described
by the General Secretary of the Deputies' Union as 'the policeman of the
mine'. Our first duty was safety. That came first – to see that the men were
working in safe conditions. But it wasn't so simple. You know that if
you have a business it has to make a profit.

The deputy is responsible for everything. If you got a man killed – I've
had four killed – he's responsible for all that. The manager would call
you into his office, and you'd have to go and see him with your cap off.
I'll show you the two extremes. One deputy is in charge of Sponny
district. There's good ventilation, a good roof, good coal. Let's call this
chap A. He's a good chap, sending plenty of coal out. He's only half a
mile from the pit bottom. Deputy B, he's in charge of Fourth. It's a bad
district – a very bad roof, a bit of trouble with water, plagued with gas.
He's only sending out an eighth of the amount of coal Deputy A is sending. Now when Deputy A meets the manager, they all smile; he's a jolly

42

good fellow, everything's happy. Deputy B's working four times harder than Deputy A and he gets all the kicks and cuffs because, from no fault of his own, he's not sending the coal out.

I've had both, but more bad than good.

If the district's in good order, they can manage without many maintenance men. If it's bad, it needs more men. More men means more cost. So actually it boils down to this. The deputy in charge of a good district is sending plenty of coal out for little cost. The deputy in a bad district is sending little coal out at a big cost.

There's such a person as HM Inspector of Mines. You never knew when he was coming until he arrived. When he comes into a district, he's generally accompanied by the Manager, the Under Manager and the Assistant Manager and they meet the deputy in his district. Now the deputy will take them round everywhere and the Inspector examines everything appertaining to the Coal Mines Act. He takes no notice of the Manager, the Under Manager or the Assistant Manager. He asks them no questions. The man he asks the questions of is the deputy. I'll put it to you this way: the inspector is in my district. It's a bad district – there are bad conditions. He's finding fault with this quite rightly, he's finding fault with that. But in all my experience, and it's been a long one, I've never heard him turn round to the Under Manager, the Assistant Manager or the Manager and say to them: 'How often do you come up this district? When were you last here?' The man who gets the blame is the deputy.

Aye, a lot of the faults should have been the Manager's responsibility, but you daren't say so. You have to keep your tongue between your teeth. In other words, a deputy deputizes for the manager. The manager would only come down if not enough coal was coming up. He'd take notice of the conditions, and then if he'd any suggestions to make he'd. tell the deputy to hire this, to hire that. One big thing, and this is my experience, when everything was in apple pie order you never got a pat on the back. But when everything was bad – through no fault of your own, but through nature – you got all the cuffs you could get.

I'll put it to you: you're a married man, you've four children. I had six, and none working. Well, the pits were doing very bad in those days and there was no dole. The thing that made me a deputy was this. When I got married, I was a workman and it was a fair wage for a pit contractor – 6s 6d a day, three days a week, sometimes four, sometimes two. The first wage I brought home was 19s 6d for three days' work. 'Well,' I said to myself, 'that'll not do for me. I'll have jam butties, but I don't want jam butties four times a day.' The advantage was this. There was an agreement between the Deputies' Union and the Managers that there was a six-day week. You had six days guaranteed – you had to work them – but there was no short time at all. That's what made me go into being a deputy.

To become a deputy, you had to pass an examination at Wigan. When you passed that, then you had to go to the manager, and if he thought you suitable, he'd put you through an examination of his own. Then you'd start – generally in the night shift under the day deputy's instruction. You had to work in the mine before you took the course at Wigan. I started when I was 14. If you hadn't been down the mines, it was useless you going in for the course.

The miners' union went from being a pup to a dog. And it's not a dog, it's a tiger today. The Deputies' Union had no connection with the miners' union. As regards numbers, we were very small. We used to pay our dues once a fortnight at the pub. If you took the average of 60 men to one deputy, you know how many members they had to us.

THE MINER FROM PARR, BORN 1893
When I got the certificate of management from the college in Wigan, I never used it. When I was taking the course, they asked me a time or two if I wanted to be an under manager. Well, you only needed a second class for doing it. He used to ask, 'How are you going on, Joe?' and all this. He never mentioned it in any way after I'd taken the examinations. The thing was, I was always on the wrong side politically in them days for anybody.

I can remember the time at Ashton's Green. We'd a checkweighman there, Labour, and a managing director, Tory, and I'm canvassing, of course, for the checkweighman. I'm told by the manager: 'You'll never get an official job in the mining industry as long as you're on that side.' I knew to some extent that I wouldn't. There used to be the old story: the husband said to the wife, 'I don't know which way to vote.' The wife said, 'Well, ask the under manager which way he's voting.' He come back and told her. 'Well, you vote different. As long as you vote different, you'll be all right.'

MINER FROM THATTO HEATH, BORN 1898
The deputies and firemen were the worst sort. They'd call you out if you'd put too much dirt in your tub of coal and you'd sometimes get sent

home. Then, the next morning, if you came with your breakfast, they'd send you back home again, but if they saw you'd brought none, they'd send you down the pit.

The Managers

MINER FROM LEA GREEN, BORN 1895

I moved from Clock Face to Lea Green in 1923. You were lucky if you got taken on. You had to all line up and wait for the manager to come. You'd take off your cap to him and ask if there was any job going, and he'd say, 'Not today.'

There's a good tale about a fellow called Allen. He went to ask for a job and didn't take his cap off. The manager was furious. He said: 'I'll tell you how to ask for a job. You sit down there.' The manager went out and knocked on the door.

'Come in,' said Allen.

'I've come to ask for a job,' said the manager.

'Well, you can't have one, we've got enough of your sort here, already.'

THE DEPUTY, BORN 1890

There was one manager, and I only hope that God has more mercy on him than he had on his workmen. We had stables down the pit – we had 90 pit ponies. All the stalls were whitewashed, with the pony's name painted in black on white. There was electric light all the way up, and we kept the horses' feed there. There used to be ostlers in charge of these ponies. No one had to be in charge of more than 15 ponies. They had to feed and groom them twice a day. These pony men used to come twice a day – once in the morning and once in the late afternoon. They all lived close to. Generally speaking, these pony men either had got too old to work at the coal face, or had bad sight, or some had had accidents.

This manager was a proper despot – his word was law. It was part of my duty in the mornings to go to the stalls and examine them. I used to pass these pony men and have a word with them. It was a matter of form. It was a good roof, everything was safe enough there. So this particular morning, I'm going to the stables and I run into a chap. He's getting old, not quite on a pension.

'Good morning, John,' I said.

'It's not such a good morning.'

'Why's that?'

45

'Read that,' and he shoved a piece of paper into my hand. It was 14 days' notice to finish, and he said 'I wouldn't care if the manager would let me stop on for a couple of months. I'll be 65 then. If I leave now, I'll get nothing and, you know, I like my pint of beer and some tobacco.'

I said, 'You've everything to gain and nothing to lose. Go and see the manager and explain the situation to him.'

'Come on, Billy. You know the manager. He's bound to turn it down.'

So next morning I came across the fellow and I asked him how he got on.

'How did I get on? I knocked on the door. He said, "Come in." I said "Good day."

' "What do you want? What's your name?" I told him what I wanted and that I'd worked 40 years at this colliery. He said, "You've worked 40 years at this colliery. Have you had 40 years' wages?"

' "Yes."

' "Do we owe you anything?"

' "No sir."

' "WELL? GET OUT THEN." '

Incidentally, he didn't tell me everything that transpired. Next day, we had to go up to the under manager's office. There he said, 'Billy, the Manager wants to see you.' I came over all shivery. It's one thing knowing what you're going for, it's another when you don't. I knocked at the door.

'Come in.'

I walked in. 'Good afternoon, Sir.' The Manager just glared at me. I just stood there. I didn't know what the Dickens to do. 'I understand you want to see me, Sir.'

'Yes.'

'What for?'

'You mean you don't know?'

'No, Sir.'

'Are you sure? Well, I'll tell you. When I want you to act as Solicitor General to my workmen, I'll tell you.'

The next morning I saw John again.

'Morning John.'

'Morning Billy.'

'Tell me how you went on with the Manager. Did you tell me everything yesterday?'

'I didn't, Billy.'

'Why was that?'

46

'I couldn't for shame. I knew as soon as I said anything to him I'd made a mistake, so I said you had advised me to come and see him.'

He's at rest too, that Manager is. Those were the good old days.

The Owners

THE MINER FROM PARR, BORN 1893

You didn't know the mine owners. The mine owners were down south; they weren't here. Pilkingtons were the only one I remember knowing. I can't remember there being any figures issued by the mine owners about how much money they were making. We got the Labour Research department going into it at the Collins Green Company.

THE MECHANIC, BORN 1896

The owners were always going to work the best mines first. When they were finished, you had to open new mines. Often they'd sell it off and the successor would have the best of what you left, which was always an inferior mine to what you'd started with. Then after ten years the second person would hand it over to another. They always worked the best mines first. On the Lancashire coalfield, it's played out.

MINER FROM LEA GREEN, BORN 1897

There was an old fellow who used to make periodical checks down the mines. Bear in mind we're going back to the 'twenties. There were boundaries to each pit, and they never went beyond that. They didn't work over what they termed the boundary line – but we weren't interested. They had the maps.

There used to be a saying that Gallis Green Colliery closed because Lord Derby wouldn't let them go under his land. We had a Manager called Foxley at Lea Green who said there was a million tons of coal at the bottom of the pit when it was closed after nationalization. Their excuse was they could get it from the other pit, Sutton Manor. They'd never been able to do that before.

Hazards and Compensation

THE MINER FROM NEWTON ROAD, BORN c. 1900

I was buried when I was 14 with a pony. We hit a low prop when we were coming out. We were buried 3 hours. The timber across the top went on the pack that held the roof up – that's why I wasn't killed. Men dug me out, me and the pony. One fellow ran away when he got me out – I was full of blood. But I wasn't badly hurt, only cuts. I've a cut on my shoulder yet.

Safety was a hell of a lot worse. They've improved a thousand per cent since then. I've had my leg broken, fingers broken two or three times, ribs broken, chest staved in, my head gashed open; three times I've hurt my knee. It's above average, that is. There are some people who've had two injuries in a year, then they might last for about four years with everything good. I didn't get a lump sum compensation for them. It was before they started giving them. You got paid weekly. If you got hurt they used to bring you home in a horse and cart. I'll not say everyone got a bad injury, but a lot did.

[The owners often refused to accept responsibility for injury. The letter below shows the sort of procedure a miner's family would have to go through to get compensation. It is written to the Executive of the Lancashire and Cheshire Miners' Federation by a solicitor acting on the family's behalf.]

On 7th December 1925 whilst Adam Pendlebury aged 60 was engaged in his lawful occupation a stone fell from the roof on his left foot. He came up the pit at the end of the turn and walked home and there complained to his wife of severe pain in his left big toe. Dr Cooke was sent for and saw the deceased the same day and also saw him later.

On Friday 18th December the deceased thought he was improving so he went to ask Dr Cooke for a certificate, but did not mention pain in his foot and he then returned home. His wife dressed the foot and he complained of great pain in it. At 1.20 he left home to go to the colliery for his club money. This was paid to him and he reported he was improving and arrangements were made for him to start work on the following Sunday.

On his way home from the colliery, he apparently felt the need to relieve himself and went behind the pumping pit. His dead body was found there the following morning lying on his back with his knees bent and his trousers down.

On Monday 21st December post mortem examination was made by Dr Cooke, Dr Unsworth being present on behalf of the employers. This is a summary of his report:

1. Injury to the left foot.

2. Disease of arterio-sclerosis.

3. A mile walk on a cold day with considerable pain in his left foot. Any pain may lead to vaso-motor paralysis of the abdominal vessels and, in a person in the condition of the deceased, sudden death.

4. Cause of death – cardiac failure directly attributable to the injury.

At the inquest, Dr Unsworth admitted that: 'If the workman felt great pain after 18th December it might accelerate death.' But his opinion was the heart trouble was of long standing – the condition of heart and blood vessels was sufficient to account for death even if lying in bed.

An interesting comment on this is that the widow tells us that her husband had very good health and was a very sober, industrious and active man.

The employers have paid compensation in respect of the foot injury for total incapacity up to death, but their solicitors contend that the death was from natural causes.

Our opinion is that we submit the case to a Medical Superintendent who will attend court and, if his opinion supports Dr Cooke, proceedings will be instituted and the case fought out.

MINER FROM RAVENHEAD, BORN 1904

Compensation was very, very poor. You couldn't sue for neglect – it was very difficult to prove there was negligence on the owners' part. Say you were injured, say you broke your leg and you couldn't work. All we got for that incapacity in compensation would be two-thirds of the difference between sickness benefit and your wages. If you were left with a limp, you wouldn't get any compensation once you got back to your job – you were expected to go back on your own job and do your own work. If you could prove you couldn't do that job, then the compensation would be very, very small, practically nothing. If men went back to work, they'd try to do their old job no matter what, even if they'd lost a leg. You couldn't prove negligence – it was all an act of God. So there was no incentive for the owners to make things safer.

If a man was killed in the pit, the amount for a widow was very little then – you didn't get anything. They'd wheel them home on a barrow – there were no ambulances. But the Compensation Act of 1911 did give them something, did recognize the liability of the firm.

When you had your fatal accidents, it was the roof and runaway tubs – they came unleashed from the haulage rope or something like that.

49

Then there were holes in the floor, where you have your roadway – it was bad walking and you'd slip and fall.

MINER FROM RAVENHEAD, BORN 1892

Compensation used to come from the colliery. You had to go to the colliery to pick it up and it wasn't a lot then. You wouldn't get above a pound a week and that was when you couldn't work at all. I get more from the colliery today than I got working. (I have a pension of £4 a week and I get my coal for 10p a hundredweight and £8·72 Industrial Disablement as well as the normal old age pension.) You'd go for compensation when they were giving you the wages. The people paying weren't in a hurry. They used to pay it at two in the afternoon and they'd keep you till four.

It was very dusty. At one time I used to wear a wet cloth while I was cutting at a seam of 2 ft 6 ins. You couldn't see anything except what you were cutting. I never had anything but oil lamps. Now they've got lamps in their hats. I came out of the pit with nystagmus. When you're down the pit with nystagmus you look at the lamp and it's going round and round like this. My eyesight will never be right – I can read now and again. You only get that working with an oil lamp. Just think, in a place like a coal pit, there's nothing – you've got a little light like that and you have to work with it. If things keep going round and going black in the middle, you can't do anything about it. You'd have to go up the pit. You'd be brought out – you couldn't see.

They didn't recognize silicosis; all over the country, men were sick with it and they didn't get a penny. Collieries have been far better under nationalization than ever they were before. An MP for Warrington first stuck out for silicosis to be recognized as an industrial injury. I know a lot who've got back pay for it. In the old days, if the colliery said you couldn't have compensation – it didn't make any difference. The union didn't help. To be honest and truthful they never bothered – they were only for their own ends.

THE MINER FROM THATTO HEATH, BORN 1898

One thing about this pneumoconiosis, it makes you more bigoted. I've been in hospital on my back twice with collapsed lungs. It gives you time to think deeper. You think, Why? Why did they do this? I've seen men killed in the pits – squashed under rock falls. And you think, Why did they do it here? Why didn't they kill them in their bedrooms at home? It would have been better.

Pneumoconiosis grows like the moss on a sea wall until you find it chokes you. I've had it since 1917. I went to a doctor about it, and he said I wouldn't live to be 45 – I'm 77. It doesn't show on an X-ray until you have had it five years – by then it's too late to do anything about it. I go out on Sundays in a car, but you can't go far because your lungs fill up with sputum and you can't breathe. I have to lie on my bed till it's all gone. That's why it's tilting downwards towards my head.

ST HELENS DOCTOR
I used to do all the coroner's post mortems, but when the question of miners' diseases came up, there was a thing called the Pneumoconiosis Medical Board. A representative was always sent to these post mortems, or we sent one to them. The representatives were specially trained men – quite unbiased, if anyone could be, doing that sort of thing. Many a time I differed from them.

Unions

Until the formation of the National Union of Mineworkers after World War II, British miners were organized in the Miners' Federation of Great Britain. This federation consisted of delegations from all the coalfields – the miners in St Helens were in the Lancashire & Cheshire Miners' Federation.

The Lancashire & Cheshire Federation did not finally succeed in unionizing the whole district until the turn of the century. Through the 1880s and 1890s, it had fought a protracted battle against more localized unions. Especially in Lancashire, there was a tendency for the miners in each town to form their own autonomous union. There were 17 local unions in 1880. But after the success of the 1881 strike, which had had various and changing demands, 11 of the 17 unions federated.

The desire to keep power locally continued, partly because there were so many different mining centres in the Lancashire coalfield – Wigan, Leigh and Bolton were as important as St Helens. This meant a vicious circle, where a proliferation of local bodies led to weak organization which further disillusioned the members of the central federation. In 1886, the federation's membership was down to 8,000.

In 1893, miners nationally resisted a cut in wages, which they had never done before. This must have helped locally. By 1897, all the area agents were controlled centrally by the Miners' Office in Bolton. But it was later than this that daywagemen were forced in by a policy of non-co-operation with non-unionized labour.

The struggle towards a centralized union was going on at much the same time in other industries. But the miners were one of the first groups of workers to switch allegiance from the Liberal to the Labour Party. The Lancashire miner, Sam Woods, was a Liberal MP in the 1890s; he condoned the massacre of miners at Featherstone during the 1893 stoppage. By the turn of the century, there were two Lancashire mining MPs, and both of them were Labour.

DELEGATE TO THE FEDERATION (ELECTED 1919)
To be appointed as a delegate to the Lancashire & Cheshire Miners' Federation, you were elected at an ordinary branch meeting. To be appointed you'd be active in the Labour movement and in the branch. You'd be noticed if you were active in the Ward committees of the Labour Party.

For the Lancashire & Cheshire Miners' Federation, every pit branch sent a delegate. There were about 170 in all. There was an agenda, so when you got there, you were determined on what to do. In any case, your branch sent in resolutions to be discussed. You only met once a month and things could happen in between – disputes could blow up in no time. Each district had a member on the Executive Committee. Officers would discuss a variety of things – such as getting inspectors to determine if a face had what constituted abnormal working conditions. There were joint conferences and joint wages boards where officers and selected members of the Executive would meet. Generally, for the Federation Conferences, delegates were mandated by their branch because of this good system of communication. Through the Executive member in your area you also knew what was going on elsewhere. The miner's agent was the principal source. He knew better than we what was going on.

The MPs were backed by the union – it happened throughout the country. That was extended so that generally speaking Trade Unions were represented by sponsored MPs. It all arose from those early days – but the miners, without a doubt, were amongst the pioneers on this. It was a way of getting their voice heard. This made the miners particularly close to the Labour Party, but even before that, you'll find the miners had an understanding with the Labour Party. It wasn't a big issue. The first Labour MP in St Helens was Tom Glover – before World War I.

In the St Helens area we had our own local miners' organization – we called ours the St Helens Central Miners' Committee. Other areas had

52

theirs so that each pit in the area knew what the others were doing. They were all great fellows, the men on the Federation. They were a very fine crew of men – quite a number of them became MPs. There were such people as Stephen Walsh, Joe Tinker, John Allan Parkinson, Gordon McDonald, all those men and a host of others became MPs.

MEMBER OF THE COMMUNIST PARTY FROM THATTO HEATH, BORN 1902

Joe Tinker was a short, quite dumpy man. I knew him quite well. He wasn't over-intelligent, but what he did know he stuck to. Although he was MP for Leigh, he used to live in St Helens. Often on Sunday, after addressing a meeting at Leigh, he'd walk all the way back to St Helens.

MINER FROM DERBYSHIRE HILL, BORN 1893

Joe Tinker, I knew him. One of his characteristics was he never put a dinner suit on. His favourite dress was a tweed suit. He was a good walker – he'd think nothing of walking to Southport for exercise. I told him, 'You'd be walking from London with a railway ticket in your pocket!'

THE MINER FROM THATTO HEATH, BORN 1898, A MEMBER OF THE COMMUNIST PARTY

The local union leaders, there was none of them any good. They were all for themselves. We used to hunt these people. Every boozer they went into, we would say what about this, what about that? These miners' leaders could spend more money on beer and treating people than what they made in the pit. When I saw one, he said 'I've had a hard life.' I asked him, 'How have you brought up eight children and you can come up here and play bagatelle and drink beer?' Tinker never did any good – he was a figurehead, that's all.

They could have organized better than they did do. All they did was collect Trade Union funds. They wouldn't organize workers as a fighting body because it was not beneficial to them – they were handling all the dollars. When the grievances came up, they had a talk to the boss before we went in. There were glasses of beer there and a cigar. We were told a pack of lies: 'I'm awfully sorry men, I've done my best for you.'

Every meeting they had, there were tallies for a pint of beer and half-an-ounce of thin or thick twist on the Union. There were only 20 people at the Branch meetings out of five pits. They'd been to the Bolton Conference. What you saw of the sheets reporting on it was so much expenses for such a body for travelling and food, and the next lot was

53

dittoes. We in the party, we had to get to know, 'What's these here dittoes?' Could he explain? Fillingham got over that by saying, 'Do you see, men, I was just going to put it to the vote whether we had two pints today.' You know miners – up went their hands for ale. They wanted two pints. We were pushed downstairs – we were against bribing them to come to Union Branch meetings.

People weren't interested. They were never given any interest from the leaders. It was always, 'Oh, I'm not going there again.' There was a Union, but it was only on the cards.

THE MINERS' FEDERATION DELEGATE

As well as the Miners' Union, there were the Enginemen, Winders & Assistants, the Boilermen's Union. There was the Kindred Trades – which catered for electricians and blacksmiths and people like that. There was the Deputies' & Shotlighters' Union, but the shotlighters were generally with the miners. In all, there would be 3,000 or 4,000 men in these unions. They all had their own agents.

Wages and Conditions

THE MINER FROM PARR, BORN 1893

From Havanagh, I signed on at Ashton's Green shaft, known as Bye Pit. I was there drawing for my uncle, and during that period came the first strike I had known. It was the Minimum Wage Strike of 1911, which I think lasted for a period of six weeks. Up to that period, the miner at the coal face never knew what he was going to take home.

They could let you down a mine, and did do, you could get to the far end, about a mile or a mile and a half out, you could stop there without a box, no wagons had turned up. You could go down for half a turn, then have to walk it home, and you weren't paid anything. That was why they went in for the minimum wage in 1911. But even then, they didn't get that if they didn't work. The collier who was paid by the box or by the ton got nothing if anything happened that disrupted the haulage. Today, he's paid a minimum wage.

MINER FROM SUTTON, BORN 1890

The Minimum Wage dispute – we saw some of the things that took place. There was a fair amount of pressure being brought to bear to get the men to blackleg. It was men from the town, men in the very collieries con-

54

cerned. They objected to it. As a matter of fact, on one occasion, mounted police were brought in at Collins Green for anti-picketing. Also, there was a tendency for some men to pick coal from the waste heaps. Ultimately, when the strike was over, this was used as a source of victimization for quite a number of men, that they'd been seen by officials in the crowds of demonstrators.

We didn't think it was successful by any means, because the minimum wage introduced was an extremely low wage. In truth, some of the very young boys at that time, especially haulage hands, didn't get anything out of it. They were already receiving a wage slightly in excess. It was a very low wage, extremely low, for the coal-face workers. The minimum for a collier was about 8s 7d a day, and his assistant, or drawer as we call it, got about 7s 6d a day. In some places like the Forest of Dean, it was even less than that, because it was held that if the men received the full benefit of the minimum wage, the firms would not have been able to keep going and they were permitted to settle at local level. That didn't do anything to strengthen the Union. The spirit was there, all the same, to get better wages. Ultimately, wages were improved over the years preparatory to World War I by the introduction of local wages which were in excess, because the local branches introduced a system of increased payments for abnormal coal face conditions. At Bold, they were considered, and even at that, the maximum in the Lancashire coalfield was 9s 11d for the collier and 7s 11d for his assistant. Later, those increases were attacked, but that took place during and after World War I.

Colliers weren't exempted from call-up. Particularly in the collieries, vast numbers were in the Territorial Army. We were called up and they had to manage on what was left. There was no such thing as reserved occupation at the onset of World War I. We were mobilized and went out to France. Returning, we were four years older, and still young men. All the junior jobs, especially haulage jobs, had been taken. It was some time before some of us could be reinstated, and even then, we had to take a long period of night shift.

All the wages following the Minimum Wage were steadily built up on a basis of the wages paid in 1911. There were percentage increases given on that, low percentages.

In Lancashire and Cheshire, the abnormal working conditions rate was regarded as a right. There were many vicious struggles at the collieries over it. This is why the miners today still want to have a national settlement. It's difficult to explain if you've not been down a mine what constitutes abnormal working conditions. One example is if a man was working on a seam and the seam underneath it had gone, then it was very difficult to remove.

The difficulty in arriving at a satisfactory rate was that there were different ways of working it out – one was on measurement of the amount of seam cut, the other was on tonnage. The commonest was tonnage – the seam thickness might vary throughout the face; the tonnage was more certain.

So when the machinery came, we had a good base tonnage set. Men didn't press unduly, what they did was 'ga canny' – that's the Scottish for 'go slow'. Most faces did this until an agreement was arrived at. The fireman [i.e. deputy and shotlighter] would come along and say, 'Come along lads, let's see what we can do!' We'd just say, 'Go to hell.' We were paid day wage rates until an agreement was arrived at. You wanted piecework, and they wanted you to go all out so that they could base the tonnage rate far lower than you would accept.

THE MINER FROM PARR, BORN 1893

There was no pay for sickness. People's conditions were very, very bad. If anyone was sick or anything like that, you had to go for outdoor relief. People helped one another. I can remember my mother sending me to my grandmother for a shilling on Thursday night. I had to go to ask her would she lend us a shilling till Friday night when my father came home from the mine. Unemployment increased just after the war, and then it didn't come to the miners for a year or two. It came to what was called casual labour. Miners were getting more than unemployment pay if they worked a full week, but you got nothing if you worked just three days. People left if they could find a pit where they could get more work.

They only worked three days in the summer, because there were no orders for coal – they couldn't sell it. I remember one railway strike about 1910 when I was working at Havanagh. They sent one or two of us up the pit tipping coal, but in general they didn't stack it because they had no sale for it. They'd possibly have lost it if they'd stacked it, like they're still doing today, with people taking it.

I don't know how people existed, to tell you the truth, when you reckon up. I remember a family living in Newton Road. My mother was very helpful to people – she always made soup and took it to people. She'd come in to help this woman when the doctor came – the very doctor that became a Labour councillor – 'My God,' he said as soon as he'd seen this woman, she was lying there taking a bit of soup, 'she's dying of malnutrition.' Her husband was there, he turned to her husband,

'WHERE'RE YOU WORKING?' (he used to talk like that).

'Ashton's Green.'

'WHAT ARE YOU DOING?'

He was a weighman with a wage of less than a pound and he had seven or eight children and rent of 4s 6d or something like that. He said, 'Get a better job than that. Get a better job. Your wife's dying of being underfed.'

That would happen to a lot, and it went on again in the 1930s, that sort of thing. Our younger children used to bring children and plead with our mother: 'Give them a butty, give them a butty.' Things like that. You can reckon the physique of children in those days compared with today – there's no comparison, and it's due to better food, better housing conditions, better sanitary conditions and health treatment.

When I started work, the hours were six o'clock in the morning till 3.30 in the afternoon. That would be 9½ hours, so that in winter, you'd go down in the darkness and in the afternoon you'd be coming up in darkness when the shift terminated. The eight hour shift was a misnomer, because it only counted from when the men got to the working face. That meant that, in my case, when I worked at Bold, I walked to the colliery a mile away. After going down the mine, I walked two thousand yards or more. Now my eight hours started when I got to the coal face. You had to be in position for when the underground rope started – that meant anything from half an hour to three-quarters of an hour down the mine before your shift really commenced. And of course this happened at the termination. The usual way of reckoning among the miners of a man's time underground was the eight hours plus the time of a winding shift. The cages which took men underground always started an hour before the commencement of winding coal, so if you counted it, they could be down an hour and a half or two hours beyond the legal eight hours of work. That's why I'm saying that the eight hour shift was always a misnomer and I still think it's true today.

THE COMMUNIST PARTY MEMBER FROM THATTO HEATH, BORN 1902

We travelled to work in the tubs. We had to keep our heads below the level of the top of the tubs – and they were less than 3 ft off the ground. We had to crouch forward holding our lamps in our hands, because if we rested them on the bottom of the tub they'd spill. Sometimes the tubs would come off the rails. Two fellows at the end were in tubs with no sides. They had to drop off when this happened and press the two wires at the side of the tunnel together to make them ring to tell the engine driver, and he'd stop the winding engine. One day when I wasn't on, they had an accident. The tubs fell off on the rock side. One fell on a protruding rock – all the others hit up against it. The men had their heads pressed against the fronts of the tubs, and on the impact the bolts on the fronts of the tubs penetrated their heads. Seven of them were injured like that. Afterwards, there was a notice put up which read to the effect that all people travelling on that run in future would have to go arse first.

FORMER BRANCH SECRETARY OF THE MINERS' FEDERATION AT LEA GREEN
I worked at Ravenhead and Alexandra – the two Pilkington pits. It was always called Groves's before the Coal Board took over. And I worked at Lea Green. I worked down all three pits at Lea Green. See, it wasn't against you leaving one pit and going down another pit. Pitmen talking in the pubs and suchlike – I always found out where the money was best. You were graded: if you were a collier, you were a collier; a day-wage man was a day-wage man; a haulage hand, a haulage hand. If you were a collier, you could start straight away. There were some what we called blue-eyed boys. They always managed to get a good place by backhanding. We've no proof of backhanding the manager – we had our own feeling. I knew nine men of one family who were always getting good places. The good places were where the coal was soft. You'd come up with some coal that was like rock. Some stayed in the same pit because they were guaranteed a reasonable place – when one place was finished, they'd put them on another. If you got a good place you'd stop there till it worked out. You wouldn't risk going to another pit where you might get a bad place.

THE MINER FROM RAVENHEAD, BORN 1904
Under private enterprise, every colliery had its own way, and if you fell out with somebody in the colliery and you said you were leaving, when they found out where you were going they'd phone there and tell them not to take you on. When I left Lea Green at 9s 11d and I wanted to sign on at Sutton Manor for 15s, they said I couldn't because Lea Green had stepped in. When I left Lea Green again I didn't tell them I was going.

THE COMMUNIST PARTY MEMBER FROM THATTO HEATH, BORN 1902
I got notice in the pit when I was working on haulage, and we were called redundant. In fact, they'd altered jobs so that they could do with four what

they'd done with eight before. The first colliery had been taken over by this other one – we went over from Alexandra to what they called Groves's colliery at Ravenhead, which was owned by Pilkingtons. There was a dozen of us to finish. If I'd been their blue-eyed boy, I'd have been kept on – I had a cool job. Now they sent me to the red hot part. It was two miles in with a 3-ft roof – just tall enough to let the tubs through. You had to get there partly crawling, partly on hands and knees. It became extremely hot, and the ventilation was very poor. One young fellow put pinches of salt in his drinking water. I only worked three days on there. It didn't get better. I gave in six days' notice.

2 The Glassworks

Glassmaking in general, and Pilkingtons in particular, did not dominate St Helens in the 1920s as they do now. The proportion of the working population in glassmaking is now nearly three times what it was then. Pilkingtons dominated window-glass production, but there were two or three factories making bottle glass and tableware. In all, there were just over 6,000 glassworkers in 1921, as against 10,000 miners. Pilkingtons were going through a rough patch, as foreign competition began to make their window glass uneconomic. It was not until they went over to continuous glass production methods in the 1930s that they recovered. In the 1920s, however, they were experimenting on innovations which heralded the end of the skilled glassblowers' jobs.

Unions at Pilkingtons had sporadically risen and fallen during the nineteenth century. They were largely based on individual trades, such as cutting or blowing. The National Amalgamated Union of Labour, one of the general unions, was formed in the north-east of the country in 1903. Several sections at Pilkingtons soon joined. From then until the outbreak of World War I, there were three branches, the blowers and gatherers, the sheet-glass workers, and the rolled-plate workers. The total membership at Pilkingtons was around 1,200 by the start of the war, but it included less than a third of the workforce and was not sufficient to gain recognition from the management. However, Pilkingtons was no exception to the national upsurge of unionization which took place towards the end of the war. By 1918, membership had reached 3,900, almost the total workforce.

It was at that point that Pilkingtons recognized the union and set up a Joint Industrial Council, which was to survive until the strike of 1970. Originally, the council was formed by nine union men and nine from the management. It was hardly established before the postwar boom in glass slumped. The company lost many of its overseas markets through the war. Meanwhile, the Belgian competition was especially intense, because the

Belgian franc was constantly sliding against the pound. Sheet glass was being produced at no profit.

Unfortunately, none of the original union members of the Joint Industrial Council is still available to describe the council's early dealings, but from May 1920 wage cuts were being implemented by management as the only way of cutting costs. There were two further cuts of 2s 6d per week in 1921. Then, with increased pressure from Belgium (including the dumping of poor quality glass in Britain), another two cuts of 5s a week were proposed in 1922, although the second was delayed until the summer of the next year.

By 1924, a labourer who had been earning £3 15s 6d at the end of the war was taking home only £2 2s. At no time did the union attempt any serious resistance to the cuts, which were usually accepted at mass meetings. But with this humiliating cut in living standards, the strength of the union was undermined. By 1924, membership had dropped virtually to its prewar level.

GLASSBLOWER AT NUTTALLS BOTTLEWORKS, BORN *c.* 1892

I was a bound apprentice at Nuttalls – you had to be bound to get a job. If you tried to leave, it was quite possible to be put in jail. You signed on a red dot until you were 21. You couldn't leave or nothing – you were a slave kind of thing till you were 21. Putting your finger on the red dot was to make it legal; your father had to be there. You worked for very little wages till you became 21. You learned your trade. It went in stages in the bottleworks. You started off as a spare lad. On night turn, they started work for half past five until five o'clock the next morning. You worked for $3\frac{3}{4}$ hours, then you got $\frac{3}{4}$ hour for supper; you worked $2\frac{1}{2}$ hours more and then you had to stay on till five in the morning. Then you had breakfast. That was Mondays, Tuesdays, Wednesdays and Thursdays. On Friday, you finished at two o'clock on Saturday morning.

In the shop where I was apprenticed, there were ten holes, each with a gatherer, blower, wetter-off, finisher and taker-in. The gatherer took metal [molten glass] from the tank, the blower blew the bottle. The wetter-off just wet the flange (the piece of glass which joined the bottle to the pipe). That made it easier for the finisher to break it off and put the ring round the top.

The taker-in used to carry the bottles on his shoulder in a forceps to the arch where they were placed in tiers. Each man would have an apprentice so there would be 50 boys running about the shop. It would make a wonderful film. The blower used to swing the metal over his shoulder. You had a knack of keeping it on the pipe without it falling off. The metal was flying about. We'd always sing the turn through.

When the blower had manipulated the metal and got the right amount of it on the end of the pipe, he put it into a mould which was the shape of a bottle. It was in two halves. The bottom half was fixed, and when you'd put the metal in, you had a treadle to shut the top over it. When you blew the bottle you'd see this faint mark down the side from the mould. If it was too pronounced, they'd throw it away. (Antique bottles won't have a line down the side, as they'd have been blown without a mould.) You'd give it to a finisher, who had what was called a tune to put on the rings. I'd blow with a tobacco pipe in my mouth as well.

Normally, the gatherer had to guess exactly how much metal to pick up on the pipe from the tank. That's where the skill came in. The blower would feel it. 'That's a bit light, fetch a bit more,' or 'That's a bit too heavy.' The blower would have two pipes, one he was blowing, and one in his other hand. The gatherer would be running to get another one – we were on piecework, you see. That was Nuttall's bottleworks. It became United Glass.

The bottles were taken and put in the arch and sealed up. It was an annealing kiln. They stayed in the arch two or three days. This was heated and slowly cooled down – otherwise, if the bottles had just been left, they'd have shattered. When they took the bottles out, there'd be anything up to fifty gross, or thereabouts. They'd be put into trucks and taken to where they were sorted into sizes. You'd have two types. One was a whisky bottle shape, and that held a quart. Then there was a smaller one.

You had to do pretty well in reckoning up, because you reckoned all your own money. They sent you word in of how many gross you'd done. You had so many pipes which you put by when you'd finished with them, and you had a tally pipe. When you had done 20 you put the tally pipe at the end of the row. When you finished work, you counted up how many twenties you had done. The bad ones they used to call the cocks. You reckoned on two or three dozen cocks in a day. If you had only a couple of dozen, you were all right. Each bottle had to be a certain weight. If it was under 14 ounces, it was too light; if it was over 16 ounces, it was too heavy. Come Friday night or Saturday morning, you used to get paid. The finisher used to go down to the office and receive the wages for all the workers. It came in a packet – we used to get down on the floor or some other convenient place and reckon all this money up, so much for him and so much for him. You were all paid definite rates. The taker-in got 7s 6d (his was the least) and a penny a gross overwork. The wetter-off got twopence overwork, and the gatherer tenpence a gross. The blower's overwork was 1s 4d.

Some made it to be blowers and some didn't. At the end of each turn, if you were an apprentice, you had some practice. When you got a bit proficient and someone left, you'd get in. The same group of men always kept together. After each stop, you'd practise. It was then we made quart bottles that held a lot more. How did we do it? You'd use less metal to fill out the same mould – they'd be no good to sell, as they were too light, but we could get them filled up with beer. There was one man who must have lost hundreds of gallons before he found out what was happening to him. In those days, they had no measures on the taps – it just ran out of the barrel.

When you went to the Glass Bottle works, you paid 3s 6d into a works fund. You paid 3s 6d when you came out of your time and when you went from gatherer to blower. This was collected by the steward. When the summer came, they'd have a meeting: 'All right, lads, where are we going this year?'

'Southport in a wagonette.'

It was always 'Southport in a wagonette' every year. The pubs were open all day, we had a good dinner and a good tea. We used to knock about a bit, go to the lake and the funfair and the bowling green. You could count the teetotallers on one hand. The horse knew when to stop. The first stop was the Millhouse on the right, just as you're going into Rainford. One of the first going into Southport was the Morris Dance. We stopped at four places at least going there, and it was the same coming back. You'd have 12 pints inside you by the time you got there. There was no water there, except the Marine Lake – you'd have to go as far as Blackpool to get a swim.

WORKER AT PILKINGTONS, BORN *c.* 1898
When I signed on, they said that with handwriting like mine I should be working in the office, but my father worked in the sheet works, and I just followed suit. My first job at Pilkingtons was as a spare lad. You were apprenticed, just as at the Bottleworks. When you were apprenticed at 14, you weren't supposed to work night shifts, but sometimes the factory inspector came round and you all had to hide.

There were three kinds of glass. Plate glass was taken in a ladle, poured on a table and rolled. It was thicker than sheet glass and was used for the really big plate-glass windows. It wasn't such good glass, and didn't take such skill to make it. Then there was cathedral glass, coloured ambers, blues and greens with chemicals mixed into the frit.

Where I worked was all sheet-glass windows. They had to be blown, then cut. The glass went to what was called the splitting palace when it was still in the shape of a cylinder. It was laid on a trestle table, split with a diamond on the end of a stick, and clipped at one end. The girls carried it off and put it in a flattening kiln [an annealing kiln]. Then they lifted it off with a big fork, and a fellow called a flattener kept rolling it out. We didn't have anything to do with that – we didn't think the flatteners were real glassmakers.

The sheet glass started at nine ounces, then there was photo glass for pictures – that was 1·6. There were different thicknesses. You had to work to a couple of ounces of metal, which the blower would judge when the gatherer brought him a draw. You could go on and think you'd done a good turn – then they'd tell you that you had a few rejects. The rejects weren't thrown away, but those who made them didn't get paid for them.

I was working with a record blower. I was getting as much in two turns with him as the others were getting in a week. There were a lot who couldn't do the job when they came out of their time – it was a skilled job, and maybe you hadn't got the physique. Not any Tom, Dick or Harry could do it. Skilled blowers at Pilkingtons were taking home the best wages in the town. I've known plenty of women who've tried to get their daughters married off to a blower – they knew they'd see them all right.

Some of the pipes used to blow the glass were 27½ pounds, and you might have 100 pounds of metal on the end of it. The pipe was on a rail, and they used to manipulate it on this. The largest pipe I ever used was 14 pounds. I was blowing and gathering till they brought a patent from America called the Glass Cylinder. They used to swing a glass cylinder till it lengthened out to the size of that tree there. Then they used to lay it out and cut it in lengths. We used to cut it with an electric wire. When that process started, we were working 12 hours. We never worked weekends till then – we started weekend work.

A lot of the time, I was in the yard. I was called a producer, making gas. (It's all run on oil now.) There's a big fire. When you drop on that fire, it gives off gas, which goes into a long iron tube, and it used to go into the tanks. You kept on taking the clinker out and breaking the fire – it was called fishing. You'd take so much out depending on the different qualities of the coal. As it kept going down, you put coal in. The gas was regulated from the tank. Across the tank there was a wall so high. They'd have

64

Above: John Foster's glass bottle works, *c*1910. *Below:* Women employed at Pilkingtons during World War I polishing the surface marks off sheets of plate glass.

Cylinder-drawn sheet glass is lowered prior to cutting; the glass would then be re-heated and flattened. This method of making window glass replaced the process described on p. 64 and was itself superseded *c*1930. *Inset:* Drawing the cylinder; compressed air was used in shaping the glass.

holes where the frit – that's the sand, glass and different things – was being melted. It went through these holes to where they gathered it. The gas was forced through flues by compressed air and came into the tank. There was a lot of scum on the surface, which was cleared off by a skimmer – if that got into the glass, it was no good.

When it got too hot, you used to go and cool down. Sweat gushed off you. You could scrape it off your shirt. You left work dripping wet, but before I got to the bottom of Greenbank my pants used to be dried and white with salt. You could drink while you were working. This is where the boys came in. If you drank water, you'd get cramp. They gave us salt tablets, and you could send the spare boy for our beer at the pub. Some of the men used to have strap (that's credit) and so that they knew who it was for, the men used to send objects they could be recognized by: a nail, a match box or a penknife. When I worked as a spare lad, I had to go down to the milk shop in Tontine Street many a time. You went down to the milk shop with three or four empty cans for buttermilk. You had a board of wood to carry them back with across your shoulders.

Most people drank homemade pop. I used to make it when I was at home in those big whisky bottles. It could be nettle or dandelion – I used to go to the brewery for the yeast. I had as many as two hundred bottles at home. This policeman used to call every night at my mother's shop and have one if he was on night turn, but he'd never come inside. This fellow came round the factory selling them from a big basket.

For me it was the underscrappers [the undermanagers] were the worst. They were in a well-paid job. They had nothing to do with the process. If they had the same job today, they wouldn't last two minutes – the men wouldn't have it. They thought they were It, and they were only staff. All the orders didn't come from Pilkingtons – you couldn't get to them – but they were getting the money. They started a pension scheme in 1924. I think they paid 1s 2d and you added 1s 2d to it. Then came short time, and if you had to draw that pension you didn't get their half, you only got your part. When it picked up, and you were working fully again, you had to start the pension again, even if you had worked 30 years.

The union was nothing, not for the glassworkers. Their Union Office was in Kirkland Street. They couldn't do anything for you. If you left Pilkington's sheet-glass works, you couldn't get another job – there was none. They monopolized sheet-glass making. They merged with Chance Bros of Birmingham. The union didn't put in any pay demands to my knowledge. They wouldn't have it in those days. I packed it in with the union after 12 months – I thought it was a waste of money. If it was organized properly, maybe it would have been all right, but who was going to keep you? If you were on strike, you had nothing, unless you had good neighbours.

DELEGATE TO THE TRADES & LABOUR COUNCIL (AFTER HE LEFT PILKINGTONS)
Philips was the name of the man who formed the union at Pilkington's offices. He and his two daughters were sacked after he had organized them in the office. They never got back. That was the time when labour was cheap. There was no organization to fight to get him back. They were all toffee-nosed who worked in the office. You had a job to talk about trade unions against the bosses they worshipped. They didn't find out about his organizing, or they would have sacked him earlier, don't worry.

Tom Williams was the General & Municipal Workers' secretary. He lived in St Helens. Although he was a member of the Trades & Labour Council, he never attended any of the meetings. He didn't take any part in the trade union activity in the town. He was not interested so far as trade union work in St Helens was concerned. His idea of doing anything was sitting round a table with the bosses. He set up an Industrial Council with Pilkingtons, and no other union would have any part of it. I worked there for a whole year. The only thing we used to see from him was a notice on the board saying: 'On and from such and such a date, the Industrial Council has agreed to a 5% reduction in wages.' When you asked him about it, he said that the management were trying to force 10% cuts, and keeping to half was a distinct victory.

The union was very weak, mainly because of the type of organization. There were 12 branches of the General & Municipal workers. They never met. They were supposed to have a meeting every three months, but these were just with the chairman, secretary, treasurer and two or three committee members – perhaps half a dozen altogether. The glassmakers had been in the National Amalgamated Union of Labour. Williams came from that union. Previous to 1914, Pilkingtons had a very heavy record of breaking strikes.

66

3 Engineering

ENGINEER, BORN 1891, WHO WORKED MOST OF HIS LIFE FOR PILKINGTONS
Daglish's made pumping engines for the water works and winding engines
for the collieries. They made hauling engines for the collieries, that were
for hauling the boxes to the main line below. That was for the locality of
St Helens.

Daglish's was the main engineering firm in St Helens. But there was
also George Varleys, an engineering works for Pilkingtons, supplying
machinery for grinding glass. These things were 10 ft in diameter and 6
in. thick – huge – like mushrooms. The main face underneath was in
sections of blocks 6 in. square. Sand and water were forced through that
face on the glass; after that, it was polished. Then there was Pritchards,
who did mostly moulding – Pilkingtons had only a small moulding department for making brasswork.

Daglish's was going down. I suppose the run-down of the mines had
something to do with it. When they made these engines, they lasted
donkeys' years and they could always be repaired. You could always put
new parts in.

Mr Daglish, he was a sarcastic character. He said a man wasn't experienced till he was 30, and you had men of 40 pulling their hats down over
their ears so as not to show their grey hairs, because Daglish also thought
you were past it at 40. With heavy engines coming out of the works, you
couldn't take them along the canal bank, in case the weight of them broke
the bank and sent them into the water. Horses took them through the
town. One day, one of Daglish's horses had died, and he got a young one.
It was straining and pulling on the engine to get it out of the yard – it
was starting off that was difficult. The horse was leaning right over forwards. Mr Daglish came out and said, 'I say, lad, you'd better look after
that horse, it costs money. I can get men for nothing.'

My eldest brother was 13 when he went to Daglish's in 1901 and learned
to be a moulder. My second brother, Mathias, started as a turner. He took

the rough casts and turned them to make them smooth. He worked on winding engines and bridges – there were a lot of Daglish's bridges in the town, and there was one in Sutton. He's still got a lathe now and turns things for the local garages, especially old car parts that they can't get any more. Our Harry was the next one. He served his time as an engine fitter. When he'd fitted the engines together, he'd put steam pumps to them and work them in the shop. The next brother was another moulder – with iron, whereas the others worked with brass.

I was a pattern maker. I started in the drafting office. Say we wanted to make that poker, you'd start with a plan, go to the planing machine, cut it in shape and make it in wood as smooth as glass. Then the moulder would press it in black sand – which was special, as it stuck together. Every engine part had to be made like that. We had to make mahogany teeth for every cog wheel. We'd mark it out on a drawing board until we got the right number of teeth. We put all the cogs on a plain wheel, and every one of them had to be exactly the same. That wheel would have to be pressed into the sand. The moulder's box would be put on the sand with four handles to lift it off. There was a little gutter to let the iron in at one end, and another to let the air out.

The iron was in the furnace, with coke, then metal, then coke again and, on top, pig iron made into bars at the iron works. That pig iron was the highest quality. They were all heated together until they melted. A big steel spout ran from the furnace, covered with fireclay to protect it, with a plug at the bottom so that the metal would not run out till you were ready for it. The crane had a bucket lined with fireclay so that it would not melt when the metal was poured in. The furnace keeper looked in and if he saw the metal was melted, he tried it with a rod until it was right for using. The crane man took the ladle to the spout of the furnace and the metal ran out white hot. The crane took it to the mould casting, which had been skittered with black lead (like lead from a pencil, powdered). You had to do that to get the cast smooth enough. If you hadn't a good surface, you wouldn't get a good casting. He turned the ladle out by a handle – being a great big handle, it was a good lever. One man would be watching till the metal came out of the air git. That mould was full of metal then. It was left for half an hour – the metal would turn to solid, you couldn't do it any harm. The crane would come and pick it up, and the pieces from the feeding git and air git were broken off. The casting had to go into the lathe, which was anything from 12 to 24 ft across. It had to be bolted on. My brother used to turn them; he had to run all round it to make it true.

68

You know that big wheel at the pit with the cable on? They cast it in segments, eight or ten – that make a wheel 18 ft in diameter. Then, there's a groove wheel for a steel cable to run on. They've got a complete wheel with no spokes. They make a solid bearing for the centre, and that has to be machined. It's laid in the moulding shop in segments. Then they get ordinary pieces of steel 2 in. in diameter for the spokes. They are laid on the moulding shop floor. The segments are drilled for the pieces of steel to fit in. Then they pour molten metal over, and that seals all the spokes to the casting.

My dad was a foreman engineer. When they started on a cylinder for an engine, it would be the length of this room; they bolted it down on a big steel table. They had a big spindle that went through the centre of it. That fitted into the lathe – the boring bar travels cutting all the way through. It makes it like glass inside, but if it stops at all it leaves a mark on the cylinder, which then has to be thrown away, because it would never work properly. They used to put four belts on, with steam engines, to make sure that the cutter would not stop. My dad came through when this man was boring a cylinder and leaned over to have a look. One of the belts broke and lapped round his arm, flung him to the roof and catapulted him into an 80-horse-power steam engine which ran the whole shop. That killed my dad when I was 18 months old and my brother was 13.

In those days, you couldn't go into Daglish's and start work. You'd have to be a bound apprentice. You used to work for your indentures till you were 21. Your wages went up about a shilling a day once a year – 3s 10d when I was 14, 5s when I was 15 and so on. Through World War I, I didn't get any more, and there were girls getting three and four pounds. When you turned 21, they put a flag out for you; they had a big bell and they tolled that. You had to buy every foreman a cigar. You were given your indentures, then you were set. But rather than their paying me 24s, I had to go to the dole house. They were getting the job done cheap, and when it came to paying you a tradesman's wage, they'd send you somewhere else. I knocked about doing all kinds of work, like sharpening butchers' knives, so I wouldn't have to get dole.

CLERK AT DAGLISH'S, BORN 1890

Just after I left school, I was down at the abattoir – it was by the parish church – getting a bladder. Then I saw a boiler coming out of Daglish's foundry and there was a weighman waiting in the office to weigh it. I thought, 'Oh, I'll stand by and watch this.' As I was standing by the gate,

George Palmer came out of the office. I knew him, as he went to St Mary's Church – my family were regular attenders there, and my parents were the first couple to be married there. He came over to me and asked if I was looking for a job. I said 'Oh, what for?'

'We've got a vacancy here for an office boy.'

'No, thank you very much,' I said, 'I don't want an office job. I want to serve my time as a joiner.'

'Now,' he said, 'you know me. Why don't you go back and think about it? Tell your father you've been offered the job.'

I went back home and saw my father: 'I've been offered a job at Daglish's foundry.'

'You what?' he said, 'You can't have. No one gets offered a job there, you have to pay a premium to get in.' That was money paid for your training and apprenticeship. Anyway, my mother said, 'Now look, you're only 13. You've plenty of time to learn to be a joiner. Why don't you go into the foundry over the winter?' Somehow I was soft and said I'd take it, and I went back and started work on Monday morning. I worked there for 29 years.

The foundry was – perhaps I shouldn't say this – like a prison. It was very strict. We had one of the finest engineering works in the country. Dicky Seddon served his time there and he went out to New Zealand, where he was the premier.

We made all the corporation pumping engines at Knowsley, Eccleston Hill and Kirkby. I used to go out to them all. My wife's grandfather worked there. He made all the heavy wagons to take the boilers. When our boss was going out there, I used to go with him in a big red Talbot. Nobody dare touch it. There were two of the Daglishes – they were some kind of half-brothers. Mr Harry Daglish was not a very nice sort to know – he was too snobbish. On Saturday mornings, he'd come down on horseback. One time, his horse was lame, and he came down by bus; he made it known all over the town that he thought St Helens buses were dirty, filthy buses. He didn't work; he used to go into the office and do all the costing and estimating.

Mr Robert Daglish supervised that all the jobs were getting done. He was too greedy, grabbing. He had an order for seven boat-shaped tanks for Knotty Ash. He told me to get the cost out for each of the tanks. I had to cost out each piece of plate, nut and bolt, and work out a price. He used to double it. That doesn't pay. The Daglishes got at loggerheads with the mayor of St Helens over the repairs at the waterworks. They sent

70

a fitter to put it right. Phythian, the mayor then, kicked up a shindy at the cost. He came down to the foundry and really wanted to know what was going on.

You daren't smoke if you worked there – you daren't even talk in the yard. If the boss came by when you were talking, he would ask if there was something wrong. They thought you were wasting your time if you were talking. If you were two minutes late, you were half-houred – that was having half an hour's pay deducted. Work started at six o'clock. A bell rang at eight for breakfast, and another rang at half-past to start again. If you weren't in after dinner when the door was shut, you were half-houred.

The highest wage used to be £3 per week, and the labourers got 18s going up to a guinea. There was 40s for boilermakers and pattern makers. The head foreman only got £3 per week, and he used to keep The Grapes Hotel at Prescot.

I remember Collins, the grocers, bought one end of Daglish's works. Mr Collins said, 'You know, it's a shame this firm is breaking up. I was doing work in Russia and I saw an engine coming on the road with "Daglish's Foundry, St Helens, Lancashire" on it.' It was a wicked shame for St Helens when it closed.

The men were very good, and doing the work, but on Monday mornings they'd meet under a lamp in Church Street. 'Ee lads, are we going in today?' they'd say. They'd toss a coin, and if they didn't go in, they'd have a boozy day. Sometimes one chap in the office got over-fond of his booze, and I often found him asleep on the boiler.

Jimmy Oakes was the best moulder. He made caustic pots – we used to weave them. Varleys did their best to get him, and they did. Varleys were trying to get the orders. If Daglish's got a bit slack, they'd go to Varleys. The corporation took over a lot of the men when the firm went into liquidation. The place just went down and down. Everyone knew the situation was getting worse. We tried to keep together in the office by only working a three-day week. One day, the boss just said, 'I'm sorry, but I'll have to give you a week's notice.' That was after I'd worked there 29 years.

THE ENGINEER AT PILKINGTONS, BORN 1891

I was on the lathe in the glassworks. There were so many machines in the works that had to be kept going. We had locos running round. They only had four wheels on, and they could do short turns in the yard where big locos couldn't get round. I used to do work on them – say the steel tyres that go on the wheels, I used to bore them out with a 3-ft inside diameter.

They'd bring me a pair of blanks. When I got these tyres on the lathe, I had to bore them so many thousandths small for shrinking. In a case like that, we left about 55 thousandths. I'd get a micrometer and adjust it down that amount, then I bored the tyre out till the micrometer just fitted in. Well, that tyre won't go on the wheel; it has to be heated to expand it, then you lower your wheel in. There's a gap all the way round with the heat until you put water on to cool it. That's what's called shrinking on. You've got to think what's happening to that metal – if the cast iron's not very strong, it'll break when it shrinks.

They used to have furnaces where they heated the tyre up and pulled it out, which was awkward as it had to be handled when it was so hot. A fellow had an idea. They had a plate in the shop across the railway lines. You've got your wheel ready on the crane. They put the tyre down on the plate. Then they put a ring of gas round it to heat it up, then, when it was heated, you lowered the wheel, and afterwards got a water ring to cool it. You didn't have to handle anything – a marvellous invention.

I used to turn the rollers for the tanks – rollers for taking the glass from the furnace to the layer. If they'd got out of shape, they had to be turned up afresh. The rollers were set a certain amount apart, depending on how thick the glass was to be. They had a 5-in. hole in with water rushing through to keep it cool. That glass flowed down through the rollers to another building, and tubular rollers carried it through various heats till it was cool. The rollers had to be rebored because they rusted inside and didn't cool with the water.

We had characters then – even the labourers were characters. One chap would have a shirtful of beer at the weekend. He'd come in on Monday singing and joking – but he'd keep working. One point – everyone would help everyone else – if you were a bit behind they'd give you a help. They all knew how long they should take over each job.

We were working overtime. If there was an emergency, you had to stay till it was over, till you got the plant going again. Every hour they were losing hundreds of pounds in production. You'd be up till two o'clock. If a bearing had collapsed, we had to go round to bring the brass moulder to mould new bearings. You had to make do with the materials in the works.

The Engineers' Lockout of 1922

TWO ENGINEERS FROM PILKINGTONS

I came out of my time when I was 21 – in 1912. I joined the Steam-enginemakers' Society in 1912, and then it changed over to the Amalgamated Engineering Union. There were good members. There was a lot of old chaps there and you daren't talk or leave the room without permission. At a certain time of year on the card of the union, there was a star – you used to get a summons to a meeting. That was the election of officers for the following year. If you didn't turn up you were fined 6d.

There were two classes of men in engineering – the federated and the non-federated. The federated shops were firms like Daglish's and Varleys, the non-federated Pilkingtons and suchlike. The men in the federated shops used to get 5s a week less than the non-federated. The Federated were all in one Masters' Federation – they were always below. If the federated got a rise of 2s 6d, we'd get a rise of 2s 6d to keep that difference.

In 1922, we were locked out. The bosses came to us to say they wanted to reduce the pay – they wanted a sixteen-shilling reduction. The federated shops wouldn't accept the reduction in their wages – but it boiled down to us all having to accept it. They were locked out till they accepted the cuts. We'd nothing to fight with. I was a member of the union, but you can't fight with your trousers down, you know.

THE COMMUNIST FROM THATTO HEATH, BORN 1902

Councillor Boscow, chairman of the General Strike committee, was branch secretary of the foundry workers' union. He was a foppish type of fellow. He wore pin-stripe trousers, spats and a black velour hat that perched on top of his head – all his hair came out from underneath, he wore it long for those days. He was a real dandy. We didn't know then that he was a homosexual. He had a tobacconist's shop in Sutton in the early 1920s. He wasn't left wing – he was a chap of no opinions. He was chairman of the Trades & Labour Council, and he also became a Labour councillor.

In 1922, there had been an engineers' lockout, a national lockout of all the federated shops. They all came out – 54 unions were concerned. During the course of the lockout, which lasted a few weeks, we had a joint lockout committee in St Helens. I was a member, by the way. Shortly after it had begun, it was reported that the moulders in a foundry on Burtonhead Road were working – blacklegging.

73

So we organized a meeting in the market place of engineers and un-employed men, inviting them to go to a mass picket at the foundry. About 400 people went along, with another 200 or 300 trailing on behind. We marched a mile to the foundry in Burtonhead Road. What surprised me was that Boscow turned up to the meeting and took part in the march. I was at one side of him and a man called Philips, who was another Communist Party member, was on the other, so he couldn't evaporate and disappear. When we got there, he halted the march. There was no gate, just two wooden posts sticking up. He went into the office, a little cabin. When he came out, he said, 'They won't do nothing.' That's all he said. I think they'd been a bit offensive to him – he took offence easily.

I stood on a heap of stone and shouted, 'Surround the foundry and prevent anyone from getting out.' We had to surround it to picket, as there were no walls. It came on to about five. I spoke to a chap I knew who was working inside – I had to shout to him across an industrial railway line. 'Are the moulders working?'

'They left here at three, when they knew you were coming.'

'What are you doing working?'

'It's not my affair. I'm just a labourer.'

'It is your affair. You're blacklegging.'

'If I am, I'm getting too old to start.' He went for his jacket and left.

This gave us some idea they weren't there. At five o'clock, the hooter blew and they started to shut the place up. Three men came out and started to walk down the road. The crowd hooted and booed and shouted 'Blacklegs!' and followed them down the road. I thought they might have been sent out to entice the crowd away to let the others out, so I gathered together about 20 men and waited by the entrance.

Soon, it became clear that the place was in complete silence. It was locked up. These two or three hundred people followed the three men down Canal Street and Bridge Street to the top of Ormskirk Street. Two of the men lived in New Town, close to where the football ground was. They weren't going in the nearest direction as they were trying to get rid of the crowd. They went down Duke Street and Boundary Road till they got to New Town. The crowd went and demonstrated round their houses; chalked Blackleg on their doors. They called on another fellow who was nominally shop steward. It meant that they had to go up to Croppers Hill. They were coming down Liverpool Road when I met them. I stopped and spoke to Boscow and asked him how he was going on.

The following day they sent summonses to Boscow on six charges: intimidation, besetting, persistent following and others amounting to the same thing. It turned out that they'd been demonstrating against a clerk, the chief dresser and the manager. He gave a total denial that we were at Croppers Hill, even though hundreds of people knew he was on the demonstration. He barefacedly denied it. He was found Not Guilty on four charges, bound over for six months on one and fined on the other.

The following morning, two plainclothes men came up to his house and arrested him on a charge of perjury. He had to appear in the Assize Court. Of course, this time, he knew he was on a serious charge. The trial went on all day. The judge was Lord Chief Justice Ewart, famous for inventing the saying: 'Justice must not only be done, it must be seen to be done.' It went on from half past ten in the morning till quarter past seven at night. They sat late to complete the case. Coming back on the train, I asked him how much it had cost him and he told me that it was somewhere between £700 and £800. I asked him, 'Won't the union pay?'

'They'll pay for the solicitor, but I hired barristers as well. I rang the Law Society and asked for the best KC available. They said that they'd recommend Sir John Simon, who charges £1,000 a day. I said that was too much, and they gave me the next category – that was Mr Merryman at £100 a day. This man had to have a junior at £50 a day.' Then he had to pay for the police court for one day, and the grand jury for two days, to prove whether there was a *prima facie* case to answer. It cost him £150 a day for the one and £100 for the other. Then there was extra pay because the court should have finished at five and it went on till seven. He paid all the witnesses' expenses. He provided most of the witnesses with a meal at midday. At the end of it all, he was acquitted. The judge said something about the statements he'd made had been in the course of giving evidence under cross examination, and this wasn't perjury.

This was the reason Boscow was so keen to become chairman of the Watch Committee. In 1923–24, the Labour Party got a majority on the Town Council. Almost immediately, it began to take over the committees. When it came to the Watch Committee, Boscow wanted to take it over. He was duly nominated by Dick Waring. Somebody seconded him, but nobody voted for him. The result was that the Tory, Norman Pilkington, was re-elected chairman. There was a row in the Labour Party, and a vote of censure was passed on those councillors who had failed to vote. The following year, he was nominated again. This time, seven of the

Labour councillors didn't turn up. The Trades & Labour Council took serious note of this and expelled Councillor Rudd and threatened others if they failed to carry out decisions of the Vigilance Committee. The third occasion that it came up, he was elected.

4 Other Industries

Chemical Works

It's difficult to find out a lot about the chemical works in St Helens, because anyone who worked in them for long has been dead for decades. In fact, during the 1920s all the works were being transferred from St Helens to Widnes, five miles away on the Mersey. In 1921, there were only about 500 chemical workers left in St Helens.

This is why the main account is one written by the Alkali Union reporting on conditions at the turn of the century. Although it is referring to the work a generation before it left the town, the processes and conditions did not change much, as can be gathered from the brief account of someone who worked there for a few months as a youth.

THE ALKALI UNION REPORT (WHICH REFUSED TO NAME THE WORKS CONCERNED)

Imagine a huge barrel of brick and iron, some 12 or 14 ft in diameter, and 20 ft long, raised above the ground and trundling round and round, while the flames from a furnace built at one end roar through it, and light streams out at every cranny. The little engine beside it stopped, and the revolver was brought to a standstill; some of the workmen mounting a scaffolding opened the manhole. Then the furnace was slowly turned again to bring the manhole underneath, and a torrent of white-hot lava rushed into iron trucks. Passing on, we came to the salt-cake furnaces, where the men were hard at work, but here the fumes of acid were so powerful that we hastened away, coughing and choking.

Here are the slaves of St Helens, labouring through the night. Men naked to the waist, their faces wrapped up to the eyes in cloths, move to and from like restless demons in the fiery light; wielding long and cumbrous iron rakes, they sweat, and labour at the glowing mass in the furnace. The tools are so heavy you can hardly lift them, the heat so intense that standing far off you can't face the glare. But the furnace man must approach close to the door and gaze steadily into the white-hot mass. Too high or too low a temperature, too short or too long an exposure to the heat of the furnace, and the batch is spoiled. With the sweat pouring off him, exposed to the cold night air, he has to exercise the finest skill.

Salt is the grand ingredient of the alkali works. We saw how it was fed into the salt-cake furnaces where, with the help of sulphuric acid, the hydrochloric acid gas from which the horrible chlorine is afterwards to be extracted was liberated, and sulphate of soda, or salt-cake, remained.

The salt-cake men, as they are called, who have the handling of this process, are carefully selected for their strength and skill. I have met and talked with several of them since I have been in St Helens, and for physique I don't know that you could beat them anywhere. Their work is of such intensity that only the finest powers of endurance can bear up against it. They work with rags or chunks of flannel between their teeth in the hand-to-hand struggle with the flames and gas.

The gas given off cuts into their arms and rots their teeth. Most salt-cake men have teeth as black as coal. Their mouths go extremely tender. 'I've only been six years at it,' said one of them to me, 'and I had as fine a set of teeth as any man when I went into the work. Look at them now.' There was a thin black ridge, from which every atom of enamel had been worn, left of the fine set. At the pace they were going, they would soon be worn level with the gums. 'Frank wears a piece of rubber round his pipe – he can't hold it in his mouth without, for the pain. To see him eating spuds – he takes 'em like Beecham pills.' They also begin to suffer from chest complaints with deadly certainty after they have been some time at the work.

Lime is the principal ingredient out of which the bleaching powder is made. Before it goes to the chlorine chambers, where it is to absorb the gas, it is carefully treated and reduced to a fine powder. It is sifted and beaten about and slaked, and the men who have to do this work have a job which no-one would need envy. Fancy working all day or all night, as the case may be, in a fine mist of lime – lime particles about like a cloud of mosquitoes, with a far sharper bite, too. To protect themselves, the men resort to a muzzle, or a piece of rag or flannel held tightly between the teeth. The exposed parts of the skin are carefully greased, and a sort of paper mask is frequently improvised in addition to the cap. In spite of everything, the lime gets in somewhere and inflicts its bite. All the time the work is carried on, breathing is a terrible effort. To breathe through the nose would have the direst consequences. A single inhalation, and

78

the lime particles would lodge there. So the air has to be inhaled through the muzzle and given out through the nose. Naturally, nose-bleeding is a frequent complaint in the works. Twenty minutes at a spell is as much as a man can stand; after that, he goes out to recover himself, and lay in a little air for his inside and some grease for outside lining. These lime men are not able to wash: they shun water as other people shun fire. The only wash they sometimes get for months together is in the grease.

When the lime man has finished his part of the job, and the lime is sprinkled to a depth of some 2 in. over the floor of the chlorine chamber, and raked lightly over, so that the gas shall have access to as large a surface area as possible, the doors are shut, the cracks stopped up with clay and an opening is made to admit the chlorine. It streams in, and through the glass which is let into the door you can see the invasion of the green gas. A long period has to elapse before the lime has drunk its fill and become bleaching powder of the requisite strength.

The duties of the powder packer consist of filling casks with the bleaching powder. To do this, he has to enter the chamber which for several days has been charged with the chlorine gas. Though the worst of the gas has been allowed to pass out of the chamber before the packer enters it, the atmosphere is still charged with the deadly fumes. The heat is something tremendous, especially as the poor wretch who has to endure it is swathed about the head in a way that would protect him from arctic cold.

CHEMICAL WORKER WHO AFTERWARDS BECAME A TRAM MECHANIC, BORN 1897
I got to Greenbank chemical works. There was a place called the lye house for filling tins with caustic soda. They'd started closing the chemical yards down from just before the war. When I went there I got about 12s 6d to 13s. I had two sisters, an uncle and a brother all working there, filling caustic soda tins and bleach.

You've seen these chaps on the moon. That's what you looked like. You had clogs on, and spats over your laceholes to keep the chlorine out. It turned your stockings green. You had sacking like lagging to go over your legs, tied on with string. They gave you calico to make a calico jacket, but you had to get it made up at your own expense. It was supposed to protect your clothing. When it got damp it let stuff through. You had another sack at the bottom of your calico jacket. Then you had a calico hood round your head, and a muzzle. They gave you a flannel, you wetted it, flooded it till it was as thick as your finger and tied it round your chin. Then you had goggles on to do the bleaching. This chlorine gas would get

79

in your throat and your eyes. You'd get a cough – that used to be called getting slugged. It could have a permanent effect for anyone with asthma or a bad chest.

Filling caustic was a woman's job. They had protective clothing. The first morning I went there, we passed these women carrying trays of bleach. The man with me said, 'Do you know who you've just passed?' I said, 'I don't.' It was my sister. She looked like a spaceman. She worked in the box room, where they packed the powder for going to Bombay and up and down the world. They had tins – small Nescafé size – you put a spoon in each and filled them with bleach. They went to soldiers in France to sterilize the water.

You never saw managers in the chemical yards. Once, one came round and watched women packing powder and he said to the boss at the lye house, 'I'm just watching those women. That one there is doing three times more than that one. Give her half a crown a week more.' It was all left to the boss at the lye house. You couldn't negotiate a wage through the union. Everyone was dealt with individually.

THE MINER FROM LEA GREEN, BORN 1895
There were three chemical works at Peasley Cross. The workers there were poisoned – none are alive now. It was worse than the pits – it made all their faces green. One family across the road all worked there – all big men, but they never lived so long. The chemical companies made so much money, they had to do something for the people. They built the hospital – the wards are named after the firms: Campbells, Kurtz ward, McKechnie's ward. No wonder they built the wards – half their workers died in there.

Beechams

WOMAN PERSONNEL OFFICER IN THE FACTORY
Beechams started with a hundred girls. It was only in its infancy then. They used to employ men, but in 1914 we started girls because the war came. In the beginning, it was just Beechams' Pills. There were two kinds of pill: the ones we call patents, and the others were cough. The patents they built their business up with. Cough pills were very popular but they were just a side line. Everything was hand-made; it was at a later date that machinery was brought in. The laboratory did all the mixing.

The girls were just packing. Mind you, they had a very responsible job because when the boxes were filled in those days we paid a medicine

80

duty, and on every box there had to be a government stamp. The girls had to take great care putting that stamp on, because it was worth threepence or a shilling, and if they tore one, they had lost the money. It was against them if they tore any – they were considered careless – but they were very good workers (not like they are now) and they were very careful not to tear these stamps. That was government money.

You didn't have girls in the labs – our managing director would think they would be poisoned. He didn't like girls. The government said, 'You must have girls and let the men go to the war.' He didn't want them, so there'd be a row every time he saw them: 'What's that girl doing?' He couldn't bear the sight of them – he didn't think it was nice for girls to be in a place like that.

Parents were keen for the girls to come in because it was a very respectable factory. We went round the schools. I used to ring up the headmistress or headmaster: 'Can we come in and see if you've got any suitable girls?'

'Oh, you certainly can, we're only too pleased for girls to come into your place.'

I'd go down to see them: 'Come in time for tea. You'll be able to see our girls work.' I would sit down to afternoon tea. All the girls paraded in front of me so I could pick the best ones. If I wished, I could talk to them.

Why was Beechams such a respectable factory? In the first place, the Beechams were a well-established family. Sir Joseph was the founder. He became an alderman in the town, then he became mayor twice. So it was considered it must be a good factory because it was his. It was specially good for girls because there was not much other work. These girls were the cream of St Helens. There was no doubt about that. Mrs Thorpe in higher grade would say, 'That's a very good girl. She's sharp at figures, she'd do at the office.' They all had good reputations insofar as they didn't steal. The teacher wouldn't recommend a girl who didn't want to come, but they were anxious to come because it was a nice factory.

It was spacious and very, very clean. Did you know that? Of course, business ebbs and flows. This is what happened when we weren't very busy: I would find them some cleaning to do. I used to say to every girl, 'Once you get into this factory it's like a home, and I want you to treat it as such.' They'd clean anything – I didn't have to put up a fight for them to do anything. I'd just say, 'Go and get the polisher,' and the door handles would be wonderfully clean.

I wouldn't have them in if they made bother. The union man used to come, and he was the leader. He always had kid gloves on. I used to say to him, 'One of these days, when you walk in here with your kid gloves on, you'll get a job.' He said to me, 'Who'll give it to me?'

'Me. You've been in here so often and you know the place so well we'll give you a chance.' He used to come in talking and trying to get his union in, but he never managed it. Now they've got various unions.

I used to go in for a rise for the girls. Our manager used to say, 'We're here to make money, not to give it away.' I said the people had worked for it and deserved it, but they said they were building the business. Pilkingtons was no better. We talked about it among ourselves, then they'd say, 'Do you think they'll consider us?' for whatever it was. They were very grudging about giving money.

It was a family atmosphere and a family firm. Everybody knew me. I knew all the girls' families and talked to them all. Today, I know the background of all the families – but it is no laughing matter. It's a psychological matter. I knew what I was going to get from each girl. I just knew, and some of them I didn't even have to look at. It's a very enjoyable factory when you can get good relationships, when you know your people.

One time, Mr Henry Beecham put up for Labour on the council, and of course he had to make speeches on the platform. At the meeting, someone in the audience – a man – shouted: 'You want to give them decent wages before you start on this.' Someone else shouted, 'There's one thing about it – they never send them home. They find them something to do, even if it's scrubbing the floor.' He didn't get in, because the people in those days weren't in favour of having money in power. He was a gentleman, and we liked him very much indeed. He was very pleased that it was appreciated that he never sent the girls home.

Pilkingtons is truly a family business. They had the same relationship in their factory as we did. You can go to the YMCA, if you're eligible, for dinner, sit down at the table and in half a tick hear, 'Hello Jack,' and it's Lord Pilkington. 'Do you come every day? Pleased to see you. Are you having your dinner here? Oh, good. I'll have mine too.' The two families were more like competitors; they weren't friends. They had different points of view. While the Pilkingtons were philanthropic, the Beechams were show people. They've always been show people. When he was mayor, Sir Joseph caused quite a sensation. His three daughters' dresses were printed with music right across – Mendelssohn and other musicians. They were painted by their chaperone with chords out of the book. It was unique.

82

Have you ever been inside Beechams? The front entrance under the tower has got a mosaic floor and it's got a very fine mahogany staircase. Sir Joseph had them put in. It's a beautiful entrance and, lo and behold, when the new manager came in, he said, 'Can we have a carpet?' That's mosaic work done by the Italians, and it mustn't be touched. These new people have got no values. We had a beautiful bust of the founder. Last time I was in, they'd thrown that out. We used to have a piece of sculpture of two girls sitting by the seaside. One of them has cupped her ear with her hand to hear what the other is saying. She's asking, 'What are the wild waves saying?' The other answers, 'Take Beechams pills.' It was splendid. These people have got no idea of beauty, no idea whatever. It was a beautiful piece of sculpture – the girls sitting on a rock – typical of a seaside scene. They took all the Turner pictures – the manager's office was covered with them. Sir Joseph was a connoisseur of art, and he bought a lot of Turners – he had some beautiful specimens. We appreciated them because we were artistic, being with the family.

The Munitions Factory

FEMALE MUNITIONS WORKER, ACTIVE IN THE LABOUR PARTY, BORN 1895

I went down to Sutton Bond 1201 ammunitions factory in World War I. It was awful really. My first job was nailing lids on the boxes in which there were shells. They were stored at the Bond and painted. Then they went to another factory, where they were filled with gunpowder. After a month, I said to my husband, 'Look, there are some awful conditions there. What are we going to do about it?' He said I should see the Welfare Officer. I'd never heard of one, but I went and found a lady. I said I thought the girls were working under intolerable conditions, and would they give us some protection, as the girls were working out in the rain. But nothing happened. I went down to Mr Anders, who was from the Union which became the General & Municipal Workers and lived down in Sutton. I asked would he do anything. 'My word, you're just the lady I've been looking for,' he said. 'We've never been able to get anyone in the Bond interested.'

He called a meeting and we got the union going. We paid fourpence a week to this union. All the girls but two joined. I collected the fourpences. I used to go round the Bond in my lunch hour, because I wasn't supposed to do it. Some girls who saw me coming used to hide behind the boxes: 'Oh, here she comes, she's going to take our money.' There were two other girls besides me – Miss Flood and Miss Makin. The three of us went round and deliberately collected – we wouldn't have got it all, otherwise.

We got a canteen going. And we got girls working so if it was wet we had some protection in a staging. We got some terrifically large shells – twenty-four inchers – so heavy we used to put them in a truck. Some of the men got behind the truck to help push it up. I protested against this, it was no work for women. I went and said, 'This heavy shell business – I'm not stacking any more shells.' We didn't have to do it any more, so we just stacked ten pounders. They were made of steel and covered with grease to stop them getting rusty. We had to get the grease off and paint them a khaki colour. Then they were stacked, and you waited for a railway wagon, and off they went to be filled.

It was Easter time, and they were starting the offensive. We had to get out I don't know how many shells a week. When the long push started, we worked all day and all night without any sleep. We did that three times through the weekend. I'll never forget it. You could hardly keep your eyes open. We had a man named O'Brien in charge. We had to stack the 6-in. shells seven high. But he was making us stack them higher than this. I went to see the gentleman – the girls were complaining about the height they had to stack them. It was too high for women. 'Oh, I'll send the lot of you home,' he said. 'I don't mind if you do,' I said – we were so tired. We got him sacked.

Then, of course, the war ended. The union complimented me – they said I had got more women in the union than anyone else. I couldn't tell you how many, but there were hundreds. We did a good job of work. The works closed down.

The Brickworks

TWO WOMEN FROM SUTTON HEATH, BORN IN THE 1900S

You started by trucking off – going out with the barrows to the layers-down, barrows full of wet bricks. You began that at 16, and eventually you'd work your way up. My sister was laying down. She used to get the bricks in threes and put them in the sheds on iron plates with steam underneath to dry them out. There was some steam on when you were working, but even more when you were off. I did all sorts there, lovey. I cleaned in the office, I barrow-filled for the men taking the bricks to the kiln, 50 to the barrow.

84

Eventually, I was put on the table filling the barrow with wet bricks. One person used to pull a handle and cut the bricks with a wire frame – that was ten in a column. You used to put four pallets of ten bricks on a truck with two legs and two wheels. One person was each side lifting the pallet – a good 80 lb – off the table.

Then I went from the table to the die. You fed the shale into the grinder, and it went up into the mixer, then into the pug. There used to be a lady on the pug, pushing it down as it was mixed with two sets of knives. It was put through two columns and came out in two dies, one on either side. The dier had to break it off into what she thought would make ten bricks. If it was too much, the little bit at the end would go back into the pug. Sometimes, if the clay was bad, they would come out all cracked, and you'd have to throw as much as you could lift back into the pug.

The wages were £1 and coppers – that was for trucking. Layers-down got 24s. Die minders and pug minders got 38s a week – we were the highest paid women. We used to sing and we used to shout – all the old songs. At the time, we enjoyed it, although many times we'd argue: 'It's not my barrow, it's yours!' – that sort of thing. We used to help each other out if the clay was bad. We'd always have the place ready for morning in our own time. At night, you'd get a barrow and sweep and shovel up all the clay and take it back to the mill. You had to have your lunch when you could. You'd take a bite and many times you'd throw it away because it was all full of dust.

We used to be on short time when times were bad. We all had lovely polished clogs, and shawls. One time when we went to the Labour Exchange, we all sat down. Mr Bell, the supervisor, came and sprayed us with something out of a tin. The clogs made a noise – you couldn't help it on those stone steps – it must have been that that annoyed him. They tried many times to get a union – we paid, and it cracked up and your money's gone for a burton, hasn't it? It was the General & Municipal Workers, I think. People wouldn't be bothered paying – the union never got a proper hold. Plenty came for a few years, then they'd get married. Equal pay? You didn't think about it in those days – there was no Women's Lib then. After all, a man's a man, and he has to keep his family.

MAN WHO WORKED AT GREENBANK, BORN 1910
I started work at 14. This job was got me at Pilkingtons, at 12s 4d a week. As the manager was taking me in, a boy came out who had his shoulder

terribly cut, and there was blood everywhere. I was taken to where there was this broken glass tube, and I said, 'Hey! This is where that boy was cut. Thank you very much. I'm not having that.' I picked up my jacket and walked out. That's the shortest time anyone's ever had at Pilkingtons – five minutes in and out. I walked up the road and stood at the gate of the brickworks. The manager called me and asked what I wanted. I said I wanted a job. There was a boy wheeling barrows of slack up a gantry to the top of the kiln. He said, 'Can you do that?' I said I could do it with the boy in it. 'You seem to think a lot of yourself,' he said. 'Let's see you do it.' So I took a barrow of slack up the gantry. It was easy. When I came down, I said, 'I hope I'm getting paid for this. I'm not doing trials for nothing.' He said, 'Don't worry, you'll get paid. When do you want to start?' I said, 'Now.' That was because I didn't want to go back home saying I'd walked out of the job at Pilkingtons, as the old chap would have beaten me about the place. So I started work at the brickworks at 17s 1d a week. And I didn't tell the old chap. I gave him 12s 4d a week and he gave me 2s pocket money. I was keeping 5s a week, and I was as rich as Baron Rothschild. After about six months. I told him I'd finished that job at Pilkingtons and got a better one.

We had to wheel 80 to 100 barrows a day and got 17s 1d for a 48-hour week. Boys were doing that up to the age of 16. Then they put you on setting or drawing – setting bricks ready for burning or drawing the bricks out of the kilns for 24s a week. The bricks for setting weighed $10\frac{1}{2}$–11 lb and when drawn 8 lb. The bricks from St Helens are ten times better than from elsewhere. London brick is made of clay; it only weighs $3\frac{1}{2}$ lb. The bricks in St Helens, the bricks of this house, are made of shale, and a brick the same size will weigh $7\frac{1}{2}$ or 8 lb. Clay bricks aren't hard, they don't last like these.

The top rate for setting was 1s 1d an hour. The job of placing the bricks so that the fire could penetrate them was called semi-skilled. You went to the sheds where the bricks were steam dried overnight. If you were setting, you had to take eight barrows an hour, and it was double that, really, because you had to load them and unload them. You might have to run them 20 yards, you might even have to go 100, but you still had to do eight barrows an hour, that's 400 bricks, and if you didn't, that was it – you were sent down the road. And if you tipped two barrows over in the same day, you were out, too.

There were three sets of kilns, with 12 chambers in each kiln. They averaged a chamber a day. They'd empty one, fill one and burn one. If

86

nothing was coming out of the quarries, they'd dampen the kiln down and wait for more bricks. If it was raining, the quarrymen used to come out, they couldn't fill the bogies. If the wagons were in when it rained, the boss got them loaded. Then we were sent home and only got 1s for that hour's work. But they made us come back at one o'clock even if it was still raining. If you didn't come back at one, you were told not to come back next day. In winter, I've come home with as little as 18s a week. If you did three days' work, you'd get three days' dole, which was 7s 6d. But if you did four days' work, you got no dole. Even if it was only three days and Saturday morning, you still couldn't get dole.

The kilns were very hot, and at times you couldn't go in without some headgear, or your hair and eyebrows would get burned. You had to wear leather grips, just a strip of leather across your fingers and two bits on your thumbs. All brickyard workers knew what work was. There were no canteens and no lunch time, only dinner from twelve till one. If you were caught having lunch, you were sent home.

I can't say I wasn't happy on the job. I really loved my work. The best fellow I met was the one that came to a sad end – Mr Robert Heaton. He was the son of the original owner. For me, he was down to earth. If you didn't work, he'd tell you – that was why most of the men didn't like him – but if you pulled your weight, you knew where you were with him. He really understood about bricks. If he'd been alive, the brickyard would still be in St Helens. He wasn't afraid of taking his jacket off and getting stuck in himself. For the position he held, I thought he was 100% worker.

I did 47 years for them. I never clocked in late, I never had a turn off on my own accord, and they gave me a bottle of Celebration Cream sherry at the end of it. I got that because I'd done 47 years. The other men got nothing. I could have gone back and smashed it over their heads. The blokes that sorted me out, all three, are dead. They got my wish.

The Brewery

WORKER AT GREENALL WHITLEYS, BORN *c.* 1902

In the brewery the day turn used to be on at six in the morning. You had to get the malt out, which came in hundredweight sacks, and put it in the dissolving tanks. You got a dipstick out which stated the quantity of water that was wanted to dissolve the malt in. When you got that quantity you let them know on the mash tuns where the malt is left. The mixture is pumped up to the coppers, where they used to put the malt and hops to boil. There were three copper boilers altogether – the biggest one held 500 barrels.

When they're satisfied they've got enough hops, they shut that manhole and put the steam on to get it to a certain heat for boiling the brew. They're supposed to boil it just over an hour, but sometimes you were waiting for empty vessels, so you had to boil it longer. There were only two of us there, so you couldn't go away and leave it.

Hundreds of barrels a day had to be boiled within two and a half degrees on the heat. You took samples, and when you were satisfied, you'd stop the steam off and pour all the hops into the hop-backs. The farmers got all the spent hops – there's no strength in them at all. They were left overnight, and had to be shovelled down with spades into the transport.

The mixture is boiled upstairs and it then goes down into what they call a receiver, and from there it's pumped through a cooling process to get it down to a certain temperature. The yeast goes in as they run it from the receiver. It goes into the vessel in the fermenting room at 70°F or something like that. While it's fermenting for a week, it's roused every few hours. When it's mixed up the yeast is got working.

There's a certain gravity to work to in the beer. Once they get it to the gravity they want, you can't do anything till the excise officers come along and check it – what they call the declaration. You put more malt in for higher gravities. On the job, if you got it wrong, there'd be an enquiry about it. If it was too high, they'd break it down with boiling water to make sure it was the right gravity that they're tied down to.

I got a job in the brewery in what they call cleaning the vats – most people started with cleaning. It was repetition work – just do the job till it's done. We used sand and mixed it up with vitriol, you'd get the copper boilers which they boiled the beer in shined up – and they had to be cleaned inside. After a brew of beer had been let into the fermenting vessels, we had to have the coppers ready for the next day. Everything had to be cleaned and sterilized with hot water. I worked through every floor till I got to the brewing department.

The beer was all right – they had different strengths. They don't brew any stout now – it's only bitter and mild. We used to get beer free at half past ten and half past two in the afternoon. The chap dished it out in the cellar. You'd have to take a can with you. Two pints a day, that's what it used to be. One chap got sacked for pinching it – they were very keen on that.

88

5 Transport

The Sankey Canal

MAN FROM THATTO HEATH WHO WORKED ON CANAL MAINTENANCE, BORN
c. 1901

When I was demobbed in 1920, I was a labourer on the maintenance of the Sankey canal which went from St Helens to Sankey Bridges, and then another three or four miles on to Widnes. It belonged to the North Western Railway, which later became the London Midland & Scottish. There were ten locks, including two double locks. At St Helens, there are three branches – one goes to Blackbrook, one to Ravenhead and one to Gerard's Bridge. The only traffic in those days was United Alkali and the horse-drawn sugar boats up to Sankey sugarworks at Earlstown. The United Alkali were lighter boats and they had sails. They went down to Liverpool to get a cargo off the big boats. We used to go working at Garston, as Garston docks and the canal were under one lease. The slate boats came up twice a year to Warrington. They sailed up the Welsh coast.

Half past seven till five o'clock our hours were. We travelled in the company's time, which was very rare. When there were only six men left, they changed it, and they had to travel in their own time after all that. We did half days on Saturdays and got 39s 11d a week. We said, 'Give us the penny and make it two pound notes in our pockets.' But they wouldn't. I enjoyed every minute of it. We enjoyed life altogether and brought six kids up on it. It's how you look at life.

Sometimes we were building side walls. We had to pull the materials up on a barge ourselves. We had a workshop at Winnock Junction. They had built a dry dock to repair boats. The carpenters did this job – there was one boat carpenter, two joiners, one storekeeper, a blacksmith, a sawyer, (he'll be dead and gone now, Jack will, gone to the land of nod) and a foreman. We used to help them carry timber to the dock.

Say the canal bank was broken, we used to drive wooden piles in – they were called stanks. We used clay to stop the water getting out. All canals

89

are lined with clay. We made a double stank and put the clay between. Ashes were used for cindering the bank. We pulled our materials in the boat. We might have been going to Widnes or St Helens. It could take two or three days. We used to load the ashes to repair the canal banks from Globe chemical works. We tied the boat up at night on the way and caught the train back home for the night. Then we'd sign on at the bottom of Church Street at half past seven in the morning. We travelled free on the train, and then we might have a couple of miles to walk to our boat. It would be two and half miles to Bewsey. It kept us fit. We carried a basket and a can under the arm – a can of tea and a basinful of hot-pot. We had a little cabin in the boat – rough seating and an iron stove – not like boats you see in magazines now.

There were four of us pulling the boat on a long rope. It's what's called bow-hauling. You tied the bow to the tow rope. It was like walking in a sling. You used to saunter along. You'd start off the boat from the canal bank. The captain would push off with a pole. The speed of the boat was called the way – a chap would say 'We've got a good way on it.' We had all the time in the world – they didn't worry about speed. Now they're all in a hurry, that's why they go awkward. It got done just the same.

They had two steam dredgers. One used to load the boat, then we used to lug it along and take it to the other dredger to dump the load in hollow ground by the side of the canal. The weeds here took possession and you wouldn't know where the tips were now.

The canal was full of waterlilies and rushes and all sorts of wildfowl – ducks, kingfishers – you'd hardly credit it. There were water-voles – some call them water-rats, but they're voles. I've seen 20 swans at a time, shelduck, anything you could care to mention. That was a big marsh from Widnes to Warrington, mostly occupied by cattle. It's now the site of a nuclear generating station. There was the canal, the river and the Manchester ship canal. I brought a few eels home and all, out of the ditches, nice too! I've had a few ducks – fellows used to be out shooting and they'd give you one. Lord Lilford [a leading authority on birds] owned a place by Bewsey where they went pheasant shooting in the season. I've had a pheasant of his, too, a wounded one that dropped right by the canal. Now it's all built up. Some parts of the canal are filled in, different portions of it. That's why I don't think you could open it again.

One time, before I was there, it was polluted by the chemical works. Where the pollution comes from now, I don't know. At Gerard's Bridge,

Munitions production during World War I.

Above: The Sankey Canal. *Below:* Aerial photograph of industrial wasteland, with dumpings from the chemical works, 1929. Canal Street is in the background.

there used to be sewage. They built a sewage tank for the corporation. That's all gone. The locks are in a terrible state. The gates are left on Newton Common, that's the only one left.

I fell in a few times off the boats. I always wore clogs. I was running along and slipped out, over the gunwales. I fell in the day before I got married. My mate said, 'That's a bad omen, you'll have to give it a miss, Tom.' You had to go down to the cabin and do the best you could to dry yourself out. I fell into Garston Dock. It was all sludge at the bottom. You couldn't take it to the washeteria. Fancy enjoying a job like that! I think it was the country life – and especially being interested in wild life and that sort of thing.

We didn't have concrete mixers, even at Garston Dock. We had ten men to a stage, five each side doing alternate wet and dry. You'd unload the sand and cement in a dry state and make it into a five to one mixture – five of gravel to one of cement. The first two men turn the dry portion and then you gradually wet it as you went along. By the last two, you had it mixed. We used to do it like that so you wouldn't be mixing the wet cement all the time which was the heaviest. You went from dry to wet and then started again on dry. We used to do 80 mixings a day. That's the one and only time we got extra money. I went to the transport workers' official and asked him, 'Can't we be affiliated to your union while we're in the docks?' I asked him to get us put on dockers' rates. We got £5 a week instead of £2. I could give the kids extra and the wife extra.

I had to leave the canal on doctor's orders. He said something about TB and took a phlegm sample away. It came back negative but by that time I'd gone.

The railway's object when they first bought the canal was to close it. They bought quite a lot to get the freight on the railways, then they let them run down. They were dying when I first started, slowly, gradually. They could be useful now – it's such a shame to close them. The Sankey could carry anything up to 80–100 tons. A wonderful engineer built it, Edward Berry, and he's buried in the town.

I was re-employed in the traffic department, I did all the bag of tricks: parcel carrying, carriage shunting, ticket collecting, portering, working as a platform foreman. You name it, I've done it. At Shaw Street, there would be three porters each turn, foreman, shunter, two ticket collectors, four booking clerks, three parcel clerks, the station boss and his clerk, three signalmen on each of two boxes, three motor drivers and parcel men, and one horse driver. I was spare motor driver—if anyone failed to turn up I used to go on the van.

It was a big shunting yard for all the glass traffic for Pilkingtons and the chemical works. It was also a marshalling yard. All the stuff from surrounding districts used to go to Ravenhead on the way to London, Liverpool, Carlisle and the Scottish traffic. It was made up into trains in the marshalling yard – most towns had a marshalling yard. Nearly all firms had a siding into their works. The works engines brought their goods out. We only did Pilkingtons Ravenhead works with our engine, and there was anything up to 30 wagons in the morning. We did that three times a day. All that's gone, now, with motor traffic and Dr Beeching. They could do with the railways now.

The feeling of most of our chaps was that the union could have done more. No one seemed to have much interest. We had to fight for every rise we got. There were too many grades on the railway: there were umpteen of them. The bottom grade got nothing much – there was a big disparity between top and bottom. If you wanted promotion, you had to go away to Warrington or somewhere, and you had to get there yourself. They wouldn't give you a pass, even though you were working on the railways.

The Railway Company

Of course, the railways were a vastly larger concern than they are today. In 1921, there were still 2,000 railway workers in St Helens. Almost all the freight that now goes by road would have been handled by the railway company – in this case London & North Western, which had its stores in St Helens. The accounts concentrate on the jobs which just aren't necessary on the railways now, but were then.

SECRETARY OF THE SUTTON NUR BRANCH, BORN 1894
I started work on the London & North Western Railway in the sheeting store. They used to make the tarpaulin sheets for the railway wagons and the carts that used to go about the streets, and the horse cloths and rugs they used to put on them at night. There were no motors in those days.

The place was built in the 1860s. When London & North Western was formed, it took over St Helens Railway in 1859. There's still a clock at the station with St Helens Railway written on it. They had the girls making sheets out of hessian upstairs on the sewing machines. Then they used to send the sheets to what they called the dressing shop. A big machine used to dress the sheets with boiled linseed oil and black paint mixed up – black dressing, it was called. They were put in a big tank and stirred. Then, there was green dressing for cart sheets. There were six marking gangs of boys – one man to five lads. They used to mark each sheet LNW and a number. When the sheets had been hung up and dried, they were sent to various goods yards – some went to Pilkingtons.

It was a big place because, besides all that work being done, there was a general stores there – all the stuff was distributed from there. Everything they needed on the stations used to be distributed once a month. There were six different journeys for the store trains.

I started in 1908 and finished when I was 65 in 1959. The lads used to start there working in marking gangs, then they could go up to sheet repairing. Men used to overhaul the sheets when they came in. They had rings all round them, about 6 or 7 in. apart, and a rope on for men to tie them down on the wagons. They were hung up and men called overhaulers used to stand behind them in the dark, to mark where they needed patches and repairs. Then we were the sheet repairers – you'd open the sheet out on the floor and sit down cross legged to sew on patches with a needle. It was a skilled job. You couldn't see the needle going, you were that quick. You had a sailmaker's patch issued you when you started, and that wore out in time with it rubbing on the hessian. They were all women sat down on the floor when I came back from the services in 1918. My wife did it. The only men there were old chaps.

During that time, I was in the NUR. I was on the committee, and eventually became the branch secretary. The ASLEF was for drivers and firemen. Now, the NUR catered for everyone outside that: guards, porters and that. Just the foremen and some of the clerks were in the clerks' association. Jimmy Thomas was a funny chap, you know. He was pretty fair, but he had a very rough time because the NUR was in its beginnings. The job was getting these men in the union. When I first started, there were only 30 or 40. We talked to the people we were working with, and we used to give them a form to fill in. There were some awkward folk. It wasn't not wanting to be in, but it was paying the 6d a week subscription. It got to industrial action – there was a strike over it, one time. Like at our place, if a fellow was working there and wouldn't join, the job he was on was stopped until he was taken off. It came to this: if he wouldn't be in, the management would have nothing else to do but tell him to finish. It got that it was the recognized thing: 'You're getting concessions, extra pay, and you're not doing anything else for it.' That was the big argument against you, you see.

The bosses used to stand on the balcony to spy on you, and if you weren't working, they were down on you in two minutes. When I'd been to the toilet once, the boss started getting at me because I was one of the big union men, asking me what I was doing away from work, I went off the deep end. 'I've been in the trenches for you,' I said, 'and I'm not coming back to be bossed around by you.' I choked him up. He never dared say anything to me again – he was one of those under-strappers, he'd never been in the forces.

You started work at six in the morning. You'd get your check at the door, that's your number, that's what you were known by. At quarter past eight, you went home or to the mess room to have breakfast. You had to be back on the job at nine o'clock, and then you worked till you were off from one till two for dinner, and again from two till half past five. If you were five minutes late, you had a quarter of an hour off your wages. If you were half an hour late, you couldn't go in till nine o'clock, after breakfast. You had no holidays – at Easter time, we finished on Thursday and went back on Tuesday, and that week I'd bring home as little as a pound to keep the house on. We worked overtime in the summer. That was the time the sheets weren't needed on the trucks. So we stayed on till eight at night, then started again at six. Men came in from St Helens on the trams, and they'd have to leave home at five o'clock. There was no time for yourself. It was a bad time for the working class.

We had a railway strike of our own in 1919. A lot of railwaymen were exempted from the forces, but in any job that women could do, the men had to go. When all the young fellows came back, we decided we weren't having these conditions any more. We'd done our bit for the country and we wanted better conditions. The slogan was: Eight bob a day and eight hours a day. A committee of representatives of each branch used to co-ordinate efforts and bring speakers. There were big meetings and demonstrations and marches through the town centre. It only lasted about a week. We went back to work from eight to twelve, and one till half past five.

Then they started the piecework system. Of course, that resulted in men being sacked – you did more, and that resulted in a lot of redundancies. It was so much for a yard of sewing – 6s 8d for a 100 yards. You couldn't have done it if it was all straight sewing. If you got sheets with little to be done, you'd do better. Three darns counted as one yard, and you could get three darns done far more quickly than a yard of straight sewing. Mind you, when you put a darn in you had to make it waterproof.

94

When you had finished, you had to black it over with dabs. But sometimes you'd get a sheet in which needed a patch as big as our kitchen, and you were supposed to do three stitches to the inch. The checkers came round all the time. You used to work up to being a checker as you worked up your service. He had to make a guess at what the dabs would be paid at – it used to be a bit of an arrangement between you and the checker. We used to get through it pretty well.

SIGNALMAN, BORN 1900

After the war, I came back as a porter at Thatto Heath. The first train of the day was the 6.15 a.m. You had to be up to book the tickets for the workmen going to work at Wigan or Prescot. There were loads of people – Prescot had the wireworks, and over 100 would get a weekly ticket for 1s 6d. It was a busy station, there was no doubt about it. You'd get workmen going to Liverpool – there was no other form of going there in those days. I should think we had somewhere around 20 or 30 a day going there.

That was the passenger work. The porter had to clean the signal lamps. They were oil – no electric – keep electricity out of it. The porter was responsible for delivering parcels and keeping the railway tidy. Parcels used to come by train for the businessmen around the area and we had to take them to the shops around the village. Of course we used to get a copper or two – we knew who was a good tip. The railways ran a competition for the cleanest and neatest station. And Thatto Heath won the first prize for the best-kept station. There was another porter besides myself and the stationmaster to keep it tidy. At the edge of each platform, we had a bank of flowers. We were on at six and used to do till three o'clock in the afternoon, or we'd come at half past two and then we were on till 11.15 after the last train.

The porter was your first grade – then you graduated to what you wanted to do – a signalman, a shunter or a goods guard, but not a locoman. To be a locoman you had to start in the engine sheds. I chose to be a signalman – I thought it was an interesting job. I used to go in the signal box at Thatto Heath when I could while I was a porter, and I finished up working in one myself. My first job was on a little shunting box in St Helens. From there I went to a signal box called Pilkington's sidings. It was used for Pilkingtons works traffic. It wasn't a busy line for traffic – that line went up to Rainford on the Lancashire and Yorkshire railway. That was a different company. I went from Pilkingtons to Wigan No. 3.

95

Signalmen go according to the class of their box. The lowest class was class 5, then there was 4, a goods box – they didn't deal with passenger trains. They were classed on the amount of work done, the number of movements in 8 hours. That's what you had to go for. The difference in pay was about 5s a week. The bottom class started at about £2 10s a week (goods boxes could have been a bit less). Eventually I came back to St Helens Junction No. 1 box, with 64 levers. The only time you got a vacancy was when a person snuffed it or retired; that moved someone up.

I was in the signal box when you had to pull levers, not press buttons. There were three signal levers for each train – there was the distant signal to tell the driver that if that signal was off he was right through to the next signal box. A driver could pass a distant signal at danger, but that was telling him he'd have to stop at the home signal ahead. If it was a passenger train, you could bring him into the station on the home signal. But the train couldn't leave without the third signal, the starting signal.

You knew the times of all your trains. All trains are passed on by bellrings. Signalmen have 30 or 40 different bell rings to know. Express trains have different rings from other passenger trains. There are various kinds of goods trains with different rings depending on whether they were dispensing goods at different points or whether they were going straight through. You had to be careful if a goods train came between passenger trains. You mustn't delay a passenger train or you're up for trouble – especially if you delayed a mainline express. You knew your timetable.

The Trams

The tram company had passed into public ownership by the 1920s, but the old managers still had a licence to run it. These accounts come from a conductor, born in 1901, and a maintenance man, born in 1897.

MAINTENANCE MAN

They were 100% organized at the tram sheds. They had to be, actually. The men in charge were very dictatorial in their attitude. The chief superintendent, called Kavanagh (a little fellow), was a nasty piece of work. He'd started out as a blackleg during a strike of tram men, so he got promoted. This promotion remained when the council took over the undertaking.

I went to the tram sheds in 1920-21. The union had started getting better conditions by then. When I first got there, the union due was

96

sixpence a week, but at that time they wouldn't allow the union man to collect it – he used to be turned away from the gate, so he'd be waiting in the street or somewhere convenient when the men got paid.

I was asked to work night turn – twelve o'clock to eight. You got no extra pay for it. As the union went on, it got a bit better organized and put in for extra money for working the night turn. There was a Labour council then, as there is now. They gave us an extra penny an hour, but straight away they changed it to working from four o'clock in the morning till dinner time, 12.30, so that they wouldn't give you that penny an hour; they called it a day turn. The union again fought on that, so they had you coming in from six till two, and called it a day turn. Eventually, they ran the night turn from twelve till eight, and you got that penny an hour.

I was interested in my work – I looked after the brakes on the trams and trolleys. The company was the best thing – the men I worked with. There used to be four of us, working in twos, on night turns doing brakes. It was a pleasure going there at nights, and turns flew by. The drivers were coming in by four o'clock.

Even before I was there, tram drivers got 4½d and conductors 4d an hour. What they had was what they'd call a spare list. If you were on it, you went four o'clock and waited to see if anyone missed their time. If they did, you got the job for the day, and when the proper driver came late, he got nothing. He'd have to wait, then perhaps he'd get a turn at dinner time. That would be late finish. But he wouldn't get paid for his time waiting. People on the spare list would stop at the tram sheds overnight so that they'd be the first to get a spare turn in the morning if a driver didn't come. Labour was that cheap then – at Pilks and the chemical yards there were always people standing round the gates. If they wanted anyone, if they saw someone who looked a likely lad, they'd beckon him out. It was slave labour – they say Britons never shall be slaves – they've always been slaves. You just had to stick it – it made you look after your job.

CONDUCTOR

When I started [in 1925], you started as a spare man. You were only guaranteed 32 hours. In summer time, spare men would get 48 hours easily. In winter, they'd go short. There were a few who remembered spare men not getting paid. There was a big turnover. Spare men would come in at twelve at night, look at the rota and find they had to be back for the shift at four. The trams had to start that early to get the colliers to

97

work. Their shifts started at six o'clock and winding began at five. I'd half an hour to walk back to Thatto Heath, and so that meant you sometimes got only three hours' sleep. If you failed to return on duty on time, it was recorded on your crime sheet. The most serious crime on a tram was a missed fare. The first offence was three days' suspension, the second six days, and on the third you were dismissed. The Labour council didn't want to know how things were run. If you didn't turn up for early duty, they never said anything to you. It wasn't till after I'd been sacked that I knew these reports were made.

They were all open trams over a certain height. The conductor had a tiny roofing space – the only other protection was on the stairs going to the upper deck. You'd a stick of tickets – if it rained they stuck together and you were liable to tear them, or give two. If you gave two by mistake, you had to pay the difference. When you left on a duty, there was a tin box with fifties or hundreds in it – so many at 1d, so many at 1½d and so on at a ha'penny a time to 4d on the route up to Prescot. You were expected to know all the various stages: 1½d to Dunriding Lane, 2d to Portico Park, 4d to the King's Head. Those tickets were numbered on two sides, and had a space of ⅛ in. in which you had to punch the number corresponding to the stage where the passenger got on. So an inspector getting on knew where the person should get off. But with the tram joggling and jerking, you could punch it as much in one place as another. If the inspector found it, you were called up the next morning to explain why you'd punched it in the wrong place. If you said the tram juddered, they'd shout at you, 'You're an experienced conductor and you still make mistakes like that?' They went on in a tirade. The fellows said, 'Let him talk. He'll wear himself out, and he'll let you go.' But I wasn't like that – I had to retaliate. 'You can't say that,' I'd say. 'Look here, in any court of enquiry, a person who's asked a question is allowed to answer.' He was stunned, and he had it in for me after that. There was a lot of this bully ragging. He was a Roman Catholic and went easy on some of the other Catholics.

Most of the trams ran on single lines, and you had to wait in a loop to let another one by coming in the opposite direction. Sometimes you'd try to get to the next loop before the other tram came, but they didn't usually try this unless they thought something was holding it up, as if you met in the middle you'd have to go all the way back again. Sometimes, they'd come off the rails, and it was a hell of a job getting them on again. They had wedges and crowbars to try to get them back. The wheels weren't static – they were on bogies – and the trams were a terrific weight, about 20 tons.

THE MAINTENANCE MAN
When you were first taken on at the tram sheds, you had to sign a form to say you were willing to learn driving and conducting. This was in case someone didn't come in in the morning and they needed someone to take the colliers to work. It was a trick, though: if you signed it you never got paid while you were learning. I never signed it. When they asked me to go out, I said I wouldn't as I hadn't signed the form. One day, the manager (his name was Bell) called me. 'About that conducting and driving, have you been out yet?' I said I wasn't doing work for nothing. He said 'I think you'd better finish up then.' I went to the branch secretary, and he told me to write a letter, give one copy to him, and keep a duplicate. He sent it to McLean in Manchester. He said to the manager, 'If he's not reinstated, there's going to be a strike.' The manager told me, 'The decision is that you can have your job back, but you've got to learn to drive.' So I said, 'Fair enough, if I get full pay.' And I got my conditions. I went on conducting, and I was finishing a round from Ashtons Green when there was someone waiting for me: 'Kavanagh wants to see you.' (He was the traffic superintendent.) When I found him, he said he wanted me to go back to my old job. I lost a fortnight's money, but I got full rate for learning. I fought the case for everyone, they all got full rate after that. I won that.

Road Transport
THE TRAM CONDUCTOR
There were no motor cars worth talking about. The only one I knew was the one the doctor used. We always ran out into the road, we never hesitated at the kerb. People did get run over by trams, horse-driven cabs and lorries. It's hard to think now how someone could manage to get run down by a horse doing five miles an hour. They used to be prosecuted for speeding on bicycles going down Croppers Hill.

A DRIVER BORN IN 1894 (WHO STILL HELD A CURRENT LICENCE IN 1975)
When I was demobbed, I don't know how long I didn't get a job, but in October 1919 I started as a steam-wagon driver. With steam engines, you had to keep the fire in and see that you had plenty of water in to be

ready to move off. There were 20–30 tubes in the smoke box leading back to the fire, and the driver had a second man stoking it up. If you didn't keep the water at the right temperature, you were soon in trouble. There was a glass tube alongside the firebox; a water gauge flew up and down. Now, if it got below a certain level in the boiler, it would melt the lead plug. You'd have to stop to put the new plug in – you'd have to put your fire out and put your ashpan underneath to catch it in.

We had a speed limit of 8 m.p.h. and 5 m.p.h. with a trailer. You could have got 12–15 m.p.h. out of it, but you'd have to keep firing it up to maintain the steam. There were only three forward gears and one reverse. You had to stop to change gear – you'd shut your steam valve off. The regulations were that you had to stop for safety's sake. Some gears were more powerful than others, but you could start off in any of them – doing that with a petrol motor, you'd stall.

I drove steam engines from 1919 to '24 or '25. We'll say it was within a ten-mile radius of St Helens, Liverpool to Wigan – you could call it local. I was carrying beer for a brewery – it's not there now – called Barkers of Huyton. We used to have to be at the brewery at eight o'clock, and that meant leaving with the engine at six. I was working for a private haulage firm on contract to the brewery. There were no more than ten or twelve of their pubs in the whole area of Wigan and Ince. The beer was very good, but the roads were damned awful. The landlord would ask you, 'Would you like a drink?' We didn't drink pints, just a wee tot. We'd have an odd glass or a packet of cigarettes. We didn't believe in drinking on the road, though there were no penalties, unless you were incapable.

We had to do all our own loading and unloading, drop the barrels down to the cellar, stillage them [lift them up and make them fast on trestle tables], and then tap them. I just had a second man. We got paid £3 or £3 10s a week. Better wages than most – but the hours! You could get in any time from eight in the evening to one in the morning. You had to stop every so often to pump out of the brook with the hydrant. They stored 50–60 gallons. The more pressure we used, the more water we used.

We broke down very often. It was not the engine's fault. There were two crossed chains under the boiler, one from by the left wheel to the right side of the boiler and one from the right wheel to the left side. When you wanted to turn left, you turned the wheel that way, and the other for right. I always had to carry a spare set of chains. I broke one a week. That was caused by bad streets – if you got a wheel in a pothole, it would jerk and snatch. They only broke in Wigan – it was the worst town in the country for streets. We put a spare chain on, and when we got back home, we used to take it to the blacksmith and get it pierced. You could put one on in a quarter of an hour, especially if you had had spanners with you and all the tackle.

We did away with steam wagons, and got a petrol wagon – round about a five tonner, with solid tyres. The petrol wagon saved a lot of time. I could go twice a day – I was back in Wigan by dinner time, picking up my second load. The steam wagon carried 40 barrels of beer, 22 on the wagon and 18 on the trailer. The other only carried 16 or 18.

I stayed with that contractor seven years. Then I went working for another firm of four brothers. They had a lot of carrying for different firms, any district. The brewery had given up, and the old contractor had only enough work for him to carry on with himself. We were carrying different kinds of material – six or eight wagons of glass a day for Pilkingtons, big 6- and 7-ft drums for BI Cables, UGB bottles. We had to do the unloading ourselves. This was long distance, Birmingham, Leicester, Nottingham, London, up and down the country. On my own, mostly. As the years went on, we got trailers and bigger wagons. We had the first Mammoth that ever came to St Helens – that would be before the '30s.

In the late 1920s, we were allowed 11 hours to go to London, and our expenses were £2. Out of that, you had to buy your lunch, pay for your digs and pay to put your wagon up at a garage. There were different kinds of digs. I used to keep a record of the places I could recommend from 'The Handy Book of Pull-ins and Accommodation'. At Chelmsford, there was Mrs Goodchild – I used to recommend that to anyone who was going down. They were good digs, mostly transport drivers and travellers.

When I first started with that firm, they had only two wagons. There were very few cars on the road. We had it to ourselves. We would drive all through the day and night. We used to go to the petrol depots. We carried a book and kept a credit account – the bill was sent to the firm. Time was our own as long as we got rid of the load. Going out in the middle of the night, with nothing on the road except me – I used to love it when it was coming daylight at three o'clock. I can tell the time by daylight. We had all the pleasures of the road in those days with oil lamps.

I can remember a time when we were snowed in going over Shap. We were stuck for three nights and two days. I was with two others, and we walked up and down to keep ourselves warm and told jokes. We only had a flask between us. Eventually, we were dug out by the men from Penrith Corporation. They had to open the road. When they got there, the snow was piled up round the wagon as high as the walls of this room.

6 Trades and other Jobs

Joinery

JOINER FROM THE TOWN CENTRE, BORN *c.* 1905

When I started, we had no machines. We got into a new yard in Denton's Green. The boss bought a whole lot of new machinery, but the neighbours objected to the noise and the boss dismantled it all. We went back to hand craftsmanship. We had two men who couldn't read or write but were really great joiners.

It was all handcart work to take materials. I pushed as much as a horse. You used to zig-zag up the road to get up the brews [hills]. Anybody who saw you struggling would give you a hand. It was a hell of a job going downhill – you had no brakes. You had to brake by binding the wheel against the kerb. The apprentices did that, though if you were going out to fix a job with a man, he'd give a hand. The wheel once came off in Duke Street. I got it caught in the tram lines, and the tram couldn't get by. When we had something heavy, we used to hire a carter and send for a horse and cart for all the tackle – picks, spades, planks and scaffolding.

Inside doors were all panelled in yellow pine. They were magnificent. They used that much of the wood, there's no more left. You could cut it with a butter knife. With a big contract, you could do as many as 200 doors together. The joiners would get going on the inside joinery work, and it would be made months before it was needed. They had to be knocked together slack and then left for six months or more while they shrank. Then we used to mortice them up – frame them with the top and bottom rails and the panels – then leave them until it was approaching the time when plastering was finishing. Then the joiners would go round to do the last fixing, to hang the doors. The lads in the shop would be wedging them up, then knot them, stop them, prime them and paint them. Knotting was covering the knots so that paint would stick to them, stopping was filling any cracks with a red lead and putty mix. Then you had to prime them with a lead primer, paint one coat and they'd go on the job practically impervious to the weather. It was a beautiful, interesting job, the nicest job there was. Jesus was a joiner and my father was a joiner.

We'd go up and cut the floors of a house down and lay them on the joists upside down. They were there for at least a month while we dried them off. When they were dried, we'd lay down six at a time, put clamps on and push them up so tight that they bent in the middle before you laid them.

I know a builder, Joe Yearsley, who was known to have timber in his yard for 40 years. When he came to use it, there was no danger about it. Now they're using wood that was growing in Norway last summer. Well, shareholders want bloody dividends next year. I've seen an old foreman turning planks over in the stack, selecting one plank to make something with. He'd go right through the stack of timbers till he found what he wanted.

The housing situation was as bad as it is now, if not worse. It was hungry times. You'd be working away, whistling and happy as a lark, and you'd be finished. On Christmas Eve, the boss came round at half past two and said, 'You're finished.' On Christmas Eve. It was one hour's notice, and the union got a concession and made it two. Joiners used to get two hours of what was called grinding time – to grind your chisel and axe to go to your next job with sharp tools.

There were two unions for joiners – one was the General Union of House Carpenters & Joiners – and they merged to form the Amalgamated Society of Woodworkers. I've known them to be on strike in St Helens and working in Liverpool. They weren't nationally organized. We were affiliated to the Liverpool district. If a joiner had a complaint against his boss, he told the local secretary immediately, or he knocked off work and rang the district office, who would send out a walking delegate to visit the job where the dispute was. If they could locate the officer, he'd be down to investigate the dispute and settle it up with the boss. If the man was at fault, the delegate would tell him he hadn't got a leg to stand on.

In those days, the militants were coming up. They were good men who were fighting for the rights of the working man, but they were looked on by the employers as men not to employ if they could help it. If you were a joiner out of work, you signed on your national Labour Exchange, but you also signed your local union book, which was kept in J. P. Morris's ironmongers – every joiner bought his tools there. You used to get 2s union pay – 12s a week off the club. Some of the poor buggers couldn't get a job. They were pretty well on the dole. They could only get jobs on the big schemes. Quietly, they had a blacklist – the employees didn't know that.

We used to black a shop if there was a man working there who was not in the union. It was in the trade journal. You'd turn over the page, and on the back you'd see a black hand with a list of the places not to work. The union was responsible for keeping up the standard of craftsmanship of the people working. The wages compared very favourably with any other skilled tradesmen. Unfortunately, the building labourers were very skilled men too. They should have been paid as much as a tradesman, the bricklayers' labourers. We were scaffolding with fir trees, spliced and held with clove hitches – self-tightening knots – the labourers knew how to do it. Two bricklayers working up a scaffold needed labourers to carry them up bricks in a hod in those days (there were no pulleys) and I've seen some who thought nothing of laying 600 in a day. Imagine three of them laying 600 bricks. In 'slavery' firms, where men were anxious for a job, the bricklayer's labourer would be labouring for three men, instead of two – the same with plasterers' labourers. Oh, they worked hard. 10d an hour they used to get when I first started, and some tradesmen were only getting about 1s 3d. It was 48 hours we worked then.

With rain, they were knocked off – they weren't paid till they came out of the cabin. Once we got to a church we were building in Liverpool for eight in the morning, and it's not stopped raining at twelve o'clock. Then we went home. You played cards in the cabin, but you didn't get paid till you came out. Joiners weren't so prone to that. That was mostly the poor bricklayer. You wouldn't work when it was freezing. The architect would come out: 'Stop those men!' The mortar all disintegrates when it thaws. They were hard days.

Electricians

ELECTRICIAN FROM WINDLE, BORN 1901

I worked in Pilkingtons as an electrician. There were some very hot jobs, where you worked with a pair of clogs and a vest. You had some extremely dirty jobs if you worked round the furnace hall. It was dirt of a sooty nature, and round the polishers it used to be wet. We did repairs to lights and that sort of thing. At that time, World War I was on, and the firm was making a mint at the same time as there was a reasonably sized staff.

At the end of the war, the tanks where metal was put came into being as we know them today. That was the beginning of a reasonably busy era for us. We had to wire up meters and controls. They used to say that they liked to bring their own electricians up, as they were domesticated, if you know what I mean. They brought in continuous grinders and polishers to smooth the glass until it was up to the standard for plate-glass windows. With the advent of continuous grinders, the machines were separate, as far as the mechanics were concerned. Every one was separately driven, which meant a fair amount of work. There were 13 grinders on a machine, and 26 polishers. One could be stopped by itself. Electricians were the most vital men, with plumbers and fitters.

You were an apprentice from 16 till your 21st birthday. When I came out of my time in 1922, the wage was £3s 6s 9d for a tradesman. It wasn't a bad wage really – when in my indentures I got 12s 6d in the last year. It was reasonably secure. In those days, all the fitters were members of the union – since the war, more or less. The money was 3d a week for apprentices and 1s 3d a week for tradesmen. When you joined, you always had your right of say in the union. Apprentices could speak, but they couldn't vote. There was an auxiliary section of fellows half-way between labourers and tradesmen. They had the right of speech and voting. There was one branch for the town – St Helens Corporation, and one each for Carrington Shaws, Nuttalls (now UGB) and Pilkingtons, then a few odds and ends. They had electricians in the mines, and they weren't properly organized – they weren't in the electricians' union, and they weren't in the miners' union till a good deal after.

The masters had St Helens Group of Manufacturers. When there was any negotiation, a worker would be elected from each shop – it might be the shop steward, it might not be. We also had a representative on the Trades & Labour Council. The masters were tough. They never gave anything away easily. We've gone in for a rise, they've offered a penny, and we used to get three ha'pence. On a 52-hour week, that was a big rise, more than 6s. You never thought of percentages – it was pennies we bothered about.

We used to have plenty of walkouts. Quick walkouts were pinpricks, but they kept people on their toes. Mind you, losing an afternoon's pay was something in those days. It was more like lightning strikes. The only time we had an organized strike was the General Strike.

Baking and Deliveries

MEMBER OF THE MANAGEMENT OF SWIFT'S BAKERY

The flour came from mills in Liverpool in a steam engine and trailer. There were 140 bags on that, 140 lb each. They weren't sacks – sacks proper were 280 lb. People used to reckon that the whiter the bread the better, but all the chemicals that made it white were put in at the mills. Of course, it's not really good for you – brown bread's much better, but we didn't bake much of it. We mixed the flour, water and yeast by machine. The bread was baked on trays of 144 loaves in tins. We had five ovens, and each bake took 50 minutes, so you could reckon on 750 loaves an hour.

We supplied nearly 50% of the bread in the town. The only one that topped us was the Co-op. We sent our vans all round the town, and we went as far as Liverpool. We sold them at 3s a dozen wholesale, and now it's more than 3s 4d for one loaf. People used to buy up to six loaves at a time – you'd see them coming out with them in their arms. At that time, they ate far more bread and bought it fresh every day. Then we kept two butchers in business supplying us with pork steak for pies. Nowadays, they just use sausage meat. It used to be wheeled in on trolleys like they use for carrying dirty rugby clothes.

BAKER'S DELIVERY GIRL, BORN 1910

I joined the bakery at 15 when I left school. Leonard Swift was well known then. His son Tom taught me to drive. It was a T-type Ford van. There was no gear box in it, and you had to hand start it – I've still got a bit of muscle in my arm. You had to let your hand brake down very slowly and press on the accelerator. I was 17 when I started deliveries. You hardly met any other traffic – you were a millionaire if you had a car. You could go for miles over the cobbled streets and turn corners without being afraid of bumping into anything. The only rule was to keep to the left-hand side of the road.

You'd get lost in the fog. You could go through a street thousands of times and if the fog came down, you'd get lost. It was like a blanket. I remember once in the fog, going down Church Street, there was a canal at the bottom there. I used it a lot as my round was up at Peasley Cross and Sutton way. I got out to see where I was and I had my front wheel right over the bridge – what a shock I got.

You got 17s a week with all the responsibility of driving the van. You worked all hours. At Christmas with the bakery, I used to be out till two o'clock on Christmas morning – I took parcels and turkeys. I used to be jiggered for Christmas. I'd spend half the day in bed.

The Shops

There were 3,000 people – equal numbers of men and women – working in commerce in St Helens in 1921. This was the only area where there were a lot of self-employed people – not just in the corner shops, but also in premises which sold their own products like the cobblers. It was in the '20s that the Co-op, in the vanguard of the big shopping chains, began to challenge the authority of the corner shops.

DAUGHTER OF A CORNER-SHOP OWNER, BORN *c.* 1895

We lived in Robins Lane and had a grocery shop. We had an outdoor licence and sold beer at 4d a quart. Children used to come for a penny gill on Sundays and we gave them sweets. Walker's beer, we sold. Inside we sold nearly everything but provisions. Only on Mondays it was quiet; on Tuesdays, Wednesdays and Thursdays we sold fish. We sold cigarettes, at 2½d a packet (cinderellas, they were called) and tobacco at 3d an ounce. We sold writing paper at a halfpenny a sheet, penny bottles of turpentine, headache powders, pills, and settles powders at 2½d per packet. All the shelves used to be packed with dry stuff like sage and thyme.

My mother got up at five o'clock in the morning and bought all her wholesale stuff at St John's market in Liverpool. The horses brought the stuff back here – there were a big horse and a little pony. The horse brought the boxes of oranges, and the pony brought the cabbages and that sort of thing. We bought the fish from Mars – they had a wholesale market at the back of the Savoy. It was a big sale and started at seven o'clock. When it was Ash Wednesday and Good Friday, we were very busy – we used to say they were our harvest – we'd come back with nothing left in the cart. We used to sell a few rabbits too, what they called frozen rabbits – they were cheaper. We hung the rabbits on rods and thawed them either side of the stove. This stove was old fashioned with a hole at the top, and you used to put a fire underneath. I used to skin the rabbits, hundreds of them. We used to get 2d each for the rabbit skins, and that was our profit. I took them in the cart on Thursdays to the rag-and-bone place that they turned into the Co-op.

We had a good round with our two carts in those days. You went to people, not them coming to you. Even Charlie King, who just sold bananas, did a round – he was known as the Banana King. My brothers stayed half days from school working for my mother. When they left school they wanted to go out to work, and they were all taken on at Bold Colliery. Their wages were more than my mother's. We had to sell both horses when the lads started working – there was no one to do the rounds. They kept leaving school – there was only two years between each one of them and they'd soon all left. I had three sisters and one of them did a round in the cart at Burtonwood. She got married from the shop – we all did.

Our business went flop because the Co-op opened on Robins Lane. They used to slope us and they'd take their money to the stores. They got three shillings back in the pound there. Sloping is the word we had for people who had stuff on credit and wouldn't pay. There was my mother getting up at all hours and getting nothing for it. Most people round us were colliers and railwaymen, and there'd be a lot of sloping when the colliers were out on strike.

My mother didn't pay me – we were lucky to get our keep in those days. But she always had us well dressed. When I married my husband she said: 'You pay his board and I'll keep you for nothing.' If I wanted to go any-where special I had to ask my father. My father was very strict. I wouldn't dare give him back again. If I had my life over again, I would have gone out to work, too, like my brothers did. I worked jolly hard and I got nothing for it. Most of the people didn't who worked for their own family.

THE DOCTOR
Another thing they did – all the little shops were run on tick. I've seen quite a few of them start up and after a year or so disappear. When they left, they left with all the customers owing – they left broke. Tick and bad debts were very common. If a new shop started up, all the old lags went there. It was mainly cooked meat shops – brawn, black puddings and tripe.

WOMAN, BORN DURING WORLD WAR I
The real business people used to sell soup perhaps three times a week, or hotpot. You'd take your dish or your jug if you wanted soup. These women were very enterprising. There used to be a place in the Liverpool Road. She baked meat and potato pies, smashing, great big pies.

They gave me a twelve-month trial period to see how I settled in and at the end of that they decided to send me away to a factory in Leeds, which did a lot of trade with Tyrers, to learn about suits. The first day I got there I was taken to the manager and he showed me the cutting room. It was a sort of mass production of suits. They had one pattern with 10 or 20 layers of cloth underneath, cut with a saw. A customer came in wanting a suit and the manager said 'Now, watch how I measure this gentleman as I want you to check my measurements to see I don't go wrong.' That's how I learned to measure for suits. Each day in the factory I spent the morning in a different room, and after a week I went back to St Helens.

Just after I went back, Al Critchely came into the shop. He was the main fishmonger, like Spavins is today, and very well known locally. He said he wanted a new suit. I asked him to choose his cloth – I had the shivers all over. I took his measurements and then I rang Mr John to come down. 'Oh, Mr John,' I said, 'Al Critchely's just been in for a new suit. I took his measurements, and I'm sure I took them all wrong. What'll happen if it doesn't fit when he comes back?'

'Now, don't worry,' he said, 'if it doesn't fit, I'll measure him.'

'But that'll be a lot of money to waste on a new suit.'

'Oh, we'll put it in the sale,' he said.

All that week I couldn't sleep a wink. When Al Critchely came back to try his suit on, I daren't hardly look. I called Mr John to come down and help me. 'Well, Mr Critchely, how's your new suit?'

'It's the most smashing suit I've ever had,' he said. And from there I never looked back.

My father was brought up in the business with his father. I started when I left school at 14 years of age. We did shoe repairs and clogs. In those days, a lot of clogs were worn both for industrial purposes and just generally. Practically all the miners wore clogs – other footwear that was available wouldn't stand up to the rough treatment. The miners wearing clogs wore a hollow in the centre of the soles. If they were on the coal face and doing a lot of bending, a pair of clogs would last 12–18 months with resoling. In the early days they cost about 6s 6d for a new pair. You could get new bottoms for 2s 6d – having them reclogged, as we called it. Some clogs had two or three lace holes, but a lot were just what we called clasp clogs – with a clasp round the ankle. They used to have sides of leather, and we had patterns to cut the uppers out with. A clog was made with two pieces, and had a wooden bottom and irons to protect the wood. They were all hand sewn – we didn't have machines then.

From cutting the uppers out, closing them and right through, it took about an hour and a half to make one pair. My father did most of it. The trade was beginning to ebb even then – I don't think you could say it was a good trade. You got a living out of it. You could make a bit extra by working extra hours with a bit of personal sacrifice. I worked from eight till six when I started. The general trend was to work long hours. It was the expected thing. You went into your father's trade, and not long after I was set up came the big depression, so you had to stick to what you had, but at least with your own shop you could please yourself how much you put into it.

The clogs were losing ground rapidly till the beginning of the second war. Children used them in the war as there were no coupons on them at first. At schools, when you got a lot of children clattering on tiled floors, of course, they made a lot of din. You could hear colliers going to work in the morning at half past six. A lot of other workers used them, brick-workers, and men at Pilkingtons. As a matter of fact, some of the men still use them – the glass splinters can go through rubber. There's no cloggers really left now.

There was that feeling of goodwill between customer and shopkeeper then. Your main business was in a radius of half a mile. There were a lot of cobblers' shops – you couldn't walk many streets without coming across one. And there were backyard repairers – doing a bit in a back shed somewhere. From Sutton Manor to Sutton, there's only one cobbler now and he's doing very little – he's 65. In that same area, there used to be ten or eleven. A little place like Peasley Cross, which was never thickly populated, had two or three.

I've seen children in their bare feet. The Education Committee used to help out. The Police had a Police Stocking and Shoe Fund. The children could get a voucher for a pair of clogs. We had a contract with the Education Committee. As many as there were in the family, they got a pair each. There was no Family Allowances. But these children got hardened to it because they had to. You'd see poor children with patches on their backsides. There was nothing thrown away, they had to use everything to the very end.

There were at least two dozen branch shops of the Co-op, all administered from the central premises in Baldwin Street. The grocery warehouse was there at the time, too. In those days, we had our own dairy which used to sell milk taken round in churns. We had horse-drawn vehicles for deliveries. Groceries, dry goods and parcels were delivered to all districts of St Helens. We had our own bakery in Eccleston Street, where it was generally admitted the Co-op sold the best bread in town. There was no argument over that.

It was one of the most successful Co-ops in the north-west. We had a coal depot in Eccleston Street. They delivered coal in all districts of the town, too. We had a pork department in Henry Street where they manufactured all kind of sausage goods, boiled hams and things. We had a big trade in all pork departments, and that at a time when it was generally considered bad to eat pork when there wasn't an R in the month.

We had a very big building department, which also comprised a vehicle shop. We built several shops, too – it was quite a comprehensive building department.

All the boys started in the flour room. There were no prepacked foods then. Everything arrived in bulk, and it had to be weighed out and packaged up. This is what the boys did with the flour, potatoes, corn and other foodstuffs. They graduated to counter work at 16 years of age. I couldn't tell you the wages of the boys. The gentlemen's wage was about 62s 6d. Of course, shop assistants did proportionately better than they do now. It was all counter service; there was no self-service. It was all male staff up to the end of World War I. There was a shortage of male staff, with the fellows going into the forces. In those days, the average Co-op assistant was far better off than in private trade. The conditions and wages were better. It was about then that we got employees on the Board of Management. We got that through trade union pressure – at that time it was the Union of Co-operative Employees. Until then, anyone but employees could apply to be a member of the board. They had to be shareholders, of course. Dividends on produce were about 3s in the pound, and in some cases there was an 8d bonus Co-op voucher which you could spend in any of the departments in the main store.

In those days, as long as people had a shilling and signed an agreement saying they were willing to pay the minimum share of a pound, they could join. They used to take a shilling out of the dividends to pay off the share. The Co-op dividend paid all their quarterly bills. People relied on them for paying for the children's clothes. They could invest in the Co-op and receive interest, so some people left their dividends in. Only one person in the family had to be a member – it's tightened up since then. There was a membership approaching 40,000 people. They could get anything from the Co-op. They could even get buried.

Of course, this was a big industrial town, but the Co-op's success was mainly due to damn good management and foresight. Everything had to go before the Board. We bought in bulk wherever it was the cheapest. We sent scouts out to other markets to see where the best buys were. The Board were a mixed lot. They were brought from all walks of life, provided they believed in the co-operative spirit. They had to be fully paid up members to be on the Board of Management. The Board were elected at the quarterly meetings by a majority vote. If there was a controversial item on the agenda, any important business to be discussed or an election, the hall was full. They may have got 300 or more at a better meeting.

If you were a tradesman like Mrs Cottington, you were rich. The neighbours would be hard up waiting for the dole. They would come and ask you to get them bread and milk. You'd go to the Co-op and supply all your neighbours, then every quarter you'd get the divi.

BRANCH SECRETARY OF SHOP WORKERS' UNION, BORN 1893
After the armistice in 1918, I was in a little shop called the Cash Clothing Company in Bridge Street, St Helens. From there, I found my way back to the union branch, and in 1919 I took over the job as secretary. I've got the TUC gold badge – there's only one awarded every year. It's given for outstanding efforts made by rank and file trade unionists – not paid officials. I reckon I must be the longest serving Branch Secretary in the country – 56 years, 1919 to 1975. I still go collecting dues every fortnight. We haven't a great lot of members. Now most are contributing through their wages. For the decade 1960 to 1970, I ended every quarter without any arrears, and there's not many that can claim that. If I gave it up, I think the branch would die – there's no one prepared to do the collecting. They'd go to a meeting all right, but not do the collecting.

Members from the branch used to elect me. We got good meetings. They don't now. They're getting these rises too easy today – then you had to fight for what you got, 3d in the pound commission, or something like that, and you had a good week if you took £30 in the shop. When I joined the union, as a manager you'd get £1 for a 54-hour week – sometimes they put you as assistant in charge instead of manager. The shop was

112

open till 11.30 on Saturday to do a bit of business when the pubs came out. It was clothing and outfitting – ready made.

Well, of course, in the town – what would there be – about 50 or so members. Contributions were 3d a week for sick pay and unemployment pay. You wouldn't get very much, but it was something. Only in the big towns, where they had a membership of 700 or more, did they have a full-time organizer. We had to rely on voluntary workers. We only had those 50 out of at least 500 shop assistants in the town. I've seen big changes, from £1 for a manager to £35 for an assistant. To me it's colossal but it's nothing compared with industry – it's really poor.

They didn't want to know you. It had to be done on the quiet. You hadn't to let an employer know you were in the union or you'd get the boot. It was not until 1935 we got anything like a wage, when it was 35s for 50 hours. In 1913, we managed to get half a day. Before that it was five o'clock at night, your half day.

We did get people from Burtons. There were one or two multiples like Melia and Pegrooms, but they've all been swallowed up. Mostly they were small shop-keepers, and that made it more difficult to unionize, with one or two assistants in hundreds of different shops. It was all the centre – Bridge Street, Church Street, Liverpool Road, The Market – we had one or two in the Market and Westfield Street.

Members were coming and going. You'd make members, they'd transfer to another town and you didn't know if they'd just lapse. You only could hold members by personal contact – like the insurance agents. They were called on religiously every fortnight. To get new members, you'd have to pick an apposite time when the manager wasn't around. Two or three of us would go together – one would come from Liverpool. Then we in turn would go to Liverpool. It was all voluntary labour – the price of a cup of tea. We gave up our half day to do it. We've been ordered out of shops more than once. One manager threatened me with a boning knife – for bacon. It's not long but very sharp. If I'd run out I'd have got it in the back. As it was I was scared stiff and stayed in my corner. We were only telling a chap to come to the meeting when the shop closed. When I got out the fellow outside said, 'Hey, what's the matter with you, you look the colour of bad fat.'

Our meetings were at a little coffee place in Bridge Street – we had a little gas flare lamp. Some time after the war, we got a meeting room for 1s a meeting in the Labour Exchange. When we couldn't get a room to meet in, five or six of us used to go up to the top of a tram – it was open

113

top then – and get off the tram at Speke. We'd come back on the next one that left and finish our meeting that way. Then sometimes we went to a café where we could get a cup of tea and a bun for a penny till they thought we were roughs.

The Coalman
MAN, BORN 1877, WHO DID A COAL ROUND FOR MANY YEARS

I got coal from Pilkingtons old colliery that they pulled down. I used to put it on a lorry, go through the weighing machine and then go out and sell it. I was always willing to work. First of all, I had no trade. I had to look for trade. If I didn't, I'd never have got any. I bagged all my own coal – it was all one grade of coal. There was one man – he could pack the bags on the wagon in a way you couldn't count them. He would smash them together and make three fit where two would go – he had the strength. They were robbed out of tons of coal, Pilkingtons. The man on the weighing machine was the brother-in-law of one of the baggers. He could say there were 39 on when there were 59. How they found out was that they got a piece of wood to count each bag – and that time he had two more than they thought.

You know Parson Peter's Church in Parr? You know the big place across the way – a hall? My horse carted all the brick for that. Afterwards I had no work for it. I couldn't keep it – I sold it for £20. If I'd have kept it I'd have had to feed it, I'd have been losing. I had three horses and a mule. I took passengers to Southport in a wagonette with the mule. He used to lie down in the Broad at Southport when we got there. The best little horse I had was Ginger. I bought Ginger off Jack Snidd – he was a bit of a gypsy, came from Southport. He was a bit drunk one night and said 'I'll tell thee what, you can have him for four pounds.' Well, I could put seventy bags behind him so I got him.

Seasonal Farm Work

Before the council's building programme, many of the miners' terraces straddled along the main roads at the front, and faced straight out on fields at the back. So you didn't have to go far to pick up seasonal work on the land.

We used to go pea picking. We'd be there at four o'clock and you'd only get sixpence a hamper. You'd be there till five at night. Then we'd go home with the peas we'd kept, go upstairs to the boxroom. We had these peas and pepper and salt and a bit of margarine, and watch the sun set. If you were good at it, it took you three-quarters of an hour for one hamper. I saw my husband at five in the afternoon and asked him 'How many's that?'

'When I've finished this will be my first.' That was only sixpence. He'd been eating them all. Pea picking was quite common – it depended how far you went. There was an old poor woman, she used to do all kinds of farm work. Spud picking is damn hard work. By 1926, they'd got these plant machines and didn't need so many people.

In Service

In the 1920s many families still had at least one servant. In 1921, 2,200 women had jobs in some form of personal service, 1,400 of them directly as servants. This accounted for a quarter of all female employment in the town. But as with other jobs, most girls just did it for a few years until they got married.

WOMAN, BORN *c.* 1906, IN SERVICE UNTIL SHE MARRIED

Girls either went into service or on to the pit brow where I come from. In the first place, I went to school in Liverpool to be properly trained. That was when I was 13. I suppose my mother must have paid for me to go, but when you're that age you don't really think about those things. They taught you how to answer the door, as you announce people the way you stand on one side, how to lay the table, how to pass everything round, how you passed things on the left-hand side, how you moved round the back of people, how to pour out the wine – you just had to have a steady hand for that. Then there was the afternoon tea, you used to have to take in on a tray. If there was a lot there, you had to mind how you walked. You learnt how to fashion the serviettes – there are two or three different ways of making them – lilies and bishops hats are two – instead of just putting them out plain on the table. The course lasted six months and afterwards they picked out what you were best suited at. I was best at being house parlour maid, not in the kitchen. I don't know why, maybe it was being small. In those days, you needed proper training – you couldn't just walk into a house parlour maid's job without it.

The first house where I was in service was in Canning Street, Liverpool, which was a very different Canning Street to what it is now. There was a nursemaid and a cook as well as me. They were just four people – husband, wife and two boys. As house parlour maid you had to look after the dining table, dining room and all kinds of cleaning work – it was like a butler's job. I had to serve breakfast, lunch, afternoon tea and dinner. I got one night off per week and one day off a month. I lived in and I had to be back by nine o'clock when I had a night off. It was about a pound a month and I had to provide my own clothes.

I had to look after the dining room because it was my place to keep clean – and the pantry too. The cook and the house nurse divided up the rest. I saw to the table cloth and I had to do the washing up. I wouldn't say it was hard work. At nights we used to sit in the kitchen for an hour or so before taking in the last meal at night. We had the same food as them. They didn't have any fancy concoctions – just plain fare.

I don't know what kind of business the family had. But I was in a good place compared to what others had. Sometimes they'd be in a big house and they'd be the only maid. It wasn't the hours you worked – you were at it all day, on duty till you went to bed. If they had friends in, they wanted attention. They didn't entertain to a large extent. I imagine eleven o'clock was the latest you'd be up. They weren't very entertaining people. They were quite staid.

There was a nursemaid as the boys were only small. Eight o'clock the breakfast was – the two boys had to do half an hour's practice on the piano before breakfast – one in the drawing room and one in the nursery.

I wasn't treated in any disrespect. You knew your place. The two boys were always called 'Master Richard' and 'Master Andrew'. We used to call their parents Mr and Mrs Hall. They used to call us Cook and Nurse, and they called me Long or it might have been Agnes, I can't remember. They would come and speak to you during the day. They were what you call the gentry. Those who'd just made their money and then tried to live the gentry life, they were the worst people. I was never in service for one of them.

Part II

The Town

Employment in St Helens, dealt with in Part I, by no means accounts for what everyone was doing. Three-quarters of all women weren't at work. That was a remarkably high proportion. At the time, the only place in Lancashire with more unemployed women was Barrow-in-Furness. Most of the south Lancashire towns employed women in the textile mills, and St Helens had none.

In spite of the introduction of the Old Age Pension by the Asquith Government before World War I, there were few people who survived to retire on it. Only one person in a hundred had reached retiring age in St Helens in 1921 – which, if nothing else, was an unpleasant testimony to the conditions of life and labour in the Victorian era. If a man wasn't at work, then, it wasn't often because he was too old, but because there wasn't a job. Unemployment in St Helens in the 1920s was well over 10%. It is easily forgotten that with big families and high death rates, children constituted a high proportion of the population. At that time, 43% of the town's inhabitants were under 20 years old.

Life and work for these sections of the community varied more than it would have done for workers in the factories and pits. Recording these conditions is more subjective, particularly when it comes to talking about neighbours, and so on. The accounts given here are restricted to those of jobs and pastimes which were common, and opinions which were widely held.

1 Children and Education

HUSBAND AND WIFE, BOTH BORN DURING WORLD WAR I
Children played out in the streets. There were all kinds of games. Marbles, which we called pin-stoney, was one. You'd have a cardboard box with three little openings in the side and one on top. You'd throw a stoney in at the top and try to get it out of one of the other holes.

We used to have books and cut pictures out and put them in the pages. You'd open it and put in a pin. If you put it on a picture, you got it, but if you didn't, you lost your pin. You'd see people with rows of pins in the collar of their jacket.

You had seasons. There was a skipping-rope season; top and whip was always a winter game, pin-stoney was cool, and ring games for girls were played in summer. Ring-stoney is still played. They chalk a lot of rings of 5, 10 and 15 on the pavement and put a stone in each, which has to be hit with a ball. If you knocked it clean out of the ring, it was 50. We played 100 up.

You know the old tub-and-pail lavatories? They used to have a little door at the side, where the men who emptied them used to pull the full tray out and put in an empty one at what they called the 'midnight wedding'. Children'd wait to hear someone come down the yard and sit down – then they'd get a stick and tickle the person's behind through this door. If it was a female, she'd get shocked and scream. You'd run off as fast as you could, before they could find out who it was.

Another trick we used to do on dark nights – we'd tie a stone to a cotton string, pin it in the window frame and take the end of the string across the street, where we'd pull it so that the stone kept tapping on the window, and people would come out to see who it was.

You'd be singing carols as boys, right in someone's doorway, then all of a sudden they threw a flat iron at the door. They used to heat pennies and put them in kids' hands to make them dance. Only sadistic people did that!

I used to like when the street photographer came up and made all the children in the street pose – the more children the better. Then, the following Friday, he used to come back to sell the prints. You don't see them any more – everyone can afford their own cameras.

We used to have two eggs between four of us. It was a fine art to divide them exactly in half. If your father had steak and onions, your mother would make a pile of flour gravy and you had some of that. But jam butties and chips were the thing in those days for us poor people. You could ask for a penny of treacle or jam – it would be poured out from a tap. Your bread used to be weighed. The loaves were all hand made. If it wasn't up to weight, they'd cut a bit off another one, and most likely you'd eat that on the way home.

Some neighbours used to brew with dandelions and nettles and herbs from the countryside, and there was ginger beer as well. They used to sell it on Sunday morning for a penny a big bottleful. They used to have a special way of stopping it. It went off like champagne – we cut the string with scissors, and the stopper would fly off. It was the yeast that made it so explosive.

If you were caught stealing an apple or orange, you'd be brought up at the town hall with your father, and you were fined. There's no comparison with young people today – there's no discipline now. I'm not an old fogey, but there's no respect. On the whole, parents were stricter. Your mother had only to say, 'I'll tell your dad about you,' and that was enough. Also, if a neighbour said, 'I'll tell your mother,' I wouldn't go home. If you'd been cheeking your neighbour they wouldn't take it.

Children are always the same. You'd go down the town, you'd see a stack of milk – you got children pulling the bottom one out so they all fell down. They'd run after you. There were more police about – we were frightened of authority. The schoolteacher was allowed to cane you, the police would give you a flick with the glove, and they were allowed to do it.

THE JOINER, BORN *c.* 1905

My brother and I used to get 1½d every Saturday to go to the picture palace. There was one film and lantern slides. It used to be a gymnasium. You climbed on the bars to get a better spec. There was a cinema at the top of Helena House, the Co-op building. It was 1d to go in and ½d for two ounces of toffee. We used to give one of the halfpennies to a friend. He had no money, there were too many of them, seven in the family. If we gave the two halfpennies to him, the three of us could go in. The children's idol was a fellow named 'Pimple' – in the same year as Flora Finch. He was a fellow like a clown. He came on in a series each week – 'Pimple at the North Pole'. Then there wasn't enough film to go round all afternoon. The lantern slides used to come on – pictures of plants, flowers and birds, then drawing-room scenes. Sometimes they told a story.

MAN, BORN 1897, LATER THE TRAM MECHANIC

Before I left school, I was a Sunday morning milk lad for the Co-op stores from eight o'clock till one. They started canvassing for customers. You went with a float, a dandy, which had big wheels and a flat bottom. The churns would go on there. You had a two-gallon can and went down the street measuring out pints and gills into people's jugs. You could get milk tickets from your branch. I got 4s/6d for that. It helped to finance the house.

Every afternoon after school, I went to Jim Pratt in Westfield Street. He was a master boot repairer. That was supposed to be learning the trade – on 3s a week. On Saturdays, he was up there till eleven at night. You were a slave finishing off shoes and boots. I learned a bit, and when I left school I went full time there for 5s.

TWO SISTERS FROM PARR, BORN 1906 AND 1908

There weren't any boys made to do housework. I know one or two girls that had plenty to do when they came home. Boys could do what they wanted. It was always girls left in charge to get meals ready. I always used to say, 'I'll make sure my boys do their share, if I have any.'

As children, we never seemed to be in the house. We went down to this wood – it must have been a mile away. We were there all day – we'd just go back for a meal, and then back to the wood again. That's all you did in summer, take a jam butty and a bottle of water. Half a dozen girls would go together. Half of them would be without their shoes and socks on the old rough road past the colliery. Often, we went down to the canal and dangled our feet over the edge. We couldn't swim – I suppose we're lucky none of us fell in.

We used to play hopscotch on the flags, and ball on the side of the houses, and we played shuttlecock. You don't see any of that now. We could put a rope right across the road and be skipping in the middle of it. You'd only have to get off when something came by, which wouldn't be so often. There'd be these steam engines coming by with bales of cotton on the way to the mills. There was no sport at school, only drill, till we got older. Hardly any school did sports – Merton Bank had hockey, and that was thought progressive.

We ate a lot of stew and a lot of vegetables. We had what was called 'lubbies' – you'd get your stew cooked and put your potatoes in with it. We wouldn't get many chops, or anything in that line. I always remember stews – that was dinner time at twelve o'clock. Most kids going to school used to get toast and porridge, but I think a lot of them turned out without. This girl had fainted at school, and the next day she told me, 'The teacher sent for me, and she asked me what I had for breakfast. I said I'd had an egg, but I hadn't.'

With cookery, you could bring back what you made. I got my dinners for 3d a day at school. Three out of five days, it was just soup with bread. Two days, it was hot pot, once without a crust and once with. We stopped at school because we had too far to walk home.

Schools

HEADMASTER OF A CATHOLIC SECONDARY SCHOOL

1923 was the year I took my job at Holy Cross. When I took over, Holy Cross was an all-standard school for boys from seven to the leaving age, which was 13. (It was soon raised to 14.) In our particular school, which had just had an inspection and got a good report, there were about 450 boys split up into 11 classes, two each for standards one to five, and a top class for the last year. Each year was split up with the better boys in one class and the rest in the other, about 40 each, and there would be about 50 boys in the top class.

The conditions were such in the town that they wanted to get to work as soon as they could from school. There was nothing for children to do if they stayed on. There was no incentive to stay at our school. The only instance to stay on was a particular individual who didn't want to leave school – we couldn't get rid of him. He went to college, and by a strange quirk he became a teacher at St Annes. As for the actual subjects taught, all the classes did all the fundamental subjects – Maths, English, History, Geography, Art and a certain amount of Sciences. But the building didn't allow of much movement about.

In the days when I started, we'd only the big hall of the school, which was partitioned into three. It was a big room, which would be 70 or 80 ft long and 40 ft wide, split by these partitions with glass doors. To get to the middle section, you had to go through the outer ones. Then there were three other rooms in the passage up from the street to the main hall. So you had two classes in each room, with two teachers. You daren't put two teachers in there who hated each other; we put people together who could get on. What happened, in effect, was that they didn't do a lot of talking. They could arrange things so that there weren't two people talking together all the time. We had no teacher accommodation or staff room at all. I had my desk in the first room – anyone coming in could come straight to me with whatever business they had. We had no playing fields – we had to go by bus at our cost to playing fields open to everyone.

We had a Dickens of a job if anything interfered in the class. I'm always bumping into old boys and girls in the street. There's one thing they remember – the discipline. It was strict, but not too much corporal punishment was used. I've only been in one tight spot – after the school became mixed, a big girl had been cheeky to one of the women teachers. I was determined to make her apologize, and she faced me out for 20 minutes. In the end, I won. I didn't think I would, but it would have been fatal to let her get away. We used the cane – perhaps more than I was aware of. It was mostly the personality of the teacher. I got a few stewpots, but they didn't stay long. Some of them found it a bit difficult for a year or two. They gradually got advice from the older members and slowly acquired the necessary control. The strange thing was this: the two strictest teachers were a man and an Irish woman, and I've never met one of my old pupils who didn't ask if she was still alive. It wasn't so much the punishment, but she could wither a kid just by looking at him. The man ran most of the sports – he acquired a hold of the boys. They had to keep the right side of him, or they were out of it. At that time, the only place to play was out in the street – we didn't even have a school yard.

When they started doing Intelligence Tests, the man who started them, Balogh, said that if you drew a graph with age against intelligence ratio you'd have a top 10%, who'd be very bright, and the bottom 10% no one on God's earth could teach to read. They're still human beings, they do something, but they are unable to learn to read. They are the people who come into the court and the magistrates hold up their hands in horror: 'This child can't read!' But five or ten children in a hundred have never been taught to read, and they are the ones who come up in court. As a result, they never progress. There were only two or three in

123

our classes at school. We were fortunate, although there were plenty of poor readers.

Children came up to us at seven. I don't know how the primary schools managed it, but they could read then. I've been to visit these schools, and all the children could read. I don't know what they did with the ones who couldn't – perhaps they'd be away from school for the day – but they don't attempt it in primary schools now. Of course, there's an enormous difference from one family to another. In a good home from that point of view, the kids learn to read at home, where the parents take an interest in the child.

As for a schoolboy doing odd jobs, if the kid's got the right attitude to school it has no effect on him. People worked, particularly paper boys, but I wouldn't like to say it had any effect on their education. We had people working at night on odd jobs, but I didn't know exactly what – it wasn't my job to look too closely. We had no one working in school hours. The average attendance in all the schools in St Helens was 93%. If it was over that, you got a half day's holiday on one Friday a month. There's a school at the top of the road here that always got it.

From the start of rationing during World War I, the kids could get their breakfast at school. Any child who was suspected of being underfed could have it at school and didn't have to pay for it. The local authority paid. They always had milk, porridge, buttered toast and occasionally something else. There was a certain amount of preserves and jam. There were other kids who used to bring their own breakfast. There were very few cases of kids being hungry.

All the children wore clogs. There were no children in bare feet – I had to insist on that. I do suspect that some teachers kept a couple of pairs of slippers for kids who hadn't any. In some cases, it might have been that they couldn't afford it, but mostly it was laziness. They'd been in the habit of walking barefoot, but when footwear was comparatively cheap, it wasn't necessary. If they didn't wear clogs, the attendance officer used to make enquiries about it. In real cases of need, they were supplied. Our children had proper clothing – circumstances during the war were such that the way children were clothed improved. They were always well shod and had quite new clothes. You look at photographs of 80 years ago – they look as if they were dressed in their grandmother's cut-downs.

The appointment of teachers at that time was not up to the head, but to the management committee of the school, the board of governors. It's

124

very rarely that the authority interferes – there has to be something drastic for that. The managers let the chairman (in our case, the parish priest) do the appointments. He followed the authority's procedure, advertising the job and interviewing the candidates. I was a member of the governing body; as a matter of fact, I was the secretary. My view was important in the appointment of other teachers.

All the finance of the school, the salaries of the teachers, all the staff who were employed in the school, repairs to the buildings, were all paid for by the authority, but in the case of new construction, the managers had to pay a certain proportion, 40%, and the authority paid 60%.

In my time, the ordinary school day lasted at least five hours. Religious instruction was given from nine o'clock until twenty to ten, and from five to four until quarter past, but it was outside the 25 hours' school instruction. The extra five hours for religious instruction were the same every week, although there were odd occasions when there was something special. When a manager died, there was a question of the children going to mass, but that was taken off the time for religious instruction.

There was no distinction at all between Catholics and Protestants. Some of the best schools were Catholic, and some of the worst local authority. The only difference was the question of holidays of obligation – when they occurred on school days, we had a holiday. I've never come across any antagonism – we had nothing political in the school.

WOMAN, BORN AROUND 1910, WHO WENT TO A COUNTY SECONDARY SCHOOL
Our headmistress was Miss Thompson, a fair woman – a John Bull type. She was a good woman, Miss Thompson, provided that you did your duty. She wouldn't stand any messing.

I went to a higher-grade school. Now, that was a council school – there were only that one and Rivington Road at that time. My father would have you go to a council school – all the others were church schools, where you learned all the religious doctrine. We had half an hour of religious instruction every morning, and learned about the gospel, St Paul's journey and so on. Protestants would send their children to council schools, but Catholics wouldn't – they were learning catechism and all that sort of thing.

We did needlework and art – the church schools didn't do them really. We had two art classes a week. She was a lovely lady, the art mistress. I did batik work. We used to have an exhibition every year just before Christmas. I used to paint on wood – you had to do your own designs,

125

and I remember I drew my initials. The boys' school did woodwork – none were mixed then. I remember making a bowl with *papier maché* and then painting it. We were taught to sew – I made a smock and a teacosy.

While half of the girls learned shorthand and typing and different things, the other half went on to the Oxford School Certificate. If you got through, you could go to Teacher Training College. I never got it – you had to pass French, and I was hopeless at it. We had a class mistress and a teacher for each subject. It was one of the new schools that had university graduates teaching. Lessons were about an hour, and arithmetic was the last lesson on Monday afternoon. We didn't do trigonometry as the boys did. We had geography – I was sick of doing relief maps, so I don't know as much about that as maybe I should. I was very fond of history – that was because of my father. I rather liked school. I was just turned 17 when I left, but at that school you'd get quite a few girls would stay on. One sister was trained as a shorthand typist, one was trained as a hairdresser.

WOMAN, BORN 1906, WHO WENT TO MORTON BANK SCHOOL
They had three teachers looked after the laundry, cookery and house-wifery at school. These three teachers lived together, and two girls would be in the dining room, two in the kitchen, two in the living room, and they told you how to clean them. We had to get their dinner – they got waited on, they'd tell us what we had to do.

If you got a form signed, you could leave school at 13. They had to say you were needed at home. One said her mother was ill, and when she left she got a job at Pilkington's.

2 Women in the Home

Boyfriends? We daren't be caught looking at a lad. I was locked out of our house at quarter past nine. My dad thought that anyone who came in after that was no good. I had to go to another mate's house. Then I had to get up early the next morning and go back home to change and get ready for work. You daren't turn your head one road, except he'd say 'What the bloody hell are you looking at?'

WOMAN FROM CLOCK FACE, WHO WORKED ON THE PIT BROW
We had coal fires, and there used to be a stool at the side. I'd come out of Sutton Manor pit and sit on the stool from Friday to Monday. I scarcely knew what it was to go through the door. My mother drank beer, and my sister went for it. We had a dust up when I went with my husband, because she didn't want me to go then.

Once, I got back late from town on Saturday because there wasn't a bus. My mother said nothing, but when I went to work on Monday morning she packed my bag with six slices of bread and margarine and a bottle of water. I went a full week on nothing but bread and margarine. When it came to my first miners' demonstration at Blackpool, I'd planned who to go with. My mother asked 'Have you got a ticket?' I said I had and she took it off me. I went to Clock Face Bridge and watched them go, and I went to Clock Face Bridge to watch them come back – that was my Blackpool. I got that way that I was shushing when I got my first home. My husband'd say, 'What are you shushing for?' I'd got so used to it.

DEPUTY IN THE MINES, BORN 1883
I used to do a lot of walking when I was young, and I met many other beautiful people in this town. What they did for children then! Five ladies took an interest in girls and formed the Girls' Friendly Society.

My wife went there. They taught them different kinds of knitting, sewing, crochet and all domestic work. They learnt how to nurse – all a girl needed to know in those days. The girls were delighted. The five ladies were Miss Evelyn, Miss Edith and Miss Christine Pilkington, Miss Alice Campbell, who later married the vicar of St Helens, and Miss Moles, a dressmaker. There were many voluntary helpers from different spheres of work.

TWO SISTERS FROM PARR, BORN 1906 AND 1908

There wasn't any work for girls. When we left school, we went round, four of us together, looking for a job. We went to that old workshop that used to be in Church Street, although my father didn't want us to work. Eventually we went into domestic service. If you did get a job, the pay was terrible – I had a friend who used to joke: 'I work at Bishops, they pay us in threepenny bits.'

Nearly always, if you had a baby you left work. They wouldn't keep married women on in any case. The only one I knew worked in the fields – she was a gypsy. If the father worked at Pilkingtons, they might have a chance of working there. I think it was acknowledged that they finished work there when they got married, though. They were all single who worked on the pit brow.

WOMAN BORN DURING WORLD WAR I

Mothers could do all the baking and cleaning and cooking, and just have time to go out with a clean pinny on in the evening to sit on chairs in the street and jangle. That was their whole life. They couldn't get ready to go out – there was no social life.

The men were horrible. Even with the poverty, they always managed to find their money for a drink. I think the men today are much better – you'd never see a man go shopping, and I never saw a man in a chip shop till after I got married. Now they can clean the house or change a baby's nappy, they're much better husbands. Men were tyrants in the old days. There was an awful lot of wifebeating and the women were the underdogs. I've seen my mother do washing in the rain all day with a sack over her shoulders for a family of 14 for 2s. Then she went down town to get something extra for a meal for him – like fish. I've seen my dad pick up the fish and throw it on the floor and say 'I don't want this. Get me something else.' And she'd have to – the food had to be there.

My mother slept in the outside lavatory at times. The men that didn't drink and behaved like that were the worst of all. My father was a generous husband, as long as he kept off the drink. The wifebeating came from the Victorian era. When it happened, women went to neighbours' houses. Then the husband would come and kick the door down to get the wife out. So it got that neighbours wouldn't put them up. It was just a way of life.

DOCTOR, BORN *c.* 1895
As a family grew up, the woman got the wages. She gave the husband his spend. She bought his clothes. Then she portioned out for the credits – not wireless and TV, but so much for clothes, so much for the doctor, coal, groceries and insurance. It was all portioned out at the weekend; the wife did it as she got it.

WOMAN BORN IN ELLESMERE PORT IN 1877
We'd been married three years when he tracked back to St Helens. My husband started his career at Ashton's Green, and I'm going to end mine here. I couldn't go out working – it was really hard scrubbing and washing until I was 86. I had four children of my own and four of his, so I had eight.

When we came back, we went to Robins Lane, near by the park. I don't know how I managed. I can truly and honestly say I never owed anyone a farthing. I must give the due to my husband – he was such a hard worker, a blacksmith till he finished.

I was a good cook, like my mother. Sunday's dinner consisted of a roast, vegetables and pudding. We used to come in to St Helens on Saturday to get bargains – they *were* bargains in those days. Big fish cost 3d, and a leg of mutton for 2s 6d used to last two or three days. How we were badly off was we couldn't go holidaying. My husband never had a holiday in his life. We couldn't have clothes as we'd have liked, although we kept ourselves nicely.

In our house, we had a front room, that we called the parlour, and a kitchen and back kitchen. We also had a big garden wh ere we grew vegetables – we could give a stick of rhubarb to anybody. We had beans, peas, potatoes and an apple tree. But someone bought the land off the landlord and we had it no more.

They built a smithy up the garden. My husband didn't shoe horses; he used to make axles for motor cars. We began to be well off. He always worked by himself – he used to go round the country after work at the colliery. He was a great walker, and anyone that looked like farmers, he used to go and ask if there was anything they wanted doing. His father was a blacksmith in Cheshire, so his name was well known round there. We both came from good families.

God and Nature gave me a gift – I was an elocutionist. I remember reciting the Tay Bridge Disaster when I was young. I found Bible study fascinating, and I went on the platform. I was secretary of Women's Work for 20 years – WW, we call it. The Methodist Church is very good for taking that up. What we made went to help the poor, especially overseas. I was in the British Women's Temperance Association, too. As I never went out working, I did a lot of voluntary work, going and looking after the sick. They called me in at the last – I was just able to make the patients comfortable and look after them. I never worked for a farthing.

WOMAN FROM PARR, BORN 1902

I had nine children, there were seven with them across the road – the Rigby's – eight in Mrs Eadey's, five in Mrs Dibby's and seven in the Tuckers'. There were four next door to me here, five the other side of me, and the Longs had three next one to that. Just count that up and you'll have a shock! You can imagine all them playing outside in this small avenue of eight houses. We used to have some falling out over children – that which you can't avoid. When it was raining, you'd have them inside and they'd play ball on the inside wall. The place was always upside down. But I put them all to bed by seven o'clock, that was the only way you could manage. It was hard on them in summer, they could look out and see other children still playing.

These days, you don't have to have a family if you don't want. There was nothing we could do to help us. My mother had 13 children and his had 12 – that's the difference. I don't think they're as happy now as we were then. As I grow older, I'm thankful for my big family – they'll do anything for me. I never left them, I stayed in for 20 years – my husband only stayed in once a week, while I went to the pictures. This is what I believe in. They had a home life here, and they were all brought up to go to Sunday school – morning and afternoon. They went until they were 14, and then if they didn't want to go I didn't force them; they were old enough to make up their minds.

You usually had toast in the mornings, or bread and jam – you'd nothing else. Then it was potato hash or potato pie, anything that's cheap. I was a proper home baker, and every Sunday I used to do a good spread – I used to like custard pies. We always had a vegetable garden;

130

now, that used to help a lot. As to milk, you couldn't afford more than a pint a day – it was just put in tea and that. Otherwise they never had any milk for years. There were two pints on Sunday because I used to make a custard pie. We always managed a few eggs. It was a struggle – I'm better off today, and I'm on a pension.

Widows, they relied on poor relief – they were lucky if they got half-a-crown. It was these people that suffered, the older people – they were too old altogether. I remember my grandfather was 80 and up till 1922 he was only getting 10s a week in relief. He'd been on the railways, and he was a proper gentleman. He used to sit there in his smoking cap (they used to have those basket chairs), always his collar and tie on, with his jacket and trousers. My grandad lived with my mother for years, I never remember our house without him.

Home Management

SHOP WORKER

Hire Purchase, as we know it, was unthought of. They paid for furniture at a shilling a week, with a man coming round collecting on Friday night, and it was marked in a little book. There was an old woman cleaner I knew – I saw her outside a hardware shop, and she said, 'I've just finished my bill for a polished fender, £2 at a shilling a week. I've got so used to paying it off, I've ordered something else.' They were paid on Friday or Saturday. They shopped on Saturday, and on Saturday night, they could get a lot of throwouts at half price – the shops stayed open till ten o'clock.

THE TWO SISTERS FROM PARR

You saw them going to the pawn shop with the clothes they wore on Sunday. I remember, one lady always had a pair of shoes with long laces that she carried in every week. There were two pawn shops at the Finger Post. You could leave things three months. They'd have to pay more when they went back to get their things out of pawn – the shops made their money that way. That's how you lost – you'd lose coppers every week on them things. Then they gave you a ticket. You'd never get anywhere near the worth of the article, so if it was left in for the three months, they'd make a profit. People used to say 'The suit's at uncle's,' when it was at the pawn shop. There was many a fight when they couldn't get things out at the weekend – they should have gone when they got

131

their wages, then they'd put them in again on Monday. We only wore good clothes on Sunday, and Saturday night. The wives could afford to pawn because they knew their husbands wouldn't want the clothes – you had clogs on all week, but you wore shoes for a Sunday.

THE WOMAN BORN IN WORLD WAR I

They'll tell you that in the good old days you could go down to the market on a Saturday night and pick up a rabbit, some turnips and a few carrots for a shilling. While we were grovelling for the leftovers, there were carcasses of mutton hanging up in the shops. It was all wrong to go grovelling to get a rabbit and some turnips for a shilling only because it would have gone off by Monday. It makes me fighting fit when they say things were better then.

THE DOCTOR

They weren't good housewives. They depended on cooked meat from the corner shops. I'll tell you another thing about the Lancashire folk. They always did their spring cleaning on Sunday. The last thing they did was the doorstep. You used to see them all along these rows of cottages finishing off the doorsteps at twelve o'clock before the big Sunday meal.

ONE OF THE TWO SISTERS FROM PARR

People weren't as house proud because they couldn't afford it, though they did a lot more scrubbing. My step was as white as could be. You were scrubbing half the pavement, too. Flags were as beautiful and as nice as inside. We had a tiled floor, and we had to scrub that every day. The kitchen and back kitchen were done every day of your life; you got a bucket of water to them. Everywhere was dirty, especially with such big families. We had oil cloth down in the parlour and had to wash it every week, but the biggest part had bare boards.

THE MINER FROM PARR, BORN 1893

There were no mechanical contrivances in those days to help the house-wife. Everything had to be done by sheer hard labour. They used a tub and a dolly to dolly the clothes – that was bang them about in the water. You'd lift the dolly up and down. It consisted of four legs attached to a round piece of wood with a handle to it. The legs were used to stir the water and clothes, making them swill round in the tub. You turned the dolly round with a handle through the top of the shaft.

132

All the houses had a boiler, in some cases built in an outhouse attached to the house. The initial work when you commenced washing was to carry water in buckets to fill the boiler. Houses with only two down and two up had no outbuildings, and the wash boiler was in the back room of the house in what would be the kitchen, and the heat was supplied by a small furnace underneath the boiler. You had to get a fire under the boiler and start the water boiling – you could use hot water in your tub. Afterwards came the mangling. The old fashioned mangle had to be turned by hand; it was used to squeeze the water out of the clothes which were being washed, but they were mangled again when they were dry.

There was someone who used to have an enormous mangle in his back shed, which was weighed down with two big rocks. He used to charge people to come in and mangle their clothes after they'd finished washing them. His house got knocked down, and I think he had the mangle put away in a museum somewhere.

THE TWO SISTERS FROM PARR

A lot took washing in – that was a usual thing. My sister-in-law's mother made her living washing for other people; now he drank – we didn't know him then. Their mother had to work – she kept them going, because if he worked he spent it all. Somebody had a shop, and customers asked about doing the washing. She washed for someone who had a bakers. Mrs Billinge had six loads a week – two bosses at the pit, and other families. The washing had to be fetched and taken back, and after that they only got coppers.

The washing came from the better off. We lived near a pub where they always employed somebody to do their washing. They'd a big basket – the same basket we used to carry bread in. Two would have to carry it, one either side of the basket. I've seen it piled high with sheets; they were beautiful carried in those baskets.

Washing day was the day you'd notice the dirt in the air. You'd be careful if it was a bit dampish – you wouldn't peg out white clothes. You'd wait until all the big chimneys' fires were lit. You could put plenty of line out. We didn't have a yard; we had big stumps at the back of the house. You pegged them right out at the back of you.

It took some drying. If you had a good day, you were all right, but there was nothing worse than a wet washday when you had to do the drying inside. Some washed in the back kitchen, but you had to hang the washing in your living room. If you'd only two rooms, you'd call them your kitchen and your back kitchen. Where we lived, we had a parlour, kitchen and back kitchen. There were ten of us fetched up in that, only there was always somebody in service or somebody off. The dampness in the kitchen was awful. My husband never wanted to be near the house if there was any washing. That was because his mother had had to wash for a living.

Mrs Shard used to do washing at one time. Her husband worked at pit. The colliers worked in pit drawers, and to clean them you'd get out your board and scrubbing brush. It was lovely when they turned out white after they'd been boiled. The ironing was done with a flat iron that you took off the fire. Mrs Walker – all her family were blowers at Pilkingtons – she used to talk about the washing. The things they had to wear, they brought them all home to wash.

Before I was 14, they'd leave two tubs for when I got back from school. When you started at half past eight, you were washing till half past five, easily. Then you'd swill the big washtubs out and scrub the suds down. You'd be surprised at how that cleaned the bricks. It was hard work, washing day. My mother used to get a meal ready half-way through.

You'd two big tubs. You started with white clothes. You had them the right side and scrubbed them, then you turned them to the wrong side to look for where the dirt was, like under the armpits. You'd give them another good wash, put them through your mangle, and put them in another tub which was rinsing water. After that, you'd put them in another tub to boil. You'd have to watch it to control the fire underneath. Then you'd do your coloureds that didn't need boiling. When your white ones had boiled, you'd put in your towels and your sheets. Then you had to swill it out, scrub your bricks down and empty your boiler out. We've seen mothers when the girls hadn't done them to satisfaction who'd make them do it again. My mother was pretty even tempered, but next door she made them pay for it.

You'd have to blue the whites, or starch them. I bet you don't know what bluing is now. It was in a bag you put in the water on the end of a stick. You soon got to judge your water – you hadn't to make it too blue. Then, when they came out they sparkled.

I used to love to see a row of washing when you had nice, white table cloths. You had them all in a line in your living room. It was a work of art hanging them up on your line so they all looked nice. Somebody would pull them straight with you. They used to be taken to the big mangle in Chancery Lane, but you paid a copper for the use of it. When they'd been under this mangle, the sheets would be flat, you see.

I used to go to a little house up off the main road at the back of a farm. They had no taps. There were seven living in that house, and the tap was on this big wall facing the house. They had to carry every drop of water from there to the back kitchen to wash with. They'd no mangle, and they used to have to wring everything with their hands. You had to keep tipping water away and fetching clean. We had a tap in the wash house and we were well done to. Their sheets used to be pegged up on the line in the front room, dripping on the floor – it must have made the walls damp. I suppose they got used to it.

Sheets we bought and hemmed ourselves; they weren't white, they were all unbleached. From that end we used to go to Earlstown Market. A lot of people bought second-hand clothes there. My mother always had a machine and had a go at fixing you up with something. She used to sew a lot of skirts up, and they used to sell parts of a shirt all ready cut out. Annie Smith and a few other dressmakers would make you a frock or two if you bought the material. Then you'd have a go at little blouses and that sort of thing.

There was a woman, Mrs Hall, who lived opposite us, who'd do a bit of sewing for coppers. That's how they made a bit of money. She'd run anybody something up. She had a big machine. Mr and Mrs Brown had a plot at the back. They sold flowers for sixpence. There were some who made pop you could go and buy.

There were several places in the town to bake bread. You made your own dough and took it to the bakers. They would give you tallies to take back when your bread was ready. The farmer used to ask us to do it, and twice a week we would take his dough over – it would make about 12 loaves. There was a bakery in Boundary Road, and you could smell it 100 yards off. The crust from that bread used to crackle in your mouth. We'd a brother on the farm, so we used to do errands for the farmer – for taking the dough we'd get twopence a week.

We'd a big plot and plenty of hens. Joe would help look after them and my father would buy them. The people next door would always shout over the wall, 'Can you spare me an egg?' We'd always a nice roast at the weekend. We were lucky being the youngest. Even in the 'thirties you could still get a rabbit, an onion, some potatoes and a cabbage for a shilling in a big old shop at the bottom of Liverpool Road. On Sunday night, the Billinges would get us a pan of fried potatoes left over from Sunday dinner.

But there were some people you never knew anything about. There were two or three died round us in childbirth. There was one woman whose husband had a white-collar job, and the doctor said she died of malnutrition. There were others who died in childbirth through malnutrition – they'd give what they had to their children.

3 Housing

There were two kinds of building – either speculative, or a house that was drawn up by an architect, where you'd tender for the job.

The spec builders would get away with murder. There were all kinds of ways to cut costs. Because they were building on dry soil, they thought they could afford to leave the damp course out. (You can see that's been done if an inside wall shows a capillary mark.)

They'd skimp the walls by putting the minimum amount of plaster in the rendering. The ceilings were lath and plaster. A labourer would beat hair out and mix it into the sand and lime so that the plaster would stick to the laths. Then they'd cover it over with skimming. They could make a bag of plaster go twice as far as it should have done – but later the skimming used to crack.

Instead of using 1-in. floorboards, they finished up with $\frac{13}{16}$ in. Out of a plank 3 in. thick you could get three finished boards at $\frac{13}{16}$ but you could only get two if you cut them to an inch. They fiddled the joists – they put $2\frac{1}{2}$ in. instead of 3 in. To fiddle drains, they'd put bends in instead of junctions and seal them up with clay – they wouldn't mix sand and cement in the spigots. They had the inspectors well greased.

With the roofs, as any slater will tell you, they used the cheapest thing there was. There were very cheap slates called Portmadocs; they were rubbish. Then there were other, beautiful hard slates from North Wales. Tun slates, the big, thick ones, went in an aristocracy – king tuns, queen tuns, princesses, countesses, coming down smaller. The king tun was 30 in. wide and 40 in. long – gigantic things, some of them. Some slates were sold by count and they were stretched out. To get them even thinner they used to split them. If a bloody bird landed on them they'd break.

They used to nail things together instead of joining them. I knew a builder who had a painter working for him. I was talking to this painter away from his work and he told me he'd never seen a man like that builder.

'He can make a gate quicker than I can paint them!' The builder was bashing things together in a jig.

There was no over-all control. The only thing that was inspected was the drains. The rest was up to the builder. You could buy a house for not much more than £290. Standard brickwork, they stretched that to the maximum. There should be 96 bricks to the square yard. A brick is $2\frac{7}{8}$ in. high, so two bricks and mortar should be 6 in.; there should be 12 courses in a yard, and a brick is $8\frac{7}{8}$ in. long, so four bricks and mortar make a yard. That means there should be 48 for the outside skin and 48 for the inside – roughly a hundred a yard, allowing for breakages. These fellows could stretch it to nearly $\frac{3}{4}$ in. of mortar. They could do a yard in 87 bricks. They'd lose a course in every four or five. They'd save a couple of hundred bricks – which is how these houses were built.

On a respectably supervised job when I was a lad, I was given a rod. We had a rod marked, specifying how many bricks there were in 6 ft, which the supervisor would sign. He'd come out on the site, walk up to the brickwork and put the rod on. That's how the supervisor worked.

If you were working on a Pilkingtons contract, a clerk of works would be on the job and he would inspect everything. I've known a clerk of works break a firm of plumbers who were putting three pounds of lead instead of five for lead damp courses. Of course, lead isn't very good for damp coursing because it cracks. But on the valley and flashings, and round the chimney stacks, on roofs it specified five pounds lead, and they put three. When there was no clerk of works on the job, that was the type of thing they did. On this job, the plumber got caught.

All of the residential property in this town was built like that. When we weren't busy in the yard in the afternoon, we'd go round to the property in Speakman Road, and it would be built in the men's spare time.

Lowe House Church, the Jesuits built that themselves. Father Reilly begged every penny of the quarter million it cost to build. The senior tradesmen gave bells; Joseph Swift (you know, the baking family) gave one, and his name's cast on it with a rhyme. There's a carillon of 52 bells there; they used to play hymns and songs on them. I lived right opposite, and they'd wake you in the morning. There's the clock with *Salve Regina* on the front – it used to strike the pilgrims' hymn from Lourdes. Pilkingtons gave them the clock up in the early 1920s. Before they were hung, the bells were laid in the yard. They used to have a fair there with the bells all on display – people used to give money for them. I forget the names of the priests, but they collected, borrowed and begged every penny for that

Two photographs taken during the building of Lowe House Church (see p. 138). *Above:* Laying the new foundations before demolition of the previous building on the site. *Below:* Priest supervising the work.

Above: The Peace Day Procession passes the Town Hall in July 1919; Father Reilly (farthest left of the four men marching) leads the girls.
Below: Pilkingtons works outing, a day trip to Blackpool.

church. It's a magnificent building, put up entirely by local labour. I can't think of any other that's worth calling a building that's been put up in my lifetime in this town.

The council were very good – they built good houses. Of course, there were exceptions when they were a bit unlucky with the ground – there's a lot of subsidence here – but the standard was very good. They had some first-class supervisory staff. The first staff clerk of works, who had himself been a builder, was on the job all day long. That man was there watching everything. The queues for the houses were miles long – everyone put their names on the council list. They were made and jumped for joy if they got a council house.

In general, houses were very bad. Some were one up and one down, back to back. There's a row of them standing now in Denton's Green, facing the very yard where I served my time. But today they've made them two up and two down by blocking the back door. Half-way along the block there was a passage to the back where the privy was. Everyone had a key to his own closet. You had to go out into the street, down the passage and cross the yard, even when it was raining in the middle of the night.

THE TWO SISTERS FROM PARR

Windlehurst was the first council estate, and Parr was built in 1926. The corporation started building all their houses with bathrooms – they thought they were giving you a treat. They'd give you a fireplace in your front room. There was a back boiler that kept your back kitchen warm, and your oven was back to back with it. So an old lady in one of those houses was never really cold. Most ordinary houses had no bathroom. You had a big iron boiler in your back kitchen with a little fireplace. You had to ladle the water out into bath tubs.

Colliers used to come home four or five abreast as we played about in Newton Road. When they came home, they stripped off and washed in a good big bowl of water in the sink. In fact, my mother's sister-in-law used to carry a bowl to the fireplace and fetch all his clean things for him. Then she used to rub his back down and take all the dirt off for him. You had to have big jars and kettles then. If you had a large family, you were always queuing for the kettle – there was trouble if you were going out together.

With the old house, you had an oven at the side with a big top where you could put anything to keep warm – on the range, as they called it.

139

You did have a mantelpiece, but it was so high you had to get a tall step ladder to reach it. To control the temperature, you let your fire die down a bit. You could always warm it up quickly; you were never without a fire. Round us, there was a lot of coal picked. It was the best thing in the world for a cooking stove. You had an open fire with a little bar that dropped over, and you did your cooking on that. There was a hob on the side that would always be warm. You could put the bar over the fire and boil the kettle in an instant because it would be warm already. You could cook puddings and pies in the old oven.

Your sink in the kitchen wasn't a white one like you know now. It was brown, very shallow, and you had a cold tap on it. There was no gas. My father went on at my Auntie Lizzie to have gas, but she wouldn't hear of it. Finally my father paid for it. They put gas in the living room and the front bedroom upstairs. She had four children in a two bedroomed place; she got a corporation house when her fifth was born. My father said the children would be pulling the tablecloth and having the lamp on the floor. The lamp was stuck in the middle of the table, and you always had a cloth with fancy tassels on, which the children might play with. My aunt only had the lamp from the living room – you carried it with you if you wanted to see upstairs. She went to bed in the daytime in summer. In winter, all the rooms would be dark, except the front one.

THE MINER FROM RAVENHEAD, BORN 1904
Usually a landlord would own a row comprising 10 or 12 terraced houses: two up and two down. Very few people owned their houses. I didn't know anybody who did. £20 was the deposit for a house, and nobody could afford it. You never seemed to know your landlord. There was always a rent collector who collected for whoever owned the houses.

If the rent collector missed you, he put a notice on the door. There was very little resistance – they didn't think they had any rights. [Tenants' Associations only started just before World War II.] They just paid their rent. You had to plead with the landlord if you wanted any repairs done. They'd give you a shilling or two for wallpaper. Repairs weren't so dear, but they often weren't done – toilets especially were awful.

THE MINER FROM PARR, BORN 1893
The mine owners had a fair number of houses in this locality, about a hundred just in the Parr area. On the outskirts, Clock Face, Sutton Manor, they owned in effect almost all the entire villages. They were built for miners at the time when the pits were sunk, and then again, they

had their own houses which were built since the last war to attract miners into the mines.

I suppose that when the miners left the mines they'd have to leave the house, if it belonged to the mine owners. I can't remember anyone's being evicted. I do remember evictions from normal houses. Where the tenant's not gone himself, I've seen doors and windows taken out, or sacks put over chimneys to smoke him out – all sorts of actions taken. They'd not paid the rent, apparently.

DEPUTY AT CLOCK FACE COLLIERY, BORN 1883
When these houses were being built, I lived opposite and watched them going up. I went to the manager and asked him for one, because the place I was in was getting too small. He said, 'George, you can have whichever you like, but I'd have one near the bottom, if I were you, because the ones at the top won't get any water in the summer.' So I moved into this house in 1914 and I've been here ever since. I always had water, even in the middle of summer. But a friend of mine lived in the top house and had to come down for a bath. There wasn't enough water for the source to supply all the houses. The rent was 6s 6d, and it's gone up to £2 – it's only gone up in accordance with the rates. If people stopped working down the pit, they were supposed to get out, but they didn't, and no one bothered. They were built for miners by Wigan Coal. They were a good company, and I don't come from Wigan!

Neighbours and Overcrowding

THE CANAL MAINTENANCE WORKER, BORN c. 1901
Money never bothered me. At that time, we were all in the same boat. The fact that no one had much, made people more friendly and neighbourly in those days. In sickness, they'd all gather round. They'd lend you sheets or material if you were stuck for something. They concerned themselves with each other more. Everybody knew everybody else. I had enough of friends with six children, the wife and the garden. Plenty of fun with them. People were more satisfied with the simple things, then. In the evening, we had enough to do looking after the kids and getting them to bed. Then, with my garden, that was my world. It went down the side of the house and round the back. We grew lots of vegetables, but mostly potatoes. When they grew up, we didn't need to bother. I never used to go out – never had any money to go out with anyway.

People aren't neighbours like they used to be. I remember, when my grand-mother was ill, they drew up a roster – there'd be someone there all the time. Last week, I was cleaning the front room, which I do for my wife on a Monday, and big black car drew up outside. It turned out that someone five doors away had died over the weekend, and we didn't even know.

I lived in Central Street. Don't let them fool you with all this stuff about what a great community it was. You'd have eight or ten families in a street, and they'd all be related somehow, but there might be another family just as big. There'd be a lot of feuding going on. You'd have friendly neighbours so long as you were in with the family; otherwise things could be pretty rough.

Mrs Rylands had a shop next door to us. One day she heard us ask for a butty. Our mother told us, 'I can't give you one. I haven't got any bread.'
'Don't worry, I can give you some bread,' she said.
'Yes, but I can't pay for it, Mrs Rylands.'
So she went off and brought us bread and milk. Others were bringing beef and butter and all sorts. We weren't stuck for anything. There were only 2 houses in the terrace, and Mrs Rylands had got them all to put to-gether to help us. My mother had never had her pantry so full.

You did a little bit more going into neighbours' houses. They never made tea, then – they never thought of it. I've known them come in during the afternoons. Next door to us, there was a woman of Irish descent who'd go in from morning till night to neighbours – she'd be there for four hours at a time.
The women helped each other more. They were at home and had a lot more time on their hands. If anyone was sick or needed any kids minded, someone would say 'Send them here.' We didn't have prams, we all had a shawl for carrying babies. I always nursed mine in a shawl – it was lovely to feel the baby was warm.
On Newton Road, there were fights on Saturday night, among women as much as men. They'd be swearing so that we daren't come downstairs. Three families used to have it out, shouting what the others had been doing. They used to go out to do their shopping late, getting bargains, and come

home last thing at night, taking this shopping with them into the pub. Mrs Billinge would have a drink before she came home. The trams stopped in Broad Oak Road, and they had a good walk.

Husband and wife hardly ever went out together. There was one couple who went out twice a week – I remember them, so it must have stuck in my mind. Some people used to get a jug of beer taken in to them. They always had children, and somebody had to be at home.

THE MINER FROM PARR, BORN 1893

After 1926, when the pits were being closed here, the population of this town collapsed – Ashton's Green, Collins Green, Southport, Havanagh all employed hundreds of men. In 1928, this town held 113,000; recently, before we were increased by local authority extensions, our population was only 104,000 for the same area, despite a tremendous number of extra houses (14 or 15 thousand having been built by the local authority alone). So that's surely the degree of overcrowding – the number of families living together – in the early part of this century.

In my carly childhood, every family seemed a large one. There always seemed to be a big number of children in every house. Personally, I was one of ten children. That seemed to be about average in the terraced property in which we lived. Not only that, people also took in lodgers. One wonders how they managed to exist at all.

THE MINER FROM FLEET LANE, BORN c. 1905

We had a family of 17, my mother's family, and my stepfather had four kids. Old Tony Platt made a special table, so 12 kids could get round. There were three bedrooms and up to five in a bed. There were the two wenches in the back room, my stepfather and mother in the middle room, and three beds in the front room, one with five and the other two holding four each. Most of us were on day turn, but some were going to school.

When we were going to Sunday School, mother used to sit on a chair and brush us all down one after the other. As you were walking along, you didn't know if it was a regiment or what. On Saturday, we used to get 20 loaves to last till Monday. Me, our Tom, our Dave, our Tim, our Judd and our Bill were working, so there was enough money coming in. On Sunday, they'd start peeling the potatoes and veg and, when they'd finished, they'd start doing it again for the big ones. Grandfather had an organ, and we used to go into the front room and sing while mother got the tea ready. You never bothered about being too crowded; you could always get a house if

143

you wanted to – we moved ten times. There were always ten in a bedroom then.

WOMAN, BORN AROUND 1910
It was the fashion in those days to have big families. If you didn't, your neighbours would skit at you. You could overhear neighbours: she blaming him because they had no kids, he blaming her. There were always four or five children of the same name in steps up the school. They just had them because it was the natural law. They didn't have family planning – they just had them. Some of our greatest scientists and poets were the seventh or eighth of big families brought up in poverty.

Sanitary Conditions

THE MINER FROM PARR, BORN 1893, WHO WAS ALSO A LABOUR COUNCILLOR
AND BECAME CHAIRMAN OF THE HOUSING COMMITTEE
The vast majority of the houses in this area were two bedroomed and had outside lavatories. It'd be microscopic the number of baths that people had – or what's called a modern amenity. By today's definition they were slum houses, but the fabric was often good. Many would now be receiving grants for renovation and modernizing by the local authority.

THE JOINER, BORN c. 1905
The toilet was called a dib hole. Both households were throwing all their kitchen waste into the midden where they both had a toilet. When it was full to a depth of 3 ft of filth and shit, the midden man used to come along with his legs wrapped in sacking. He'd climb in and spade it all into tubs. With the old system, it filled up in three months. The bloody flies in there would drag you under.

Well, you see, people looked upon it as part of life, like walls where the paper was peeling off – they didn't understand the reason for the damp. They thought it was coming through the wall, not up it. They had one cold water tap in each house and that very often burst in winter. There was no gas, never mind electricity. We had candles. I set the house on fire once so that the fire brigade had to come. I had the candlestick in my right hand while I pulled back the curtain to get my jacket out of the recess in my bedroom to go to an Oddfellows' meeting, and the candle must have caught the side of the curtain. They started putting gas in the main rooms, but in the back you'd carry on with the old lamp and candles.

The lavatories were just outdoor midden or tub and pail – what we called the ashpit type. You put the ashes in, and that was the lavatory as well. It was cleaned out periodically under council direction by what we called the night soil men; they generally came down at night. There was a specially constructed vehicle for emptying the tub and pail because it was liquid. For the other, there was just a normal cart. The midden was emptied by spade, with plenty of chloride of lime put down, into the nearest cart. Some of it went on the fields, but most from that period, especially at the end nearest the town, was just piled on the muck-tip like any other debris. You wouldn't know the place where that dump was today. A lot also went to fill the clayholes at the brickworks where I first started work. Now that's Parr Industrial Estate. There's coal been extracted from it, there's clay been taken, it's been used as an industrial tip, a municipal tip for all kinds of rubbish, and today it's a model industrial estate with new buildings on it.

There wouldn't be main sewers then, and even if a place was sewered it didn't mean that all houses were immediately connected up to it with flush toilets. The local authority brought in a bye-law after 1924, giving grants to the private owners of houses to convert to flush toilets.

Most people had mains water, but there were odd numbers with an outdoor mains supply and quite a few houses with toilets in an open yard behind. Toilets of the type I'm talking about were built touching up to each other along the back wall that enclosed the houses. Neighbours passed each other running backwards and forwards to the toilets. With terraced houses, you had to go down the tunnel entrance to the back yard. Of course, some of the houses were back to back – not too many when I remember, but a lot of them had been.

You know, there were houses up here that weren't converted till after the last war. When I used to come past in an early morning, round about seven o'clock, on the way back from the colliery at Bold, the heaps from the ash-pit were still on the flags. There's no back passage to this row of houses, so the night soil men had to wheel it in barrows from the back of the house and tip in on the flags. When you came by, you couldn't walk there. It was human excreta, you know, that I'm talking about.

Not only was there the open lavatory in the back yard, many of the people when I was young kept a pig in the yard, and the greatest entertainment we had as children was when they killed the pig on the land behind the cottages. We all knew who was the best pig killer in the area. What happened was that even if we didn't get to know that a pig was being killed, we soon heard from the screams when the knife was inserted, starting at a very low squeal and rising in a crescendo, then gradually dying away again as the blood poured out. The pig was first taken out of the sty in the yard and tied to a trestle and the blood was caught in a bucket as it dripped away from the wound. It was used, I suppose, for the making of black puddings. Then they proceeded to scrape and clean the pig, all in public view. The children were generally nearest to it in the hope of getting the bladder when the pig was cleaned. It used to be blown up and tied so that they could play football with it. Hot water was poured on the pig as it lay on the stretcher immediately after it was dead, and the bristles were scraped off.

On some occasions, the pig was taken to market by dealers, but in the main it was sold retail from the owner's house, cut into small joints and so on. The owners made black puddings and sausages. Often, a pig would be killed just before Christmas to give the owners a bit of extra money to celebrate with. No one had fridges then, and if you wanted to keep any of the meat, you salted it.

This was stopped by the public health and the local council – new bye-laws were brought in, I suppose, to stop the practice. Another aspect, when one comes to think about it, was that the manure was stored in heaps immediately behind the cottages. All adding to the general health hazard, because children played there. It makes one, looking back, not wonder at the high death rate among children in those days, and of the whole populace, for that matter.

One of the ways in which we, as children, earned half pennies or a few sweets was by taking the peelings or any vegetable waste from the house to people who kept pigs. They were always open to receive any waste of that kind, which they cooked up with the pig-meal.

THE JOINER, BORN *c.* 1905
I've seen bugs in houses, when we worked in demolition. Once, there was an outbreak of typhoid, and the houses had to be stripped. We took the gable ends out from these houses in Greenbank. It was the Irish quarter. They were unwanted, outcast; there was all kinds of filth amongst them. I've seen fellows in these houses, and there's lots of people will bear me out, sleeping six in one bedroom with two mattresses on the floor. The day turn got up to go to work, and the night turn lay down on the same bed.

For cooking facilities, did you ever see a washing boiler? The women in the lodging house cooked in that. They used to get spare ribs and cab-

146

bage and turnips – five or six gallons of it, these fellows used to eat. There'd be no oven or cooking stove. They used to cook over the fire – grill and braise on it, even.

The bugs were up the back, in the wall, on the ceiling – everywhere. They used to say that at the time of the coronation, in a street not far from here, when they put a flag out for King George V, the bugs came out along the pole and dragged it in.

I think it was the conditions of damp and abject poverty, with plaster infested, and the lack of personal attention – not realizing that these bugs wanted attacking. You had to get special candles and spray everything with formalin. Then you'd put a tray of water in the middle of the room, put a saucer on it with one of the sulphur candles, stop up the windows and doors, light the candle and get out quick. The sulphur fumes and the formalin made the gas that killed the bugs – it would have killed you and all. It was bad enough squirting the walls, the formalin alone brought tears to your eyes.

When we went into the houses we were debugging, we had elastic bands round our trousers to stop the flecks, as they were called. At school, they used to come inspecting nitty heads with hair clippers, and they'd take off all the hair, there and then. Then they'd go to the mothers and take *their* hair off. Bald as a cat, they'd leave them. You used to see mothers in the summertime, with their kids kneeling down in front of them, combing their hair over a piece of white paper. Lice would be falling on the paper, and they'd crush them with their thumb nail. It was always the same ones who had them – you'd see flecks jumping about on them. I've seen a woman with flecks jumping round her eyes.

There were rats everywhere. Running through the heart of St Helens was what was called the stinking brook. It came from Eccleston, entered a culvert in Lingholme Road, ran under Boundary Road and turned left to Kirkland Street. It was open there. Then it went between the houses down to the bottom of Westfield Street, where Beechams is sited. All the sewage and everything went into it; the people in those houses threw all their rubbish in. I remember playing on the centres – every ten feet all the way down the culvert there was a wooden arch to build the brick roof on. They put planks from one arch to the next, and the bricklayer laid his bricks round them. That's when the open brook was covered in.

There were rats running up and down the place and in all the houses in Napier Street, New Cross Street and Talbot Street, which all led down to the brook. At Tyrers clothiers' shop – I worked there, doing shopfitting – I had to run down the shop knocking them off the counter. The girls used to wait till I came. We filled the rat holes in with broken glass and cement, and the buggers ate that. They used to be in my workshop. I called in the Town Hall ratter, a fellow named Blakely. I had a little wire-haired terrier, a good ratter. He said, 'Take your dog away. Mine won't work with it there.' The bitch still wasn't pointing, and he said, 'There's no rats there.'

'What do you think I called you for, then? He'll tell you where they are.'

I let the terrier in, and it wasn't two seconds before he killed one. He killed 48 in one morning.

I had a friend with a grocery in Peasley Cross. Rats had been seen crossing the road and going into the cellar there at night. We went down there one Sunday morning, put the ferrets down in the cellar and stood at the top of the steps. Like a rat, a ferret hasn't got a backbone. It can squeeze itself into very narrow holes and it can wrap itself up and turn round in its own run. The rats came out of there in an endless stream that day, the dog killed them as fast as he could. We were there from half past ten till half past one, and he caught over 70. Frank was up there with a walking stick and leggings. He didn't half lash them. It was 25 or 26 the first time. They'd quieten down, there'd be a bit of a lull, then we put the ferrets in again through the window. One ferret wouldn't come out. I took the window up and saw it was practically a skeleton. It had started eating the rats it killed, till it got slow and sleepy, so the other rats turned on it and ate it.

4 Health

THE ENGINEERING CLERK, BORN 1890
My brother, who'd joined up, brought the flu back with him. Six of them landed in Liverpool and came back to St Helens by taxi. My two sisters came over that day, for tea. On Monday, we all took ill. When I came home from work, my sister was coming from the doctor's. I said 'What are you doing here?'

'Jimmy's in a terrible fever. He's talking about shooting the Germans.' He'd had a bad time in the thick of the third battle of Ypres.

That was the last time I saw those girls. Five of us took to bed, and all were dead within a week except me: my father, two sisters and my brother, that was. The doctor said to my mother, 'I'll tell you when to tell him about his brother and sisters.' He told her he'd done all he could for me, my chest and nails were black, and the inside of my stomach was rotting. The stuff coming out of my nostrils was thick black. He said if I was still living the next morning and had 6½ hours sleep he'd give me some hope. They did everything for me. They put cloth on the knocker, so I wouldn't be disturbed. Daglish's sent up a bottle of brandy; a neighbour put some of it with milk in a feeding cup and they got me to sip it. She made a note of the time. I slept 6½ hours, and I was still living in the morning.

One day someone came into my room and asked if it was all right to open the window to put the flag out, as armistice had been declared. 'Has John come back, or has he got an extension?' I asked. But they didn't tell me. Then Daglish's sent up a pheasant one of them had shot. I said, 'That's good, make sure the carcase is sent up to father, as he always likes picking it.' That was when they told me about my father. At that time, they were burying people in their hundreds by torchlight. While I was still in bed, I said I thought there was something wrong with the cemetery, so many people seemed to be going up there.

THE JOINER, BORN *c.* 1905

Once people went into consumption hospital, that was it. TB was a killer, because of bad housing and malnutrition. I've buried dozens of children after diphtheria – that's so rare now that some doctors don't recognize it when they see it.

When people had diphtheria, they used to come and disinfect your house. Every room had to be sealed, and men from the Town Hall would pump gas into the place to kill infection. They used to bathe the people in eucalyptus oil – you could tell weeks after that they'd been in hospital.

WOMAN FROM NEWTON ROAD, BORN *c.* 1900

When you were put in Eccleston Hall, you gave yourself up, because you weren't in for anything but TB. It used to be a dread place. Some got out, though; they didn't all die. I had a friend, whose son was there. They used to say you were 'on four hours' or 'on six hours', meaning four or six hours out of bed. When you reached ten or twelve hours, you were nearly better. One young man, who was on ten hours, went out to Taylor Park with his young lady – he only lay on the grass, got a cold and died. It was as bad as cancer is now. It frightened them – they used to call it the white scourge. You used to say of people, 'He's not here for long,' when they got it. That's all finished now. The trouble now at Eccleston Hall is pneumoconiosis.

THE DOCTOR

I came to St Helens in 1921. It seemed a place where there were opportunities for medical work in an urban population. What I didn't notice was that the chimneys weren't smoking, the pits weren't working and it wasn't a lucrative place.

You had to buy yourself into a practice. Usually starting as an assistant with a small share of the practice, you proceeded, gradually getting a larger share until you had it all. In my practice, there were three doctors; others were mostly in ones, but friends tended to help one another.

You were all at each others' throats to make a living. Sometimes a doctor was blamed for something that went wrong, and there'd be a breakaway. If a doctor was canvassing or scrounging for patients, there was a row. They weren't friends deep down, although they were maybe on the surface. There was an awful lot of petty jealousy, and that spread to the wives – enough said! The St Helens Medical Society is one of the oldest in England. There, the doctors were friends; they met frequently in winter. Some were members of a book club and they exchanged books, not just about medicine. It was a mixed society and included some of the Pilkington people and some from United Glass.

There were more family businesses in the town, like Nuttalls and Carrington Shaw. We knew the heads of these businesses, like the Daglishes from the foundry; we met them socially. That it was more of a multiple industry town made for a leavening of the population. I used to know a shopkeeper – a draper, haberdasher and supplier of sheets and general house furnishings – and I remarked to him that it seemed a pity so many people went into Liverpool to buy their clothes. He told me, 'This is a 95% working-class town. We stock for that population. The other 5% would go anyway – we don't stock for them.' As a businessman, he was probably right. Warrington is a better town than St Helens. Look at our town – it's too dominated by one party. Not that I'm against the Labour party, I'd say the same if it was dominated by the other.

There are more doctors now – I suppose, counting them up, there were about 20 then. Only the men were on the National Health that Lloyd George brought in. They had to pay for their families, and that was the collection system. The better-class people had accounts. If someone never paid, you could put him in the petty debt court. The commonest way was to cross him off your list. If they started badgering, they could go to another fellow. There was no liaison between doctors. If a patient with a bad debt went to another doctor, the doctor could only jaloose (put two and two together, and make four, not five). Two Poor Law doctors were appointed to look after the needy in the town.

But we're painting a very gloomy picture. There was another side to it: the medical work, and the decency and humanity that you found as you went round your patients. They were good and honest people. Those that couldn't pay . . . you cut your coat according to your cloth. If a patient contributed a small sum a week, even if the book figure was ten times that, you kept visiting. If they died, they died. You scored your pen through it. The bad debt was big, but I won't say how much. I wouldn't make us out to be martyrs – it must have paid, because we went on working. I closed my books in 1948. It was necessary to start the National Health Service in those days.

Looking back, I've had a happy working life. The type of people made the enjoyment. I can't go down town and come away quickly – I meet people I know. All the patients were friends and are to this day. You had your *amour propre* to look to – to live with yourself.

There was more competition than there is today, when they all have full lists. If a patient went away from you, it created bad feeling – we're all human, you know. I'll show you what I mean. One day a woman came in with a baby. I looked at it and, being a Scot, said, 'That's a bonny lad,' meaning pretty, petite, delicate. 'Bonny?' she said. 'Bonny? That's just why I've brought him, doctor!' In Lancashire, bonny means more plump and buxom, and that baby was rather small. I examined it for half an hour and told her that I couldn't find anything wrong. But she went to another doctor, as she wasn't satisfied, and he gave her a bottle of medicine for the baby. Later, he came round to see me and said, 'You know, you should always give them a bottle of medicine; it's what they expect.' You see, spending time on the baby wasn't good enough for her. In Lancashire, they want to know what's the matter – you have to satisfy them. The doctors were much closer to their patients. I know the Warings. They all had brains – the girls went into hairdressing and the boys went into radio shops, where the money was. They always had hens running about the house. Alderman Waring could recite me Burns by the yard. Ask the doctors of today if they know that much about their patients.

People worked morning, evening and night. We even had a surgery on Christmas night. People turned up, or we wouldn't have opened the door; they expected it. The doctor was the friend of the people – there was a personal human contact. He knew their troubles and worries. There were no health visitors or social workers then, and the doctor did maternity work – I used to do 200 confinements a year. Every other night, on average, and sometimes two in a night. My record in the flu epidemic was 100 visits, one appendix and one confinement in 24 hours. When the epidemic was on, I used to stop for one meal. I had lob scouse. That's a kind of hotpot – I had it with all the vegetables and meat in one course – and it was a big one. Then there were cups of tea for the rest of the day. Cups of tea were the most you were given when visiting.

They always had night visits. That was true all over the country. When I was doing a locum for a friend in the country down south, I had to do five or six night visits. It was terribly hard work, and constant. There was no time for hobbies and leisure. You got a fortnight's holiday a year. Otherwise there was just one half-day week; I always slept.

Cycling along the cottages, you could do a dozen an hour. One stop might take a quarter of an hour, but at the next you'd just have to say, 'Better today? Good.' And off we go. A lot more people used to live in the centre of town, and you went round there in the afternoons. Your bicycle went up against the wall, and you didn't put a lock on it. You had your bag on the back, but you could carry most of what you needed in your pockets. They couldn't do the visiting in the traffic of today, but I don't like it. It's a terrible responsibility for the receptionist to decide whether someone should be visited the same day, or whether it can be left. What often happens is that the people who shout loudest get attended to first. I know a man who was very angry that his wife had called me round late at night, but if I'd left it till morning he'd have been dead. There's no doubt patients are more mobile today, though; many have their own cars.

In this town, there was a lot of chest disease from the chemicals, soot and grime. There were the miners' illnesses of pneumoconiosis and nystagmus (which was a condition from working in the dark – your eyes went round and round). Then, of course, there were all the accidental injuries. One doctor, Robert Jackson, had a record of 100,000 injuries in his books – perhaps it's better not to take that literally, but he had the most unbelievable number. Bad injuries to the hands and kneecaps were a very common trouble in a man.

In the glass industry, it was mostly injuries. There was heat stroke on summer days, but that passed off – I can't remember its ever causing permanent debility. Of course, life was shorter; they didn't live to a great age. Glassmaker's cataract was something to do with the glare of the furnaces. There were men who had to look in to see if the metal was right, and of course they didn't have the protective clothing you have now. When the chemical works went away from St Helens, we were only left with the terrible slag heaps of waste chemicals, the odour, and the bad chests in the male population.

Another condition in miners was bronchitis. They had it till a winter cold took them off. There weren't all the old age pensioners there are today. I was never invited down the pit, except to see the conditions – not to attend anybody. But there must have been doctors at the time of accidents. There were first aid men everywhere. Blood transfusions weren't possible. With that Moorgate tube accident, you saw them coming out on drips. They didn't have that then, they were dead.

The diphtheria people had serum. They all went to hospital, some of them on tracheotomy (a tube inserted in the throat below the diphtheria adhesion, so they could breathe). Diphtheria serum was a life-saver. The disease was transmitted mouth to mouth in droplets from the breath. I don't think I'd any medicine for scarlet fever but boiled fish and potatoes when you were well enough to eat. Cases were mostly sent to hospital. You could dab them with a cold or tepid sponge to bring the temperature down, and you gave them placebos, but it was treated symptomatically. With whooping cough, they used to walk patients past the gasworks; they thought that was a cure. You gave them anti-spasmodic medicine and, when their faces were black after a spasm, you used to rush them to the front door to make them breathe with a blast of cold air. Pneumonia was treated with good nursing. Dr Cooke used to say that you had to teach a patient to *be* patient. There was a crisis in the illness. When you reached that point, you either died or woke up very weak and recovered. One reason for night visiting was to watch people with pneumonia who were nearing the crisis. I haven't seen it happen for many years. You gave injections of morphine to the people who were in pain and dying.

To certify someone insane, you had to convince the relieving officer and two doctors. Then it became a relieving officer's job. General conditions contributed towards mental illness, but I don't think it was very common. Life was too hard, people didn't have time to think of themselves. But treatment didn't exist for the cases that there were. It was said that the bill for the doctor's wine was larger than the bill for drugs at Rainhill Asylum at that time. We were never trained to deal with this class of thing – I'm glad I'm out of it.

There were rows and rows of cottage properties – there still are some. There weren't any flats or tenements, but it was ugly. There was overcrowding – sleeping top and tail, maybe three to a bed, was the usual thing. If one of them got chicken pox, they all did. There was less promiscuity, though. They used to say no prostitute could make a living.

Antibiotics have revolutionized medicine. I can remember all kinds of strange mixtures before. The juice of dandelion, called taraxacum, was used, but I don't know what for; there were all these placebos and tonics which they say are a waste of time. But Nature's tendency is to cure, not kill. Trust in the Lord was as good a medicine as any. I remember the happy things – the birth of a baby, the joy in a young mother's face. The tragedies I was inured from – they were just incidents; you can't live with tragedy.

DOCTOR'S MAN, WORKING FOR A DIFFERENT DOCTOR
The doctor said, 'You're a bit of a mechanic. How would you like to work for me. You'll learn to mix medicine and collect the contributions.' I

worked for him and I used to drive the lady out in a big MG. She was a potato farmer's daughter from the East Lancs Road. I took her to play tennis. I had to wear a white shirt, black tie, kid gloves and a blue waistcoat.

The doctor said he had a house on Broad Oak Road and asked if we'd take it. It would be a surgery for a couple of hours a day, and we lived in the flat upstairs.

I went out on Saturdays and had all the shillings to collect. Everything was marked down in a little notebook, how much everyone had paid. There were private doctors then, and they paid what they could afford. Mostly they were paying off treatment they'd had – medicine on the never-never, really. Some would tell you to call next week, but they always wanted the doctor to come out. When the National Health came, these bills finished. Some people owned £20 or £30, and that had to be written off.

When I first went there, I used to get night calls. The telephone was upstairs in our flat. I went by push bike to Haydock and got the car out to take the doctor where he was needed. There was a secretary who fixed the charges for a consultation. When the patient came to the doctor, it would be 5s 6d; a bottle of medicine was the same, and a visit to the patient's home cost 6s 6d.

The front room here was the waiting room from nine to eleven. In this back room, there was a big table with the doctor's cards in a box. He'd sit on one chair and the patient on another. He'd reach up for his cards and prescribe for them. If he wanted to syringe someone's ears, he'd get warm water from the kitchen and do it in here. At least he had a nice fire to warm his back, which is more than we had upstairs.

There would be 15 or 20 Winchester bottles mixed at the chemist in Haydock, and I'd drive them over. For baby mixture or stomach ailments, he'd call out the one he wanted, and I used to take so many drams, to which I added water. Many nights, the doctor would tell us what tablets to give so that he wouldn't have to come in.

There was diphtheria about. Children brought in would be sick all over the floor, and I'd have to clear up. One fellow came in with a burst ulcer – he filled the bucket I gave him with blood. During the flu epidemic, people were coming in all the time sneezing. I never caught it; I've got a clean card. I was always being injected with something, all over my arm. I never caught anything.

You touched on everything in nursing. It was all work because the people had very little, and you knew that, but you did your best for them when they came sick. We had to do all the scrubbing and cleaning as well as bathing the sick and looking after their sores. It was very primitive as regards hygiene.

The main thing was looking after the person's physical comfort. It was easy to be patient with them – they wanted very little; they knew very little of the comforts of life. Of course, people were always ready to help themselves if they could. I found them helpful and generous, if you would ask them – they were very kind. It was a great comfort to look after *their* creature comforts, their immediate needs. People would come in very dirty and very poor, with their feet not washed for a year, and they didn't know the comfort of clean feet till it was done for them. It was really a pleasure to see them recover, to *feed* them, because a good many people were hungry at the time. These were the people you liked to help and the people who wouldn't say they were in want till you found it out.

None of them were paying patients. There was a time when the nurses only had their uniforms paid for. I was a nun when I came here very, very young. Some of the nurses were probationers, just beginners. There was no general training – we had to do our final exams years after. These nuns who were only beginners would want to be taught a good many things. The first thing was to look after the interests of your patient at all costs – at your own cost, sometimes.

The hospital was supported by voluntary contributions in the beginning. They collected in churches, they had collectors here and there throughout Lancashire; some people signed money in their wills. Many a thing we wanted, we had to do without, but we did the best we could with what we had. Working men built the wall round the hospital in their spare time. St Helens hospital took their share, but they were better situated. We took any creed that came and, in fact, most of our patients were Protestants. We never had any religious trouble, you know.

There were only two wards: St Patrick's for the men, and St Helen's for the women and children, who were in one long ward – there would be about 20 children and 15 women. The children were in the front part of the ward. The men were downstairs. They were brought here just as they were brought out of the pit. Some were in very bad condition – you wouldn't know what you were washing. The men were very dirty. Before doing anything with them, you had to wash them, those who were not able to have baths. They used to come in badly hurt on stretchers. Any part of the night you'd get them in if you were on duty.

A good many of the nursing sisters came by boat from Ireland. They'd have to be requisitioned, you know. They came for a living if you like to put it that way; some of them made very good nurses. They came to our order: The Perseverance of the Mother of God. Officially, we're a nursing and teaching order. Some joined it before they came, and some came to join, but nursing had a draw for the young.

THE RELIEVING OFFICER

There was a chap in the market on Saturday who had what he called his surgery – he used to pull teeth. If you had a toothache, you had to wait until Saturday. He had a flare lamp which he used to stick on a pole. 'Step into the surgery, please,' he'd say. I used to laugh – you could hear the screams. It was a wonder he didn't kill anyone. The crowd was the entertainment. He was a real showman: 'Now gentlemen. I'll extract teeth. Which one of you is it to be?' He'd get his arm round the victim's neck and pull. 'There it is, gentlemen.' He'd wave the tooth under the light and drop it in a spittoon. A broken jaw was a mere detail. The blood was spattered around. But he was never short of customers.

Under Parish Relief, we had free dental care and a new set of teeth for £2. I've known people make their own out of bone and hardboard stuck together with tallow. Very often, though, they would do without their teeth – they could break nuts with their gums, they were so hard.

5 Insurance, Savings and Burial

EMPLOYEE OF THE WESLEYAN & GENERAL FRIENDLY SOCIETY, BORN 1905

In those days, the majority of working people had no money for buying a house. Consequently, their insurance was invariably for death benefits. Otherwise, if a death occurred, they wouldn't have any money. You'd call at a house and collect 6d a week. People were quite happy to pay; indeed, they were very embarrassed if they couldn't find the money.

We used to turn out at a quarter past twelve on Friday and Saturday. Friday was a busy day, as people were paid then. You'd never get any money on a Tuesday or Wednesday. If a person wasn't in when you called, you went back later.

There was no saving among working-class families – maybe one in a thousand cases, but you had to be mean and deprive yourself of necessities to do it. They endeavoured to keep up their payments. We gave them 13 weeks to recover if they got behind. When the 13 weeks were up, if it was a long time that they'd paid, they'd get a reduced amount in case of death, otherwise they'd get nothing.

The collecting amounted to about £10 a week – today they're taking £200. It provided a sparse living. The people now don't ask for 6d; they ask for £1. I was never able to adjust myself from pennies to such a large amount. I thought they couldn't afford it.

I think the people I went to were marvellous. As a matter of fact, I think it's a sad thing that affluence has taken away kindness. I went into houses where there was little or nothing and they'd say, 'My God, you look cold! Come in by the fire for a rest and have a cup of tea.' I didn't have time, but I went in out of politeness. I never had time – you had to fight the clock and extend the round, as you were paid on commission. I was the last to be on the old terms: if I didn't go out collecting, I wouldn't earn any money. I can't remember the commission, I think it was 10% in some parts and 20% in others. Well, I'm a bit vague, mind

158

you; I think I was getting £2 a week, and that would be collecting from 400 people. I used to run like the devil. I was a man who was very energetic physically and kept in good health, thank God. On the go all the time in the supposedly fresh air, if you could call it so. I attribute my reasonable health now to that.

You'd have to keep your ears open. If you heard a whisper that the daughter was getting married, you'd make a proposition. Often you'd find that the family would say, 'Our Mary's getting married, so go and fix her up.' If you saw a lady with a protruding stomach, you'd know she was having a baby that would have to be insured. It's very mercenary, isn't it! All this would be amusing if it wasn't quite so tragic, which it was at the time.

If someone died, the money was paid out as a single sum. They used it for funeral expenses. In most cases, it only covered the funeral. They could bury an old man for about £25, which was an enormous amount of money. Ten to one, they took the best part to pay the undertaker. You can only get what you pay for in this world, and they could only pay very small sums. Of course, the amount varied with how much was put in and the expectancy of life – everything in insurance is calculated on life expectancy. If you'd paid for 20 years, you stopped payments when you retired at 65, and your policy was still all right.

WOMAN, BORN DURING WORLD WAR I
One woman who ran a corner shop had a way of saving. She'd get twenty or thirty people, draw their names out in order and write them down. Each week, everyone put a shilling into a pool and you got thirty bob in the first week, if you'd drawn number 1, or in the 28th, if it was number 28. It was a way of saving. If you drew an early number, and didn't really need it, you'd get someone who was desperate to give you 5s for it and you'd take his turn later on.

THE SHOP WORKER IN A TAILOR'S AND OUTFITTER'S
You got a three-garment suit for 12s 11d. We could fit a man out for a funeral – shirt, black cap, black tie, collar, pair of socks and pair of black boots – for a pound, and we'd give him a pair of braces – we didn't charge for them. They used to draw their insurance money, that was how they were able to equip themselves. It was only with a death that you got a new suit from the insurance money. So if you wanted new clothes, you had to wait for someone in the family to die. They used to pay the insurance

money for a death certificate, provided you weren't in arrears with the payments.

THE JOINER, BORN *c.* 1905, WHO WAS ALSO AN UNDERTAKER
How could they afford a funeral? They didn't afford it. People did pay, they used to have to go on relief, or they paid insurance policies of their own. We used to keep a shopful of coffins for still-born babies in stock. Now we don't have any – if we need one we make it to order.

People were buried in poor ground. If they were really out to pay for it and anxious to co-operate by having the barest minimum, you could do a funeral complete, a coffin, hearse and one cab, for £5. The coffin was made of elm or chestnut, and it would have rings and handles. Then they would have what was termed a 'public single interment'. The grave was dug only once and kept open till it was full. They'd cover the coffin with a door and some soil. It wouldn't be long before there was another one. Each of these graves was unmarked and officially held six.

They weren't necessarily paupers, simply people who couldn't afford anything else. You could make a coffin for £2 10s. A hearse cost £1 if you were hard up – that way it was dirt cheap. Then there were some who couldn't pay that, but it was something that had to be paid at all costs. They always reckoned the dead weren't lying easy till the funeral was paid for. Even though you did get bad debts, for the majority it was a matter of conscience – they wouldn't rest till it was paid for. You had to go with them to the relieving officer to see if he'd give you a bit of a grant.

It always upset me – I could never see a parent who'd lost a child crying, especially a father.

6 The Institutions

In the state's welfare provisions during the period after World War I, the thin line between poverty and starvation was still held by the Poor Law. Instituted in the reign of Elizabeth I, the Poor Law had last been subject to major modification in 1834, when a Board of Guardians was set up to administer it in every local area. After 1834, Poor Law relief was only supposed to be granted to people who were living in the workhouse. To live at home and still receive relief – what was known as outdoor relief – was the exception. Any payment which was made was means-tested; any man capable of work was expected to do so, at the Guardians' direction, on tasks such as breaking stone.

By the end of World War I, a lot of these regulations had been relaxed. The Guardians were by then specifically briefed to ensure that anyone eligible for relief was 'sufficiently clothed, fed and lodged'. Children were no longer allowed to live in the workhouse. The rule that men had to work for relief was normally waived, although this was supposed to be done only in special circumstances. One of the reasons for this was that the Boards of Guardians were appointed by the local authorities, and where the Labour Party were gaining strength, the working class were getting representatives on the Boards.

Although the guiding principles of the Poor Law were laid down by central government, the scale of payment was locally determined. It was controlled largely by the fact that it was supposed to be raised entirely from the rates. This meant that in poor areas the rates had to be vastly greater than in rich ones in order to meet this bill. However, it also meant that pressure could be put on a local Board to get the level of relief improved.

The prewar Liberal government under Asquith had provided some very basic welfare provision over and above this. In 1908, Old Age Pensions were instituted, and then, in 1911, Lloyd George as Chancellor of the Exchequer successfully piloted two bills: one establishing health insurance, the other beginning a scheme for unemployment benefit – both dependent on National Insurance contributions. The Old Age Pension was minimal, standing at ten shillings a week by the early 1920s. From 1925, the Tories began to make these pensions, as well as the new widows' and orphans' pensions, also dependent on insurance contributions. By this time, there were over a million old age pensioners, and the health scheme covered about half the workforce – but not all their dependants.

Unemployment benefit was more complicated. Until 1920, it was only available in a few industries such as engineering and shipbuilding. The idea behind this was that these were industries where people were often laid off; unemployment benefit would tide them over from one job to another. In 1920, this contributory scheme was extended to nearly all manual workers, but it wasn't designed for the periods of protracted un-employment then being experienced. The amount of benefit people were entitled to through their contributions soon ran out. Rather than throw people on the Poor Law, the government devised the notion of 'extended benefit'. The theory was that people could continue to draw benefit as a 'privilege', even though they were no longer entitled to it, with the vague notion that it would be repaid through contributions once they were back at work. This scheme was cobbled together in a series of twelve Unemployment Acts between the end of the war and 1927 – which reveals just how unprepared the state had been to take on the responsibility for unemployment. This period was the only time when unemployed people could draw benefit which was neither means-tested nor fully covered by insurance contributions. The system was comprehensively revised after the National Government took power in 1931, when even people entitled to full benefit through contributions became subject to means-testing.

The Poor Law

RELIEVING OFFICER, BORN 1900

The Poor Law was operational until well after World War I, when Public Assistance came in. Here, it was called the Prescot Board of Guardians. The town of St Helens was split into four districts, and there were four relieving officers, each responsible for the poor, sick and aged. Those wanting assistance came to Hardshaw Street. Having taken down the details, we always visited the home to make sure the funds were distributed properly. We had a subcommittee to interview the people the relieving officer had visited. A chap who had a serious complaint could come along.

The committee were selected by the council. There were some councillors, and some people appointed *ex officio*, former teachers or welfare officers.

WOMAN ON THE COMMITTEE (PREVIOUSLY THE MUNITIONS WORKER),
   BORN 1895

It was called the Court of Referees, and I was there as representative of the General & Municipal Workers. We used to meet once a fortnight, on a Wednesday morning. There were about five of us. Mrs Shard came from Parr. Colonel Guy Pilkington would bring daffodils or other flowers and say, 'Now, you get these in water.'

The relieving officers reported to our committee. I remember, one of them used to describe some houses as sunshine houses. What's a sunshine house? One with so many holes you can see all through it.

In one case that has always been on my mind, a lady came wanting some relief as her husband wasn't working. We gave her money so that she could go to the landlord and pay the rent. She didn't pay him or get food, and when she came back we asked her why. Her husband had spent it backing horses. We sent for him, and his first words were, 'What's it got to do with you?' We soon told him. We didn't give them any money whatsoever, only vouchers. Mrs Shard said, 'We'll show you if you can do what you like with the people's money.' The money came from the town – there was nowhere else for it to come from.

MAN ON THE NATIONAL INSURANCE APPEAL TRIBUNAL, THE SHOP WORKER,
   BORN 1893

I was on the National Insurance Appeal Tribunal representing the men. When these people came before the tribunal, the Insurance officials put before us full records of every time they had gone sick or been unemployed – all their history.

There were some hard cases with the miners. Very few doctors would give notes saying death was due to pneumoconiosis – it was all chronic bronchitis and heart trouble. That was a bit rough on the widow. Even if we decided in her favour, the commissioner would often turn our findings down. When a widow came, she always had a medical representative to put her case. You had two opinions, her own doctor saying it was pneumoconiosis, and the one from the insurance unable to find any sign of pneumoconiosis, just chronic bronchitis. You can see what a hard decision it was.

The only income they had apart from the Poor Law was from the Friendly Societies, which were under the auspices of the government. Normally, if a man went sick he got 15s. That only lasted about six months before it went to half-pay, depending on contributions. If a man was earning £2 10s, he wasn't doing too badly, but if he got pneumonia or broke a leg he got 15s. Ninepence a week paid from wages into government funds earned you sick pay from one of the societies – the Catholic and Royal London were two of the biggest. Then they would come and apply for assistance.

When they came, there was a scale of assistance. The committee would interview them. We'll say they had a rent of 7s and an income of 15s from the society. The scale would be 20s for husband and wife, plus rent and an allowance for each child of – don't laugh at this – 2s, however old they were. A widow got 10s a week, with 5s for the first child and 3s for each successive child. So a widow with four children would get 24s a week. Then they should have had a widow's pension to which the husband had contributed, but often the contributions had not been paid. Then, if she had to find 7s a week for rent, she couldn't live on what she had.

Don't call them the good old days; they were bad. There were people who died without relatives; there were people just derelict in lodging houses. But there were no more paupers' graves. We arranged things with the parson, where people had died without relatives, and put a stop to paupers' graves.

We had a lot of grumblers and malingerers, but on the whole it was a job I thoroughly enjoyed. A relieving officer had to take people who were not under proper care and control, and were considered a danger to the public, to Rainhill Asylum. *That* wasn't funny, believe me; I've had some free fights. People with nervous breakdowns, schizophrenia, religious mania – things had just gone haywire with them and they couldn't cope with the world. There was a young man who thought he was someone else – there was no convincing any of them. They used to visit me afterwards, quite all right.

'Don't worry,' I'd say, 'have a week or two off, and I'll give your wife the money. I'll come and visit you.' That's the thing they looked forward to, the visiting. We became friends. It's all right now, but it hasn't got the personal touch. When I went round, they treated me as judge, jury and someone to talk to and ask for advice. I'd keep off legal or medical advice, although people used to bring their children to me. I'd tell them to go to the doctor. In those days, if you couldn't pay a doctor, you resorted to home remedies. You solved everyone's problems, wayward daughters, wayward sons, people who owed four weeks' rent and feared the landlord would turn them out.

There was the famous Romeo who went off with people's wives. When the wife wanted to go back home, she'd find herself locked out and come round to me. 'Don't worry,' I'd say. 'What time does your husband come up from the pit?'

'He'll be up at four o'clock.'

So I'd wait at the pit head as the men came up. When I'd found the right black face, I'd say, 'All right, she's played the fool, but forgive her. Who's looking after the children?' It generally worked. I wasn't surprised. I used to think what a miserable life they had – the only pleasure was the pub at the weekend, and there wasn't much money for that.

One lady had 48 years' rentbooks, beautifully kept, and signed up every week. She wasn't owing a penny. She had 10s a week pension, and all I could give her was 5s. I used to ask 'How do you carry on?' She had a beautiful clean house that was a joy to go in. I used to call regularly. She would ask, 'Do you want some tea?'

'No thanks,' – because tea cost money, and she hadn't got any. Sometimes, I'd leave a penny so she could get some, and I'd have it next time. She had no gas stove. She used to have to boil the kettle on the fire.

A lot of the houses were beautifully kept. The people were proud of their cottage property. None of my brother officers would urge them to sell anything. I used to say, 'Keep your little home together,' and they did. Most houses in a village were cottages. Some of them were deplorable slums, but people kept their house and furniture spotlessly clean. How they did it beats me. When I had to report on one house, I said 'Rent 13s a week, worth easily ninepence.' That was because they were jerry-built; they weren't built to last more than 20 or 30 years.

If people defrauded the ratepayers, I used to have to go to court. They were usually fined a pound or thirty bob for obtaining money by false pretences. If they went to prison, then the wife and children would be on my books. They didn't take it out on me. I'd see them in the street and they'd say 'I'm sorry about last week. I was a bloody fool.'

Many wouldn't come for help. I had to ask about, and I used to get information from neighbours. There were people with poverty staring them in the face, and very often, I couldn't persuade them to take public money. Some just wouldn't, they preferred to struggle on. I used to ask them, 'How are you doing?'

'Not so bad.'

'I was talking to your son. You're on the pension – at 10s a week?'

'Yes.'

'Your rent's 4s 6d. How do you manage, especially in winter?'

'Oh, I manage. I don't want any charity.'

'It isn't charity. It's there to help you. There's no charity about it. Do come round and see me.'

In those days, a son would be liable for his parents. It was difficult to comply when they were living so poorly themselves. The law said they were liable if they were earning. If they were single and living at home, their income was counted against any relief.

THE COMMUNIST FROM THATTO HEATH, BORN 1902, WHO WAS AN ORGAN-
IZER FOR THE NATIONAL UNEMPLOYED WORKERS' MOVEMENT

If a father was working with a grown-up son out of work, the son didn't qualify for any relief. It was the same if the father was out of work and the son was working. So the son, daughter or father used officially to go into lodgings with someone in the same street, with friends or relations. In a lot of cases, they never did lodge there; that's just what they told the officer. In some cases, they even went on the road because the family would be penalized if they stayed at home. So they travelled from work-house to workhouse.

WOMAN FROM NEWTON ROAD

People now don't go through what my grandmother suffered. Now, when you're old, you have nothing more to worry about. My grandmother used to strap all week. At the weekend she took her 10s pension, and she was all right for another week. If she had a shilling change, she thought she owned the world.

Eventually, they put her in Whiston workhouse. My grandmother thought the world had come to an end. Her sons had to pay half-a-crown each to keep her in – and it was terrible at that time to take that much off you. They all had children, and it was a terrible job to make ends meet. Old people now, it grieves them to go to Whiston Hospital because they think it's still the workhouse. My grandmother wasn't in for long. I'll tell you why: she had to be brought out because her sons couldn't pay. They did it through the courts – it wasn't just asked for, you got a notice. They brought her out, and my mother had her to live with us then.

I had a number of spells of being unemployed. I was a blacksmith's striker at Pilkingtons. They decided to replace the system of making plate glass. Instead of blowing it, they had a system of drawing it flat out of the tanks. The smithy was being cut down, so 14 of us were sacked. That was early in 1924, and I was out of work for nearly two years. I was the branch secretary of the National Unemployed Workers' Movement. Finally, I took a job down Alexandra colliery and had to fall out of unemployed activities, although I still kept in touch with what was going on.

If you were unemployed for too long, you went on Parish Relief. To receive unemployment benefit, you'd to have 106 stamps, but later they took the requirement down to 16, then to eight. There were between one and two thousand people on Poor Law relief in St Helens. I only went on once, and that was just for a month. Most jobs on sewerage and roads with the council lasted more than eight weeks, so that put me all right as far as benefit was concerned.

The Unemployed Workers' Movement used to hold a lot of meetings and activities. There were two or three open air meetings almost every week. We used to have a series of demands on the Town Council. The slogan was 'Work or full maintenance'. We used to try to get the council to open up jobs so people could be employed. We met groups of councillors. Labour had a majority on the council and you'd have thought we'd have got somewhere, but we didn't. We had meetings in the Town Hall. Once the Chief Constable stopped us going in there. He claimed one of the Roman Catholic churches had a dance booked for the evening, and that we would spoil the specially waxed floor if we went in. He let me go in and have a look. It was waxed – whether it was true that it had been prepared for a dance, I don't know. He wanted us all to march into the police yard. We held the meeting on the Town Hall steps instead. We weren't marching into any trap.

The number of people unemployed in St Helens varied between 8,000 and 10,000. I must have represented hundreds of these people about their benefit. The government had all kinds of ways of reducing it. There was a clause referred to as 'Not Genuinely Seeking Work'. When you went in to see the clerk in the Labour Exchange, you had to tell him there was no work you could find – he didn't ask you. They started a scheme of interviews during which you would be asked where you had looked for work. They made you go back for six days, which was a week, really. You were expected to name at least three places where you had looked for work in the morning and three places in the afternoon each day of the week. Most of those who were called for interview didn't know of this unofficial rule, and people were knocked off the list wholesale. Of course, it didn't mean that you couldn't go to the same place two, three or even four times. At first, you had to carry a notebook or sheet of paper and get a signature from the manager at each works to say that there was no work. We soon put a stop to that. We got two or three hundred men to queue at one place at the same time. The manager was soon ringing up the Labour Exchange telling them to stop. They altered it so that you had to write it down yourself. Occasionally, they'd ask to see it. If you failed to give the required number you were sent before a court of referees and duly held to be Not Genuinely Seeking Work.

We used to give out papers outside the Labour Exchange with a list of places on it, but we had to stop that when one fellow was asked in front of the referees where he got his list from, and told them. So then we made them write the list down themselves before they went in. They were allowed to read the names off the slip of paper. Of course, after you'd been unemployed for a few weeks, you couldn't possibly go every day round all these places where you knew there wasn't any work. You just waited till you heard of something going and went to see about it.

If you couldn't claim unemployment benefit, there was Poor Law relief. They used to send the relieving officer to your home. If you had a piano, a gramophone, a good cupboard, or any saleable article, they would tell you to sell it before you got any relief. In some cases, they looked to see how much there was in the larder. I remember meeting a woman in Bolton with a son who was smaller than his next but two brother down, although he was 14. She said quite seriously, 'We were on the Means Test when he was born. We couldn't afford to feed him properly.' If you had any supplies in at all, the amount was taken out of your Parish Relief. Sometimes, they didn't give you any money at all, just food vouchers that you had to take to the grocer's shop. You weren't allowed to buy any luxury goods, no cigarettes, cakes or anything like that, only bread, butter, bacon, tea, sugar and that sort of thing. They'd give you a cheque for ten bob or fourteen shillings, and that had to last.

Later on, there was a lot of struggle over this lot. We had a demonstration at the county offices in Preston. Unemployment benefit was 17s for a single man, and the top amount the Board of [Poor Law] Guardians would pay was 15s – to some it was as little as 12s. We had three contingents marching in Preston, one from Wigan, Leigh, Warrington and the St

Helens area, a contingent from Manchester, Burnley and a small one from Blackpool.

When we got to Preston, they billeted us in a parish church school. The other contingents were in similar places, and we slept on the floor. The following day, we had a big meeting in the Preston market place and marched on the Lancashire County Council on one side of the railway. When we got there, we asked them to receive a deputation of 12 people representing different county areas. They refused to accept 12, but they did accept a group of three. The Preston people were in the main road and the others in the side street. The crowd moved in when the three went into the office. The police got the wind up, arrested the three in the deputation and started to hit out at the Preston crowd. You could hear the batons knocking on people's heads. I was in charge of the Wigan section. I stood up by the street entrance with a megaphone and shouted, 'The police are attacking the people!' A number of members, mostly ex-rugby players from Wigan, filched some chair legs from the school, got in front of the crowd and confronted the police. As soon as someone hit back, the police retreated to the County Hall. A few fellows had bloody faces.

It was all rather confused then. I thought we'd better try to get away before there was any more shimozzle. I lined up three or four ranks and asked them to make back for the market place. We got all the members to fall in behind the banner and make their way. At the railway, we were met by six mounted policemen. They didn't do anything, because we were led by two policemen on foot – not that we'd have gone their way unless we'd wanted to. We started a meeting back in the market place, demanding the release of the people arrested. I went to meet the Chief Constable, who was standing outside a door behind a big iron gate. When I told him what I wanted, he asked me to come in. I refused, as I had no idea what would happen inside, away from the public gaze. He came out and said, 'It's all a mistake.'

'What's a mistake?' I asked.

'Those three aren't arrested, no one's under arrest. One may receive a summons, that's all.'

I didn't believe him. 'How do I know they're not arrested? They haven't got back to the meeting.'

But when I got back, there they were.

The Chief Constable [of St Helens] was a real vicious type – he was the one the Watch Committee sacked because Councillor Boscow had a grudge against him. They got rid of him for a few months, then had to reinstate him. In theory, police were controlled by the Watch Committee, which was a subcommittee of the Town Council. But the government paid half of the cost. It was done through the Inspector of Constabulary, who was usually a retired general or something like that. When he came round, they showed him the offices, the force paraded for him and he went off to sign the Certificate of Proficiency.

When they sacked the Chief Constable, the government demanded a court of enquiry. Though the Watch Committee refused to attend the enquiry, it was held just the same. During this time, the Inspector of Constabulary refused to sign the Certificate of Proficiency – he'd obviously been told not to. That meant that the Town Council would have to pay the whole cost of the upkeep of the police force. After a little while, they met the government again and decided on another enquiry. This time, the council were represented and brought witnesses to prove their case. It was a real washing of dirty linen in public. He was a bully and tried to browbeat everybody. The decision of the enquiry was that he should be reinstated, and he was, as the council couldn't afford to pay the whole cost of keeping up the police force.

The Bible Class

The Bible Class is a Church of England organization. It meets every Sunday afternoon in the Parish Church. Founded in 1888, it had in its heyday over 2,000 men on its books and could expect an attendance of 500 on any given Sunday. Today, there are only 50 or so regulars, and most of them are pensioners. There is a parallel class for women.

ONE OF THE OLDEST REGULAR ATTENDERS
When I joined the bible class in 1907, I was working on the trams. I couldn't attend except on rare occasions – there was Sunday working every week then at 4d an hour. Before I joined, my father had sent me to St Mary's Sunday school. At that time, Mr Gore was the secretary and Mr Bickerstaffe his assistant. My father had been a member since the start in 1888.

We shed tears in the trenches when we heard that the Parish Church had burned down. Then the bible class had to be held in the Town Hall. I persuaded my brother to come along with me the first time I went back after coming home from the war. It made me blush, and I know it made my brother blush too, when they said two men came to the class of their own accord. They even asked my brother to stand up!

170

From that time, I had the opportunity to go more often. It was a rare sight to see the men coming out of church. I was a conductor on the old trams. Nine times out of ten, we used to volunteer to bring people from Eccleston Park and back. And we used to be pretty well packed. There was a load from Denton's Green, too. That was extra work for men on Sunday – all the transport then was run by the District Tram Company. I remember one of the Pilkingtons, Dick Pilkington, who used to live at the bottom of Prescot Brow, came on the tram every Sunday – he didn't have much to do with the bible class, though he attended. The biggest part of the Pilkingtons were non-conformist.

The men in the class were church people, and it was through the church that they decided to come to the class. There were good preachers, and it was an occasion just for men. The women started their own later. During the war, men from the bible class got a letter every month to keep us in touch. We got them when we came out of the trenches and went to our billets.

There were 12 districts, each with a divisional officer who was responsible for the men in his district. The men in charge of each division had six or seven visitors to deal with. It was organized that way. My first job, when I started, was as a visitor. I got to be divisional officer for Number Four division in the town centre. I had six men in my charge. I still have my books recording the men's attendance – you can see by looking down the columns who the most regular comers were. Of course, a lot of men couldn't manage very often because they were working shifts.

We visited the sick, and any case of trouble or illness we used to report either to a curate or to a bible class official. If a fellow missed.two weeks, you'd always have someone go and see him. Everyone was very keen, but if he didn't want to come there was no one to force him. Any particular case of a member out of work, or down and out, we'd visit him to get him back on the road. They got help from the bible class committee. It was only half-crowns or five shillingses, but that was something in those days. We used to have a sick club, 'Sick and Divide', as we'd divide a sum from it each week. The curates used to see the needy people when possible. The secretary and committee allotted so much money to each district. Some were too proud to receive it. The secretary and the vicar had the say over all these things; you couldn't do anything without their permission.

Every man has a number, which he gives to the secretary at the door of the church on Sunday. The service has never altered. It is a mixture of hymns and prayers, with a scripture reading and an address. We used to have all the best men to speak – men like Bardsley – aristocrats, we called them.

We had field days to raise money – I started that off. There was a game with a steel ball which you had to roll into holes, and you got prizes, mostly coconuts, depending on your score. When we first started, we only had that game, but later on there were all kinds of side shows.

Members of the committee met every Monday and did all the business – they still do. They noted in the register how often each man came, and all about him. At the Annual General Meeting, all the officials, the secretary and other officers, were appointed. Between the wars, there were a lot of men on the list, I should say well over a thousand.

The Roman Catholic Church

ROMAN CATHOLIC FROM SUTTON MANOR

In those early years, the boys from here used to walk to the Catholic school, St Bartholomew's, at Rainhill, and the seniors went to St Anne's, Sutton. There was a denominational divide, and they kept more or less to themselves. The areas were family areas, everyone knew everyone else, and four or five families would compose a street. This was a national phenomenon, not really local, but more pronounced in the towns. It's very hard to explain. The divide was nothing detrimental to any individual. Anyone who was bigoted would make play of it, but that's all. Generally, the works owners made the political divide, and not the religious bodies. The children could mix, but there were times when conflict could occur after school – on St Patrick's day, the children would be shouting 'I or E?' (Irish or English?)

There were Catholics here before our grandfathers' time, before the Irish came. I'd say it was fifty-fifty Catholic and Protestant. You didn't get your job through your religion. Really, it was on a personal basis – if the boss knew your parents, you'd get the job. Senior jobs in the mining industry went from father to son.

Now, there is an accepted Christian unity – the parish priest from here will go to St Michael's, and vice versa, but you wouldn't have seen that in the early years. You can't generalize about attitudes in the town as a whole then. There were no travel facilities. The Sutton Manor bus company ran one bus every two hours back. From a denominational point of view, the parish priest was the only person you saw.

The Catholic Young Men's Society was very strong in the early years, and they had the CYMS clubs, which were confined to members, but they've gone by the board. There was general association and discussion in the clubs, where they had a bar. They used to meet to have bible readings.

The St Vincent de Paul society is an organization which is still going, doing the same job of work. Parishioners of all denominations gave them donations. They handed out money wherever there was sickness or extreme need. It was a practice for the priest to visit every house once a month. Some big churches had three curates, then. The priest was a very important figure – wherever he went, you saw kids run up to him. There was 100 per cent attendance, more or less, on Sunday – everybody went. The church played a very important part in the community.

THE CATHOLIC HEADMASTER

The whole of south Lancashire, right down from Preston, had always had a fair number of Catholics. Preston has more than St Helens; Wigan and St Helens have about the same. There are places where Catholics have always been strong, right from the Reformation. Once, the figure was 33% – I don't know what it is now.

When you say 'Catholics', there were many only in name. Most people in St Helens now don't go to any church – even Catholic attendances are dropping. Crowds of people only go three times; when they're baptized, when they're married, and when they're carried there dead. They still call themselves Catholics. The pupils at Catholic schools will say they're Catholic; it's the same with Anglicans, but I wouldn't say it was true of Jews.

WOMAN, BORN *c.* 1910, DAUGHTER OF THE LATE SECRETARY OF THE TRADES AND LABOUR COUNCIL

My father used to say there was no one in the town who could call him their enemy – he could talk to conservatives just as well as socialists. The only thing was that he got a bit strong against Catholics at one time.

It was true that catholicism in this town was very strong. They had a church at Lowe House. I knew a woman who, as a Catholic, went to mass on All Saints' Day, 1st November, which was also the day on which the municipal elections were always held. The father used to say from the pulpit who to vote for, and this woman voted for the candidate, a conservative. She was very upset afterwards and said she'd never do it again.

It was a very strong Catholic town. There was a lot of bitterness. They tried to get as many Catholics on the council as they could. The Catholics used to come to their own, and my husband, who was a Catholic, used to say, 'Whenever he comes, give him something.' They came round about every six weeks and I always used to say, 'I'm not of your faith.' It was to keep them – I don't know how priests live, but they seemed to do very well. I've seen Father Reilly come up with his little case to the pork butcher, who used to fill it up – I've seen that with my own eyes. He was crafty, was Father Reilly. I've known children he asked all to take a potato to school – he had sacks of them at the end of it. He built Lowe House – there was a cardboard cut-out, and you had to pay a penny or twopence to put a pin-prick in it. The priests tried to get so many of their own on the council. Then, it couldn't be proved, but jobs seemed to go to Catholics.

THE COMMUNIST FROM THATTO HEATH, BORN 1902

We used to have regular open air meetings in the market place. We were influential in the National Unemployed Workers' Movement. I stood as a candidate in Central Ward, the main slum ward, and also the main Catholic one, opposing a fellow called Marsden, who was the official Labour candidate. To be a Labour candidate, you had to be a member of the party for at least 12 months, but he hadn't. So the party disowned him after all his election material had been printed.

This ward always put forward Roman Catholics. It was held that you couldn't win if you weren't Catholic, and there was a lot of truth in that. We had a hell of a rough time. Once, a crowd of one or two hundred gathered on a piece of waste ground by Liverpool Road. I was trying to speak from a box, but they wouldn't let me. Almost all of them went down on their knees and sang 'Faith of our Fathers'. I could just see a few standing out from the people kneeling. About 20 young men, nominally Catholics, we had in the crowd burst out in retaliation into 'The Red Flag'. When we walked off, the rush carried us with only our toes on the ground.

The priest came out openly for the Labour man. There was a Father Murphy there then. I was standing at the end of Liverpool Road with three men I knew, who had been members of the Unemployed Workers' Movement. Father Murphy came up and said, 'I suppose you'll all be voting for Marsden.' No one answered. 'You'll vote for him, won't you, Patrick?'

'No, Father, I'm voting Communist.'

'Nobody can be a Catholic and vote Communist, Patrick.'

'I'll see you at Mass on Sunday, Father, but I'll vote Communist on Thursday.'

Methodism

METHODIST LOCAL PREACHER, BORN 1904

In the 1920s, the main church for Primitive Methodism was in Westfield Street. Unlike the Church of England, we sometimes have one preacher for five or six churches. We were responsible for five other churches in St Helens and Parr, and three in the fringe villages.

The church would hold about 600. It became known as the singing church, because it had a very fine choir and, not only that, very fine congregational singing. This was largely because each sect of the church would hold a special Sunday once a year when they invited top singers – we once got Isobel Baillie. There were members who had contacts in the theatre, and we'd often get people down to sing for £5 when they usually charged £25. Whenever we advertised singers, we could pack the place. If we brought in a special preacher, I've seen the place full very many times. We had to carry forms across from the Sunday school for special services.

I should say we had an attendance in those days of about 300, although the membership was about 220, with hangers-on. There was a Sunday school of over 300 scholars and 40 teachers. Now I would say most of the people who attended there – it was almost like a village – worked from the church and centred their lives round it. That started from childhood. The children always seemed to be practising for something – either an operetta, or a Sunday when the kids did their own service. We had a lot of midweek activity. A young ladies' parlour, a men's union, a young men's union and a ladies' guild met regularly, at least once a week. We had a boys' Life Brigade, which specialized mainly in ambulance work, a football team and a very, very good cricket team. Women even took their babies to Sunday school. We had a service and Sunday school on Sunday morning, a walk in the park, then another service and Sunday school in the evening.

The congregation was a real cross-section, from labourers to professional men, yet they all seemed to get on well together. Our chief steward was foreign correspondent for Pilkingtons. He spoke seven languages, and he was the son of a farm labourer from Glazebrook. One of our choir members left for Australia and became the principal soloist at Melbourne University. We had doctors, labourers, tailors and glassmakers.

It isn't generally realized that this town is about one-third non-conformist, a third C of E and a third Catholic. I think you'll agree those are very unusual proportions. I heard Jimmy Sexton say something about it when he was thanking his supporters after his election victory. His opponents criticized him because they said the Roman Catholics were responsible for making him an MP. 'Tell them from me, it's the non-conformists who decide whether I get my seat or not – they have the power.' And I think he was right. At that time, non-conformists were ex-Liberals who decided to go Labour. The non-conformist conscience, as they call it, was a force in this country. The Labour Party leadership in this town nearly all came from non-conformist preachers. I can think of at least twelve non-conformist mayors. Including the Salvation Army and the Presbyterian Church of Scotland, I reckoned up about thirty non-conformist chapels, all fairly flourishing.

I think Jimmy Sexton's opponents were right in saying the Roman Catholics would knit together a bit, but it wouldn't be organized on the non-conformist side. They were inclined to be radicals, that's the point. Funnily enough, though, some of the most famous sons of non-conformity were Tories. One branch of the Pilkington family had a connection with the Congregationalists through Austin Pilkington in the 1920s. They've had a great influence, and I'd say another political influence in the town was the Unitarian church, a small church, but I can think of four mayors they've produced.

In those days, I invited a Roman Catholic friend, who was a very good clarinettist, and his sister, an organist, to play at Westfield Street. They were in fear of trouble from their priest for agreeing. Our parents were horrified if we talked of a mixed marriage. 'Oh, my goodness!' they'd say, 'Do you know what he's done? He's married a Roman Catholic.' But the Methodists never barred anyone from the sacrament so long as he believed in Christ.

You tend to believe what you're brought up to believe, but on the whole I think the non-conformist thought about his religion more than the Roman Catholic did. In other words, he wasn't always satisfied with what his mother and father taught him. But it generally goes according to family. There was a time when part of the town was predominantly Catholic – unfortunately it was the poor end of town, because they were bringing in Irish people as cheap labour.

176

Wesleyan Methodism came directly from John Wesley and his class sects. Primitive Methodism was born through the efforts of two men who started in Staffordshire. The two churches joined the United Methodists in 1932. I wouldn't say there was a difference in doctrine, and there was precious little difference in the form of service. I think Primitive Methodism appealed to the working class in those days because it sprang from them. Even in the 1920s, there wasn't any close liaison between the Wesleyans and the Primitive church in St Helens – Westfield Street tended to look on the Wesleyans as snobbish, up in the air. You didn't feel welcome if you went up to their church.

It was from the 'twenties that attendance began to diminish. Partly, it was happening nationally, but secondly it was because people moved to the outskirts with the expansion of the town – we became a downtown church.

Crawford was a mining village with a good church, until the closure of the pits in the 'thirties, when all the young people went elsewhere for employment. The church at Sutton never really took off. I don't think it was open for 20 years in all. Crank always had a very small attendance, and when transport came easier, they attended at St Helens.

The Labour Party

Although St Helens elected its first Labour MP before World War I, the Labour Party didn't gain control of the Town Hall until 1922. By 1926, then, they had had little time to make an impact on the town with their policies, such as council house building, which have changed the face of the town since.

The policy-making body of the Labour Party was the Trades & Labour Council, which consisted of all the elected councillors and representatives from all trade union branches, women's sections of the party, and so on. Only very recently did the Trades Council split with the Labour Council.

Unfortunately, it has been impossible to find the records of the Trades & Labour Council – there are even fears that they have been burnt. They might have given a more reliable guide to the policies the Labour Party fought on to take office. This is something which the accounts below do not reveal. It is also significant that none of the Labour activists could satisfactorily explain why it was that people changed their vote to Labour. By and large, it is seen as a 'natural' process.

177

The main issues in the election of November 1922, when the Labour Party took control of the local council, were unemployment and housing. The Tories had built 52 houses in the three years after the war, when it it was admitted that the town needed 4,400 to clear slums and relieve overcrowding. Labour was fighting for a council housing programme, and also a job creation scheme.

They pointed out how the Tories had managed the main enterprises in the town. The tramways, although under corporation ownership, had been sublet to a private contractor; the pricing of the town's gas supply was manipulated to benefit local industrial concerns.

WOMAN, BORN 1895, WHO LATER BECAME A LABOUR COUNCILLOR

Dick Waring was a miner. He was one of the first Labour councillors. He was a very stout gentleman, with a big stomach. When he was first made a councillor, he went in wearing a cap, and they all laughed at him. 'You can laugh,' he said 'but you'll laugh on the other side of your faces when I've finished here.' He never turned back, ever. Thinking he was asleep, they'd start making remarks about people dropping off. 'I'm not falling asleep, I'm listening to every word you're saying,' he'd tell them.

From then on, we got a seat every year, but there wasn't sufficient for a majority – we gradually built. The men at that time became Labour people through reading books and papers on what the party stood for, and of what benefit it was to working-class people – the party nationally used to send them out. They were people who thought seriously, they were of such a brain that they could think and reason for themselves. They became councillors, not because they wanted to be councillors, but because they had thoughts that, put into being, would improve the lives of Labour people. Until we got a majority, it was a Tory town. It was only by arguing at meetings that we got any progress at all.

THE DAUGHTER OF THE FORMER SECRETARY OF THE TRADES & LABOUR COUNCIL

My father was a well-known figure in the socialist party. At 18, he was a socialist, though they were frowned on in those days because they were atheists and that sort of thing. My father was a shop steward, and was victimized a couple of times. He was a toolsmith by trade. He worked in the electricity works at the substation for running the trolley buses – that was where he finished up. He was secretary of the Trades & Labour

Above: Soap-box meeting behind an unidentified terrace in 1921.
Below: Football teams of boys (in collarless shirts) and girls (wearing caps).

Above: Carr Mill Dam. *Below:* Grove Street, the view from Pilkingtons towards Liverpool Road.

Council for 40 years. I don't know what kept him going so long. He only got £6 a year as a kind of salary; then they raised it to £30, and he gave that back to the Labour Party. My husband took it over after him. My father was really glad; he didn't want it to go out of the family.

We lived with politics. I think that's why none of us has taken it up in any way. I was once not going to use my vote, and my mother said, 'Women fought for this vote. I don't care who you vote for, but it's best to vote.' My father took a lot of interest – he used to talk to us. That's why we thought a lot. When I was at school, the Inspector said to the head mistress, 'This girl's got a lot of general knowledge.'

THE SHOPWORKERS' UNION DELEGATE
The Trades & Labour Council meetings were very well attended because people were beginning to get interested. The unions were then building up – they have command today. The Labour party was made up of representatives from all the trade unions. Any union branch attached to the party could nominate a member to stand for the council. Nominations went back to the Trades & Labour Council to be sorted out as to who was the fittest person to represent them on the council – you questioned them about why they wanted to be councillors, whether they held positions in the union, and anything like that. There were always people who were really interested. Joe, Dick Warings' son, used to be in the shop assistants' union and was nominated by them. I couldn't get time off to attend meetings, which were held during the day in the Town Hall – my boss wouldn't let me off.

DICK WARING, ON 13TH OCTOBER 1922
The propaganda of the Labour Party for years past is having its effect. The men and women of today are more enlightened and they see their only hope for better conditions is through the Labour Party. They have more confidence in themselves; they see clearly that it is foolish to send rich men and employers to make laws. Besides, they have hundreds of educated, capable men among their own ranks who know their conditions.

THE TWO SISTERS FROM PARR
When Labour took power in the Town Hall, they were fighting on housing, wages, everything you could think of. It was mostly against poverty from all directions – low wages and long hours. There was no direct housing before Labour. Those houses [across the road] were built in

1926 during the strike. That was their project: they did start all that housing going.

We used to go round collecting a ha'penny a week for the Labour Party. There were only women doing it with Mrs Shard. Anybody could pay; it wasn't just members. We went round on Friday and Saturday night with a book to show what they'd given us. It was going for the local elections – there were no Labour clubs then. The ward meetings were held in our house. We'd a good membership with women. Mrs Shard was a good worker who came in after the strike. There had been a few women members, but none stood out as she did.

THE WOMAN, BORN 1895, WHO LATER BECAME A LABOUR COUNCILLOR
In the 1920s, we had a women's section of the Labour Party, but there isn't one now. We used to meet every Tuesday and send someone as an official delegate to the monthly meeting of the Trades & Labour Council. We used to discuss the men's doings – there were no married women in work. We discussed what was going on in town and ended up with a cup of tea. We organized speakers who came to talk about the equality of women, but they didn't bother about equal pay – it was never mentioned; it wasn't an issue in those days. At the sheet works, they got equal pay all the same. Ellen Wilkinson came when the General Strike was on. She was fiery, a great speaker and a good woman's woman. You couldn't get near Robins Lane School, there were that many people. She spoke about the injustices of the workers. I remember one woman shouted out, 'Yes, but half a loaf is better than none.'

'Yes, but we've had enough of living on half a loaf. We want a whole one.' I never went to the Trades & Labour Council myself, as I had two kids at home.

THE MINER FROM SUTTON, BORN 1890
There was a Communist Party, but its influence was negligible if there was any at all. There was this great amount of loyalty to the Trades & Labour Council. As a matter of fact, locally, the Labour Party had begun to gain more influence and representation since 1921. It was slow, but it was very steady. There was never any question that socialism couldn't come through the ballot box. It was never an issue. Particularly the mine-workers – their loyalty to the socialist party cannot be questioned.

The Labour Party was only a bit of a skeleton. You didn't have the excessive activity in those days. There's a hell of a lot active these days. Then, it was just a few that kept the ball rolling – a very haphazard attitude by most of them. When they got the Labour councillors on, they were too high and mighty to talk to the common people. They all stuck to their own class – most of them were colliers. They weren't a great deal interested in other people. Underneath, the people must have supported them, even if they didn't show it. Although you got your meetings that were mentioned as well attended, the only time you got a decent number was when they were called by letter. Even when they got A. J. Cook, who had plenty of hearers, it was more or less miners who went. You see, he was one of their own people; he was a collier.

THE COMMUNIST FROM THATTO HEATH, BORN 1898

I thought Labour were rubbish. You don't see any action from them. We had lots of keen young boys come to us – 'Oh yes, we'll do this and we'll do that.' The way we found if they were genuine or not was by giving them six Workers' Weeklies [precursor of Daily Worker] to sell in Church Street. You'd never see them again – they didn't want to be seen in public like that. The Labour man is only a glorified Tory, that's all he is. Once a Labour man becomes a militant, he's no longer a Labour man, he's what was termed a Communist, but he's a Socialist really. Labour man, no. You either work or you don't – there are no in-betweens. You're socialist or capitalist, there isn't such a thing as labourism.

The Communist Party

THATTO HEATH MINER, BORN 1898

I was in the union on principle, as a member of the Communist Party. I joined the party through poverty. I've gone to work without any food. The organizer lived in Whittle Street. His father was getting decent money from a good job at Pilkingtons, and so he could afford to do things we couldn't. We used to go out at night time, chalking roads to say there'd be a meeting at such a place at such a time.

I used to love being out with the party. I've gone down the behind of Pilkingtons at Greenbank, where there used to be a canal. We went among the poorest of people. We'd only have five or six of us at the meeting there, and once or twice you'd get a chamber pot over you. They were

181

Catholics – Catholics and Communists don't bear thinking of. You know what Lenin said, 'Religion is the opium of the people,' and Marx said, 'He that does not work, neither shall he eat.' Really, I enjoyed myself. We were once out sticking posters on walls. The sergeant and police constable followed taking them off as soon as we put them up. We made a detour round by the police station. Jack climbed up on the railing and stuck a notice on the police board. The sergeant tackled us many times – he was after knowing who'd done it, because by the time he got back to the station, the poster had dried on. You had a certain amount of kick, a certain amount of enjoyment, out of fighting them.

We used to have meetings, regular as clockwork, and you'd have to put up the fellows we had to speak; they had nothing. We organized the meetings on a building site – the men gave us the key to one of these houses, without anyone interfering. They were council houses – they're there yet. We had to stop meeting there when the foreman put the police on.

THE COMMUNIST FROM THATTO HEATH, BORN 1902, A LOCAL PARTY ORGAN-
IZER

I was a member of the Communist Party from the beginning. when the Congress of 31st July and 1st August 1920 set it up. There had been a Socialist Society in St Helens – my father and two uncles had been members. It went into liquidation during the war, but we revived it afterwards. Early in 1920, a group got together under the Liverpool Labour college.

[Referring to the local election in South Eccleston Ward, traditionally Tory, against Austin Pilkington, Conservative.] We made a fight of it; the Labour Party didn't fight. I was standing openly as a Communist. We got 500 and odd votes against 2,000. If you'd seen the campaign, we were in by a large majority. We had meetings down where I lived on a piece of waste ground behind Whittle Street; we met round Thatto Heath station, round Top of the Rock, Rainhill Asylum. At Booth Street, he had one in opposition – we had a crowd of 200 and he hardly had 20. There were numerous questions asked, about education and other things, which I dealt with. We hand-printed leaflets and distributed them.

One of the men with me then had been in O'Connell's army in Dublin. He used to wear a belt studded with trade union badges. There were one or two real characters who supported us in that ward. One of them, who used to shout and gabble at all our meetings, wore boots which always seemed too big. His clothes, hanging loose, suggested that he'd been quite a hefty fellow. Whether he'd lost this weight in unemployment, I don't know.

When I was standing as a candidate, the Conservative Club was not far from where I lived. It used to be called Charlie Whittle's Gardens and must have been a bit like the Vauxhall Gardens in London. It had a building, and lots of garden ornaments, including a carved face which we thought was the devil when I was little – we pulled faces at it and ran. Most of the people in the Women's Section of the Conservative Club lived in the same street as I did. They went to a meeting at which the speaker was Flora MacDonald. She became famous as a suffragette when she rode a white horse down Whitehall, and had become one of the Women's organizers of the Tory party. She invited them to vote for Austin Pilkington, who was standing against me when he was supposed to be an independent. She accused the Communist candidate of getting Bolshie gold. One of the women who knew me shouted out, 'I've known him all his life, and he doesn't get gold from anywhere!' She didn't know how to answer that. Every time she tried to attribute something to me, they refuted it.

When I took my expense account down to the Town Hall, it was 35s. The clerk asked me, 'Where's your vouchers?'

'You don't need receipts for expenditure of less than £2,' I said.

'We've had no candidate who's ever spent less than that,' he said. 'I'm afraid you'll have to bring those receipts.'

'No, I don't,' I said. 'Look it up in the book and you'll find it's correct.'

Two months later, he saw me and said, 'About that expense account, you were quite right.'

When I was going to stand as candidate for West Sutton, I went down to one of those big housing estates. We went to the cross roads, which had big, swerving, cut-off corners. No traffic went down the road, as one turning led to a lane and others to parts of the estate. In the evening, we set up a box under one of the lamps. A policeman came up and said, 'You can't hold a meeting here, you're causing an obstruction.' There were only 50 or 60 of us and we weren't blocking the road. The policeman insisted we couldn't, but we said we could and did. I and Jack Burns spoke. They sent us both summonses. A sergeant came to see us from Thatto Heath. He said they'd take no action if we agreed not to hold any more meetings like the one we'd just had. I asked whose decision that was. 'The superintendent.'

'He's no right to do that. If he thinks the law has been broken, he has no option but to prosecute.' I wasn't withdrawing on a verbal promise. 'Tell the superintendent he can't act as judge and jury.'

They went on with the prosecution and we gave evidence. We measured the distance from the lamp to the kerb, and we also found out that the Salvation Army held meetings there on Sunday mornings. They dismissed the charge on payment of 4s each in costs.

7 Entertainment and Sport

Although people didn't have nearly as much time off as they do now, pastimes were more varied because they involved people actively far more, and required people to be spectators far less. This selection could be extended almost ad infinitum, but is intended to give a cross section of different activities.

The Brass Bands

THE MINER FROM SUTTON, BORN 1883

There were about ten bands in the town: Parr Church, Parr Methodist, Holy Trinity, Sutton Road Methodist, Ravenhead Church and Nutgrove Methodist; there were the Engineers and Volunteers, Haydock Colliery and Moss Bank. Most of the bands were split up into churches but Parr Church, Parr Methodist and Ravenhead were practically colliery bands. Most of the players were colliers. I should think there were about 28 in a band: the drum, four horns, a double bass instrument, euphonium, first, second and soprano cornets. Most of the bands were composed of relatives; at Parr Methodist, there were four brothers, and at Parr Church three brothers. They gave all their best without pay. It was like a family concern among them all.

There was one great idea – the bands kept the people of St Helens in the knowledge of music. There was the Catholic symphony orchestra, a large one at that period. I think it was attached to the Sacred Heart. Whatever happened, it didn't stop the band music. They entertained us; St Helens was a town of splendid music. When I lived at Clock Face village, there was a street behind that was built up on only one side. On summer evenings, we were entertained by half a dozen accordions, and wasn't it lovely! Colliers, how they enjoyed themselves with accordions. In those days, it was music, music, music. These men did it for pleasure, to bring happiness into the lives of their neighbours.

Other interests have dragged boys away from band music, and that is not beneficial in many ways. Clubs were one of the things that took them away. They are the biggest detriment to the interests of young people, from what I've seen, instead of bringing out the best in boys. Gambling was an interest when they started earning money. Political groups started the first clubs. There's everything there to amuse – I'm only told it, because I never go in.

BANDSMAN, BORN IN 1886

We had a flute band at school. I was only 12 years old when I started the flute. We'd a teacher who was just a bandsman. He taught us for free. I could play the mouth organ and tin whistle. Same as all the lads there, I wanted to be in the band. It was a big thing, it was that! One time we took the miners to Blackpool and marched along watched by a crowd gathered all along the promenade. We marched in front playing our flutes with the miners marching four abreast behind us. I had a brother, Bob – he's dead now – who was in the flute band marching with us; he was only four or five then. The artists at the Tower Circus were hanging over the balcony, throwing pennies for us lads, but we couldn't stop to pick them up. People would pick them up and put them in my jacket pocket.

Parson Peter's band played at Parr School. We used to practise every Wednesday night. One little episode that happened was when they built St Vincent's Church in Derbyshire Hill. On the first field day, we were asked to lead them, though we were Protestants and we knew that was a Catholic church. Some chaps said we shouldn't, but we did do. They lead them, now, every year, on their walking day. A group of church wardens were going to take our instruments off us because we played for Catholics. The vicar came one Wednesday after we'd played – we thought he was going to reprimand us. He stood and listened while we finished the march we were playing and said, 'Now, chaps, I'm proud of you. You've broken down some barriers here in Parr. There's always been some animosity. I believe there are some people who want to take these instruments away. If they do, I'll buy you another set. How much are they?'

'Well, it costs £500 for a whole new set,' I said.

'By Jove, that's a lot! I'm only a poor chap, but I've got some friends who have money. They'll help out.' Anyway, they never did take them away.

We played at the miners' demonstration at Blackpool once a year. Do you know how much the fare was? – 1s 10d return to Blackpool. It was like a day out. Ashton's Green, Clock Face, Sutton Manor, Bold

186

all joined together. We used to have our dinner there in the hall. Parson Peter's band used to lead Parr school to Sherdley Park on August Monday. Captain Hughes and his wife used to stand opposite the band listening to us. Then we'd be invited in the hall to have beer for the men and pop for the lads.

They built a club at the top of the street in 1914. I was working at Clock Face then. A chap called Anderton got £500 and bought a full set of instruments for 25 players. He was a manager at the colliery, and that's how we formed Clock Face band. Six of us who played in Parson Peter's band formed a new band of our own here. We used to go round at Christmas time, playing Christmas carols. Then we'd go to Billy Webster. He was a single chap, a solicitor, who lived at that big house, Abbotsfield Hall, with his two sisters. They used to invite us in to play for them and give us a drink.

Dancing

THE RELIEVING OFFICER, BORN 1900

There weren't the attractions of today – no radios, no television – but there were several dance halls. The Town Hall could hold 600, and it cost a bob to go in. If you went to a posh place, it was ten bob with evening clothes. There were various Labour and Conservative clubs as well.

The dances were three or four times a week – all that's gone now. There's bingo and talkies. The band combination varied. For a small job, you'd have piano, drums, violin, banjo and sax – that would be a five job for dances of up to 120 people. At the Town Hall, you'd add a trombone, bass fiddle and trumpet.

DAUGHTER OF CORNER SHOP OWNER, BORN c. 1895

I was always dancing. It used to be only 6d to go dancing. We didn't get much money off my mother, and we always had to be in by nine. We used to get free passes in those days with some of the groceries. I gave my brother's friend the pass for 6d and went dancing. There used to be a farm with dancing in a field every Monday night. Sometimes there were two or three in the band with a cornet player. I danced in Sutton Park on a Tuesday. My husband could dance. There'd be a big band there, and in the park the children came from everywhere. Out in the field, there'd only be a few of us, about 30 or 40. After I was married, I didn't do a lot of dancing.

Singing

THE COMMUNIST FROM THATTO HEATH, BORN 1902

The first meeting I can remember attending was in the Volunteer Hall, just off Duke Street. It was quite a big hall with a balcony. I think the speaker was Keir Hardy. They sang 'England Arise', Edward Carpenter's song. They started to sing it in the 1920s and 1930s.

During the Miners' Lockout, we sold 'The Red Flag' on a sheet for a penny, at Thatto Heath station. We used to get a lot of children round the meetings, and we promised them that if they kept quiet we'd sing 'The Red Flag' at the end. That was their entertainment – they were accustomed to it.

There was a pub in Thatto Heath where you could hear the best operatic singing for miles around. People would go deliberately to sing and listen. They used to sell music books; tenor songs, duets, things like 'In a Cellar Cool', 'The Vicar of Bray', 'The Friar of Orders Grey', 'He Never Wanted Anything'. I can remember going to concerts in Mission Halls where there were recitals in Lancashire dialect.

The Labour Party Gala

THE WOMAN, BORN 1895, WHO WAS ONE OF THE ORGANIZERS

The first gala wasn't very successful, because we weren't very experienced. I can see it today. If you have children, they're the attraction. They were all dressed up in paper; we couldn't afford anything else. The girls had a large marguerite on their chests. Of course, they looked very nice. We had a lorry which we decorated with crepe paper. We'd poles at either end, and we couldn't get the paper to stick – when we got it strung from one end of the lorry to the other it stretched in the wind. We learned our lesson. As we marched through the iron gates into the park, I remember Jack Stead [Secretary of Trades and Labour Council] saying 'You'll never feed all these people.' In fact, we were in a quandary. If you only have one tea urn and have to keep filling it with water it takes a long time to give everyone some tea. I remember Mrs McGee flopped back in a chair. I think we had a few barrels from the brewery to fill it with, but they weren't enough. We had to go down to the Co-op for more food as well.

Our last gala was the best. We had a swan made out of white flowers. The Rose Queen or Fairy Queen sat in the swan on a lorry, with her ladies in waiting. We had everything that you would find in the country, groups dressed as flowers or bees. Every ward took a colour, and everything in their section would be in that shade. We made a lorry with a wonderful lattice on it covered with paper wisteria flowers. One man called it a pagoda. 'It's not straight,' I said. I wasn't happy till we got it straight with wedges. Then we got a woman to sit with her back to the pagoda so it wouldn't wobble as it went along. We won the prize. We got men to wear great big heads painted with 'Vengeance', 'Be Good' and things like that. They just had little holes for their eyes. When we got to Denton's Green Labour Club, they insisted on stopping; they were that hot, they said they were suffocating.

The Women's Section met and garlanded a lot of skipping rope with green paper and flowers. The children carried it to stop them getting out of line. We'd all the kids of all the wards. We met on the Town Hall steps. My daughter went to a dancing class. She came down the steps in ballet dress and danced – she was only this high. When she was walking behind the retinue of the Fairy Queen in a Fairy costume, someone said to her, 'Your mother must be a good washer, your pants are so white.' Those were the happiest days of the time. Nothing was too much for the women. Each ward was allotted a place at the Town Hall. Our men and women looked after the children and saw they came in at the right place in the procession. We had a couple of bands. My husband was organizing, 'Get you ready, you're next,' he would say. We'd a banner nearly as wide as this room – purple and white satin, and someone had made a fringe at the bottom. I forget what it said on it.

We gave it up because it was a long walk to Sherdley Park. Some of the children walked all the way from Thatto Heath to St Helens, and then from St Helens to Sherdley Park. That was the only place big enough for us.

Theatre and Cinema

WOMAN WHO WAS STILL LIVING AT HOME WITH HER MOTHER AT THE TIME
All my mates used to go to the Shakespeare plays that used to come to the theatre, but we were never allowed to go to the last house. It used to be packed, it had a great following. Edward Dalston was a real Shakespearean actor. One Sunday, I saw him in the street. We used to go in the gods – that was the cheapest place. It was cheap, but it used to be dear to us. I went in a little money [savings] club for when Dalston came next time.

189

Before talking pictures, there used to be a gramophone at the back of the screen. There was Charlie Chaplin, Buster Keaton, all them. Pearl Buck used to drive me mad – they used to leave her every week about to be killed, and you had to be back next week to see how she got on. We used to get in the pictures for a penny. The film used to change twice a week, on Mondays and Thursdays. We always went when it changed. If it was a good picture, some used to go twice. Some of the following-up pictures used to run weeks and weeks – nearly getting killed by a tiger or lion.

Sports

Rugby League was, and still is, the biggest spectator sport in the town. There were then two main clubs, Recs and Saints.

ONE OF THE PLAYERS

They used to put on a gold medal competition – it was a good game, that. Gerard's Bridge, Sharrocks, St Helens Rovers, Sutton and Westfield Amateurs made teams up. I was playing with Westfield Amateurs against St Helens Rovers in the final. We won, and after the match we went to the Talbot Arms for a drink. Three of us were signed on for Saints – me from Westfield, with Peter Molyneux and Bill Marr from St Helens. They turned Tommy Greenhall down because he was too small. Recs picked him up, and he turned out to be an international. That would be about 1912. I played scrum half, fly half, or any of the centres. I played centre for Lancashire. I was 21 – I lost the best years in the army. When I came back, I had two and a half seasons with Saints. Then I went to Rochdale Hornets. That would be 1922. I wanted a bit of a change.

They were happy days at Saints. You got a couple of quid if you won and thirty bob if you lost. The crowd was pretty good – I've seen 10,000 there at ordinary matches. The players weren't as good then as they are now – they spend more time at it. It was all rugby then – those Derby games on Christmas Day and New Year's Day with the Recs. They were a good side. You'd get 20,000 at that match. The atmosphere was champion. Wigan and Warrington used to play alternately at home on Christmas Day and New Year's Day. I used to enjoy those matches, too.

We practised after work on Tuesdays and Thursdays at the Talbot Hotel. I was a glassblower at Pilkingtons, and we went up there after we'd finished work; we were young then. We did skipping, sprinting and ball practice. We used to skip in the Talbot yard. We got there at about seven o'clock, and then we'd run up to the park. You'd only get half a day off when there were cup ties.

Then, when there was a match on, we used to go up in a wagonette with the horses pulling it. It was lovely coming back if you were wet through! Both teams used to go up in it. We had to change in the Talbot. When we got back, we changed, bathed, got dressed and went into the pub. At the pitch, there was only an old hut to throw your jumpers in. Once we got the new pavilion, we did our training up at the ground.

It was a tanner or a bob to get in, and they used to have season tickets for the seats. £300 was a good take for a match, and that went on players, jerseys, groundsmen and things like that. We left the spending to the board of managers.

A CROSS-COUNTRY RUNNER

I lived at Peasley Cross. All the lads worked at Sherdley colliery. When they finished work, they played a game of rugby every day. Where the hospital is now, there used to be open fields. We were all young lads then. When we got back home and sat down in a chair, we used to drop asleep waiting for the kettle to boil. We'd got enough energy, though. I used to turn out for a Harriers Club. As many as sixty used to turn out twice a week from Peasley Cross. We used to go up Appleton Street, across the fields to Clock Face Bridge and Lea Green Bridge, and a mile break from there back to Peasley Cross.

THE ELECTRICIAN

There were a lot of organizations with football and swimming teams. Life wasn't dull. Quite a lot of juvenile organizations operated in St Helens. There were three or four leagues for football, then there were swimming galas at Boundary Road baths. The only sport we knew was in St Helens. Now you can't get away from it – it's gone from local to national to world-wide. Either you played, or you used to watch the local team in the local matches, from here to Wigan, Widnes and Warrington. You don't meet your friends on the telly; there was more personal contact in those days.

At the time, there were two soccer teams – St Helens Town and the Recs. The Town played where the greyhound track is now. They weren't first class teams, but they played in the Lancashire combinations – which had a higher standard than it has now.

THE MINER FROM NEWTON ROAD, BORN *c.* 1900

In the canal they used to swim. There was 10s for the winner – you had to manage half a mile for that. All the good swimmers would make a bet in the pub and go swimming in the morning. There used to be boats going along it, you know. They used to swim past them. The first time I went to swim, a fellow pulled me up drowning from the bottom – I was shoved in where it was 12 ft deep. A fellow ran 100 yards, pulled me out and pumped all the water out of me. Somebody told my mother, and she bloody near killed me. I was only a lad. You used to swim with nowt on. The wenches used to sit and watch on the bank. Bobbies used to come and give you a good hiding – and not a stitch on.

THE MINER FROM FLEET LANE, BORN *c.* 1905

We were swimming in the canals and flashes. They used to have two men cleaning and building the banks of the canal up; it was quite clean then. There were bridges every so far, and the railway used to go over the double locks. Even little kids used to be swimming. We had nothing on, and the girls used to be very shy, walking by with their heads down. It used to be a Sunday treat going out there, besides a bit of a place for courting Haydock girls and Parr flats boys – that's how they got to mix.

THE ELECTRICIAN

There was amateur boxing, but it was mostly professional. They weren't like they are today. But they used to box for side bets. There were one or two good lads in the town. They didn't have efficient backers, trainers and that. There were no boxing halls unless you arranged something at the Volunteer Hall. When the fair came, there were always sideshows – they had boxing competitions then.

THE COMMUNIST FROM THATTO HEATH, BORN 1902

They must have had colder winters, then. The dam by St Helens used to freeze over so regularly that they even built a little railway station for the skaters. It fell into disuse and was eventually demolished. People skated on the lake in the park – my uncle and aunt must have been really quite good. They used to skate facing each other, holding hands. They set up special electric lights in the park and opened it up late, so that people could come and skate. Skates had a big screw at the back which was fixed into the heel of your boot, and there was just a flap at the front which you tied over your toe. It worked all right, but it damaged your boots a bit.

We sometimes went to the Isle of Man to watch the TT races. You were in the country and you could hear them coming off the mountains, roaring away. We had good times. The boat was only about 12s then – the Pearl Castle was an old tub. We stayed in Hall Street, with the same people, every year.

There was plenty of enjoyment in all those entertainment places. We used to love jumping on and off the horsecars. There was plenty of swimming, and there used to be an old steam railway. Ramsey is a class place, now. We used to see them smoking kippers there on the beach in huts. They used to smell like coffin wood – they smelled bloody rotten, the shavings they used to smoke the kippers with. The fish were hung on bars.

You had to save up 12 months for it, and if you hadn't enough you had to be very careful. You wouldn't go jumping about supping a lot of ale. You could get a bar of rock as big as me for a shilling. There used to be a lot of folk there, a lot of Scotch folk. They had a week on their own they called Scotch Week. You'd see one playing a melodion walking on the front with a crowd following him. They'd go on the beach and form a circle, and someone with a concertina would join in. They'd 'dance on the hot sands'. There were oysters, shrimps and winkles. Oysters were only twopence apiece. Toffee was four ounces a penny. But them with children couldn't afford it, definitely not.

Dog and Horse Racing

Although the St Helens track didn't open until 1932, there was a tradition of training greyhounds, especially among unemployed miners.

MINER FROM ASHTON'S GREEN

Greyhounds came along as you reached manhood – I started to keep them then. You housed the dogs in the back yard, and that was a bit rough, but I won a few races and got myself a few quid. I started buying them cheap and selling them dear. There were no prizes you won with your own dog – it was all the money you put on it. You stop your dog for three or four weeks, until it's lost a few times and all the public think it's no good. Then you race it at 6–1 or 8–1 and it comes in. How do you stop it back? I'm not giving you that – a bit too dear! I've kept that to myself all these years.

Thousands of people had dogs. Say you'd bought yours from Ireland. You paid a fair sum for it, and stopped it going as fast as it could for a few weeks. But the Irish are getting very clever now – when you race a dog, they take the marking, which is written down on a card with your name and address. The people who go get to know who you are and what the dogs are. When you take a dog down again, they examine it to see it's the same one. Especially with black ones, people would try to slip in a better dog under the same name.

To feed them, I used to have a gas boiler with a tube at the back. You'd lift the lid and put four or five sheep's heads in. I used to cook stew, cow heels, cabbage and that sort of thing in it. After I left the boiler outside, it acted like a fridge; the food would last a fortnight. There was always a pile of brown bread in the bowls – I'd mix tripe with the bread by hand. In the morning, we used to give them glucose, sherry, eggs and rusks. You've got to have good grub if you're going to run at 40 miles an hour round a dog track. You've got to be strong and muscled up.

After breakfast, you'd go out for a walk for five or six miles and then come back for an hour or two in the pub. Then you'd go out again for another six miles, follow that with a big feed, and bed the dogs down with straw. Anyone who's working can't look after greyhounds. It's an impossibility. To keep the dogs right and make the grade, you've got to be out of work. Three dogs is ample for one person to groom, wash their feet and all that. Their feet should be washed every night. At White City, they're only washed once a week, the trainers have too many to do. You've got to see to it that they've not knocked a toe, or got glass in the pads. I bought one dog off a man for nothing. I'd had it for a fortnight, and it wouldn't show. Then, one day, walking him, I noticed that he was holding his paw up. I found he had a lump of glass under his pad that had healed over. I lanced it and cut it out – there was blood all over the place. It did about three or four races after that. If you can get an enclosed field, like at the back of Bold Miners, you can let the dogs run, but if they see a small dog or a cat, they'll try to kill it. You have to be careful to keep them on a lead, or you'll find yourself in the police court. If you can let them loose two or three mornings before a race, you can watch them run to see they're all right and not lame, but you train them on a lead.

The racecourse that closed down here was the last open one [i.e. unfenced] in Lancashire. I'll tell you the last winner there, Water Hen. The Newton Cup was run there – it's run at Haydock, now. The course was up on the common. I used to see the horses training up there. What was left was the stables near by – we used to watch the horses there as lads.

A lot of people went to Haydock – it's a good track, one of the best in the north. Its surroundings are nice, the stands are good – the view is the best part of it. It's been well managed: there are better horses, better facilities, and much safer bookmakers, now. They used to welsh in those days. Now you can send your ticket to Leeds weeks after the race. Then they used to sneak off as the last race was crossing the line and slink into the crowd. Very few working men made a fortune out of racing, but a lot of people could get by in a small way.

There were no bookies' shops in St Helens. A fellow in Warrington started up before there were licences here. Bookies used to send a man running round taking bets here, there and everywhere. The police used to stop them. They'd take them to court and send them to jail – just for taking bets. If you won, you'd find the man who took the bet – you knew where he lived and you'd go to his home. If he didn't pay up, he was in hospital, thumped. Mind you, they could thump back. There were four-penny bets, fourpenny double and fourpenny treble. You'd bet on what was in the papers and phone the bookies to get the results.

AN ILLEGAL BOOKMAKER, THE JOINER, BORN 1905

I had a bookmaker's office at the back of the house. You had fellows going round from house to house. The police would be observing these houses and catch the punters with their betting slips. We were always being blackmailed by policemen on the beat, and the men who were supposed to be detectives. A lot of the blackmailers had no more information than we had.

One of them went too thick with a man who was chairman of our association. The chairman stood up to him; he informed on the policeman to his boss, who in turn informed the chief superintendent. One night, I was having a chat with him, exchanging confidences, and someone came up to ask him if he knew of anyone else who had been blackmailed. He told him I had. The police came along for me, and I had to go down to talk to a constable at the station. He said, 'You're a builder and undertaker – you're also a bookmaker.' The fine was £100 then, you didn't have that to throw away. 'You might as well admit it, you've been named.'

'Yes, it's quite true,' I said.

'We are out to rid this force of a scamp and we shall do it with or without your help.' He then told me who'd told him. 'Are you willing to give evidence to that effect?' I agreed.

Eventually, the trial came, with ten bookmakers giving evidence. The next thing was that the blackmailer had to appear before the watch committee and was stripped from the force. My agents were raided – they didn't spare me that – but because I disclosed what I did, they told me to keep the traffic down, which I did.

They'd still come along for a fiver, telling you they were watching your agents. Another bookmaker called me into his house. He said, 'There's a man wants to see you in here.' He showed me into his front room, which was darkened. It sounds a bit like the Ku Klux Klan, but it's true. There was a man standing in the dark. He told me, 'So and so's working for you. They've been watching him – let him get picked up.' Fair enough, I told my fellow, 'Don't take any bets in the house,' they picked him up, and he got done £20 for street betting. So I slipped the informant a fiver. I had to pay fines and solicitors' fees for the agents; then the dole prosecuted and fined them – I had to pay their dole.

Once, after a fellow was caught, I went down to the solicitor: 'He's my best agent. All I want to know is where they watched him from.' He had been fined £50 and lost his dole for ten weeks; his wife had been fined £10 for assisting him. The solicitor said he couldn't tell me where they'd been watched from – it had been given in the strictest confidence. I said, 'There's no ifs about it. You were briefed to defend him. He hasn't got a penny to pay you, and if I don't get to know, I'm not paying you.' Well, he walked in front of the safe in his office and moved to the right, saying 'It wasn't from here.' Then he moved to the left and said 'It wasn't from here.'

'So it was the house directly opposite?'

'You can draw your own conclusions.'

It must have been that house, because everyone else in that street was solid – his own mother lived in the house to the right.

Some time later, the dole fetched this same agent up for working while he was drawing dole. They fined him £10 and stripped his dole for ten weeks. The same solicitor, the very one who'd defended him before, prosecuted him and I had to pay another £4.

We had our own club. The steward had two candlestick telephones in front of him. When they said on the tape that the race had started, he would use both phones to tell the first bookmakers. They would each ring the next man, 'They're off,' all down the line. One rang Parr, and the other went down the line to Teddy, from Teddy to me, and from me to Dave up the road, and out towards Eccleston. Then we'd stop taking bets.

The steward would sing out into the phones which horse had won. We knew about runners, objections, betting news, in the same way. We all had a private line from one house to the other, and divided the cost between us. Nobody could ring in – you were sure of no interference. We shared the cost of the tape, too. It was a first-class service.

We used to bet with each other. We held a meeting before all the big races and had our own call over. If anyone was in trouble with a horse, he'd lay off some of the bet. I've never made any money – the Income Tax people are still around. They were hard times; people were betting in threepenny bits. We used to have a fellow called '21 Horses' – he used to back 21 horses for a shilling.

Pigeons

MAN FROM SUTTON

Short scotching was the name for short pigeon races – you can hear the pigeons, can't you, scotching over the hedges. It was a great sight when they dropped over the roofs. They were specially trained to fly one or two miles. Each area had its own enthusiasts – the people from Sutton or Parr had their own races. They might do it from due east or due north, making out a distance for each bird from its own loft. These people, who couldn't read, knew exactly how to measure where each pigeon should be released. There was an umpire with each competitor to make sure he let out the pigeon at the right time. You could see them stretched out over three or four hundred yards of land. Another man was at the loft to click his watch when the pigeon came in. There was great excitement and anxiety as the times from different lofts came in. Everyone paid an entrance fee. There was side betting on the birds. Sometimes, you'd have a bookmaker – before they were allowed, but the police never bothered. The lofts were built next to the house. The pigeons would get exercise flying around, and they would be taken out distances increasing four or five hundred yards at a time till they would fly back one or two miles.

The Pubs

There were more pubs than shops in St Helens then. The police had to go about in twos, and they had to be burly. People just got drunk, especially on a Saturday night, and they used to fight with pointed clogs – the idea was to get a fellow down and punch his head in. Beer was strong then, and a few pints would knock you over.

Where I was staying, there was a fellow who used to get a set of the blues when he was drunk. He chucked everything, all the furniture, into the yard. I had to put a chair under the door handle to stop him getting into my room. When he was sober, there wasn't a kinder man, but he was enough to frighten anyone off drink. They had to send the policemen in fives then.

LICENSEE'S DAUGHTER, NOW IN HER SIXTIES, WHO WAS IN HER TEENS AT
    THE TIME OF THIS ACCOUNT

My mother worked from six in the morning until eleven at night. It was licensed all day; they never shut. The men going to work would call in for Oxo – some wouldn't go on to work, they'd stay for a drink.

One family, who were tenants, would be running the pub. Greenall Whitley monopolized the town then, although there were a few Walkers pubs. You paid them rent and the rates; the rest was yours. It was one of the best jobs in town. You always worked long hours, even when the pub wasn't open early in the morning, but you were certain of a living. That's why it went in the family. Quite a few people who had good jobs seemed to want pubs but, by that time, people had got good wages, and it wasn't worth giving up a good job for a small pub. For some people it's a status symbol to be a licensee. We went to the Hen and Chickens, only a little beer house, and kept that for 20 years. Then we went to the Oddfellows. They were all ale houses; that was the right name for them. As the years progressed, they had spirit licences. As children, we used to go and pay the rent at the brewery with a little book, and you'd get a week's supply of beer for £36.

They brought the beer round with horses. There were mild, bitter, and extra strong bitter they called Double X. They only sold it in ponies of half a gill – it was that strong. Those were the days when beer was a penny a gill and twopence halfpenny a pint, and you got five pints for a shilling with the halfpennies knocked off. Five pints for a bob, that's what the customers used to call it. I think the beer was 36s a barrel, although if I'm wrong I'll admit it. There must have been about 280 pints in a barrel.

My father took the business from his parents – that happened a lot. He did the cellar work, keeping the pipes clean and doing his own fining – that's adding something from a bottle of clear liquid which the brewery sent with the beer to make it ready for drinking. There were all the old-fashioned methods, with lead pipes that you used to trip over on the floor. A landlord could make or mar the beer – it's like fish and chip shops, some people keep better ones than others. It was better beer that came out of the brewery then, pure malt and hops. On Sundays, they used to come from everywhere for a good pint.

My sister and I used to do the cleaning when we left school, polishing the floors. We had to scrub the tiles; it was all tiles then. In the Hen and Chickens, there was sawdust, but that was a wood floor. The tables were black-leaded, as they were in the Oddfellows. There were spittoons, because they used to smoke a lot of pipes then, and they must have had worse chests than they do now. They smoked long clay pipes and dipped the ends into the beer to keep them cool. The spittoons were iron, and terrible to clean out – you used to have to put sawdust in. Imagine cleaning what someone had been spitting out! When the floors were carpeted, they daren't spit on them and went outside to do it. They used to spit on the fire; you used to have to clean off what stuck on the grate after bad aiming. They always spat on the fire at home. Then some women used to use the outsales as the Ladies'. But most people were clean. There was no cleaner person than a collier – you'd never find a collier having a drink on the way to or from work; they always went home first for a wash.

Mother used to cook white butter beans and spare ribs on certain nights, usually Wednesdays. Whoever wanted any could have it. It was all home-cooked and given free. We also had a stove where we baked potatoes that would be put out on the bar with butter and pepper. If there was a match on, all the customers used to get a sandwich for nothing. We used to have a lovely great coal fire. They used to come in for a good warm. They had to sit back – it was so hot. Next morning, you had to put water on it to put it out. They all grumbled when we went over to gas fires – it was the colliers' living. I can remember looking at the big black grate as a child. All sorts of things would be cooked by the customers: broth, little custards in jugs and basins, and pies. There were that many that we children were able to eat them – the customers used to bring them in for our consumption. They used to bring in little titbits for my mother when she was ill or off having children.

People would always drink in the same pub. When we were in the Oddfellows, there was old Poll in the pub across the road. She never used to bother, and the place was very dingy till someone else took it and brightened it up. That did take some off us – then we got to the stage of people using both. But we had some dedicated customers who never went anywhere else.

We had some funny ones. We also had a quantity of trouble makers, who had to be thrown out by my dad. You'll always get that till the end of time. They'd get drunk, but they never fought in a pub then; they always used to go outside. They'd take their waistcoats off and fight on a Sunday morning, after they'd fallen out the night before, to prove who was the better man. Then they'd shake hands and go in for what was termed a peace pint. Catholic and Protestant, Labour and Tory, they never used to fall out over it. I think you'd get a bit at voting time, but when it was all over, there was no trouble.

There was one man who used to come and drink the beer out of his own bottle. There weren't so many women or very young people. We had what was called a Best Room, where men and women used to go. It wasn't the practice for a young woman to be seen in a pub. They daren't come in – their parents wouldn't let them. It wasn't done, just as women didn't smoke in the street – they'd have been called hussies if they had. When there were parties, though, we'd get gallons of beer out, and the children would get a cup each. A lot of the older women drank harder than the men, but they only lived just round the corner from the pub. We never had to carry them home – we wouldn't serve them to that extent. Most of the customers used to know how much to take, anyway.

The pub was the social centre – there was nothing else, was there, really? Yet they knew how to enjoy themselves without spending a lot of money. We had a sing-song, especially on a Saturday night. We had a piano – we never used to pay anyone to play. You could get an accordion player or a fiddler, too. In those days, people made their own entertainment. There was no television, and even darts playing was in its infancy. Someone used to get up and sing a song – they were fair turns. Most people would sing, even my brother, when he was only 16. My dad used to play the piano, though the law didn't allow a landlord to entertain his customers – they used to have a man watching on the door. Songs used to last up to half an hour. We had a standing joke about sorrowful songs:

'Oh, it's that song that made our Peter leave home.' There was a man who used to sing a song called 'Greed for Gold'. Mother used to know it all the way through. One verse was about a lad who had gone to sea and grown a beard. When he came back from the sea and returned to the pub where he used to live, they didn't recognize him. The landlord went upstairs and murdered him as he slept, all for the greed of gold.

The lamplighter came in on a Saturday night, with dandy clogs all studded with brass, and he'd do all kinds of things with his cap as he danced. Another fellow used to come into the Oddfellows wearing dandy clogs, plus-fours and a bowler hat. He was a right comedian – he used to talk entertaining nonsense, really, and when he sang, it sounded like a cinder under the door. His mother used to leave him his dinner and go to bed for a rest. He'd always had that much to drink that he couldn't eat and fed his dinner to our black dog so his mother wouldn't know, but she found him out in the end. Mother used to wash on Mondays, although some people didn't go to work, and this particular man used come into the wash house and say, 'You daft bugger, what are you washing for? Lend us ten bob.' He was a right character, but a good one, though. The ten bob was to spend on beer. He'd go through our living room back to the bar and spend it. He always paid it back at the weekend.

There were dominoes and a game called tippet, which was illegal. I never quite understood it, but they used to put their hands under the table and bring them up suddenly. If the police came in and found them, the landlord could be fined. They would only play for pennies.

At that time, all the pubs were small – pokey little places – so they needed a lot of pubs to fit everyone in. There was the one opposite us, one at the end of the street, the Bull's Head, and then the Finger Post. The Oddfellows was so cramped we had to wait on every room. Sometimes it was so full that you had to pass drinks in from the door. The clubs weren't as they are now; they were just glorified rooms. Most people came to the pub every night, but late, after work. Sunday was a belting afternoon; you used to get big crowds. We had outing clubs, and they all paid their subscriptions then. It was all kept under the table. You weren't allowed to keep books – there were a lot of regulations.

They also played penalties – you'd have ten minutes when no one was allowed to smoke, or five minutes without talking or sipping your drink. There were two 'bobbies' who fined you a penny if you forgot. The money went to an outing fund. They'd maybe go to Chester races or somewhere, once a year, when they would have a salmon tea in Chester, then spend the rest of the evening in a pub somewhere nearby. That was the only day out in the year. People didn't go in for weeks' holidays. Now, their children are off to Majorca.

THE MINER FROM DERBYSHIRE HILL, BORN 1893

There was a pub in Ormskirk Street called the Hope & Anchor. It had two rooms, and the smaller one was comfortably full with 12 people in it. There were 12 of us who used to go there every Saturday night, all from different trades, one from the glassworks, a fitter, a miner – I can't remember them all. One chap, Charlie Fishwick, was a watch repairer in his spare time. Talk about the 12 apostles – they were there! Once you'd had a couple of pints, it loosened the tongue – no one was under the influence – and we had real discussions and arguments in there.

There was one fellow who was a real comedian. He used to sit in the Swan, or the Royal Alfred, on Monday afternoons. The Swan was where all the performers at the Hippodrome used to go. But if you wanted entertainment, you didn't have to go to the Hippodrome; you could just sit and listen to him. He never had to buy his own beer, though I can't remember him being paid. He didn't have any books or anything, the jokes came out of him – all good humour, nothing cruel.

Part III

The Miners' Lockout

1 Introduction

Throughout the early 1920s, the promises of 1918 were turning sour. Attempts by the engineers and others to prevent wage cuts had failed, and all the glassworkers in St Helens had suffered heavy wage cuts without a fight. Unemployment was already extremely high, while very little had yet been achieved to alleviate housing conditions. The 1926 Miners' Lockout was the last stand against the threat of even worse conditions. With the acceptance of the mine-owners' terms came the enforcement of a general standard of living which lasted until World War II. But life in the town in the 13 years after this defeat is another story.

The resistance in 1926 came from the whole community. St Helens was not typical of most mining areas where cut-off villages felt themselves politically isolated during this lockout. Here the miners were only part of a very complex pattern of employment in the town, where glassworks, mines and brickworks might have the same owner. In St Helens, the lockout stands out in people's minds as being of far greater importance than the General Strike with which it began. After all, it was the biggest industrial dispute there had ever been in this country. It lasted for 28 weeks after the failure of the strike – and resulted in the loss of nearly two million working days in St Helens alone. To get some idea of what that means, think of it like this: nearly as many days were lost to production in St Helens in 1926 as were lost *nationally* in any whole year in the early 1950s. This is an attempt to understand how such a poor town managed to sustain such a struggle and remain solid till the end.

For anyone with a belief in the Labour movement, the result of the General Strike is crushing, but there were also possibilities in it. The running of this national stoppage was taken on at three days' official notice by Councils of Action – rank and file trade unionists at a local level. Their leadership failed them. But with the lockout, the leadership was in many cases pleading almost to the end with the men to stay out. The power of Arthur Cook, the general secretary of the miners' union was extraordinary. He visited Leigh and Atherton in the Lancashire coalfield after several thousand men had gone back to work; the day after he'd spoken there, only a trickle of men were working. But this wasn't enough. The lockout revealed the point at which people can no longer be sustained by their deepest beliefs and are forced to act against them.

After the last shift on Friday, 30th April 1926, all the miners in the country were locked out of their pits unless they accepted wage cuts. At that point, the miners were being asked to accept the results of a government commission headed by Herbert Samuel which recommended wage cuts and then rationalization of the industry as the two main solutions to the unprofitability of the mines.

On Saturday, 1st May, the day after the lockout started, leaders from all the unions in the TUC met to vote on how they should support the miners in their effort to prevent these wage cuts. It was only at this meeting that any commitment was given to call out their members in a national stoppage from the following Tuesday. It's difficult to imagine how they could have avoided this. The whole labour movement realized, after the debacle of 1921 that if the miners were forced to accept these wage cuts, most other workers would also have to. The credibility of the TUC was at stake. They had lost a third of their members after 1921 and now they had to plan a national stoppage at three days' notice, even though the threat of this situation had been hanging over them for the nine months since a temporary subsidy to the mining industry had been granted.

As they planned, the General Council of the TUC continued talking to the Government. They were happy to discuss the Samuel document if the lockout notices were withdrawn. The owners wouldn't withdraw them and the government wouldn't intervene to make them do so. But there are signs that on the Sunday night the Council were prepared to *accept* the Samuel document – implying wage cuts – if the lockout notices were withdrawn. It was Baldwin who cut talks short. In the early hours on Monday morning, the printers at the Daily Mail had refused to print an anti-strike editorial. Baldwin considered this a sufficient mark of the TUC's bad faith to call off negotiations (although it could only have been a spontaneous action inside the Daily Mail offices) – the government wanted to fight.

From Tuesday morning, the fight was on. Each town set up a local council of action to organize the strike, although some of them were fraught with inter-union squabbles. Many produced strike bulletins

206

giving news of how things were going in other areas nearby. All of them kept in touch with TUC headquarters for general instructions, but local branches organized things in their area. The TUC produced its own paper, the British Worker, which had two main points to make: it was just an industrial dispute they were all engaged in, and everyone should spend the time quietly at home. The response to the strike call was almost total from the sections called out, and large numbers of others came out too. The extent of it surprised the TUC.

The government put its plans into action. It had a massive propaganda campaign orchestrated through a paper produced by Winston Churchill called the British Gazette and through the BBC (which even banned the Archbishop of Canterbury and Ramsey MacDonald from speaking on the radio). It also enrolled 'special constables' for organized blacklegging. At the beginning of the strike, nothing was moving. But by Saturday, 8th May, the government was beginning to use force in strategic places. Enormous consignments of troops were sent into the docks in London to unload cargoes and bring out food supplies, although in other parts of the country, particularly the north-east, the control of supplies and transport was firmly in the hands of the strikers. Every day, more people were coming out, and the strike was getting stronger. But, on the ground, things never got beyond skirmishing. The struggle was won and lost by the TUC General Council and the government.

After three days of the strike, Lord Samuel came back from Italy and talked to the General Council, without holding any government authority for what was agreed. Effectively, he was a face-saver for the TUC who revived their hopes of calling off the strike by agreeing to his memorandum. They were now definitely prepared to accept his recommendations – for them, a cut in the miners' wages was all right so long as reorganization of the industry was guaranteed. When they agreed this with Samuel, no member of the mineworkers' union was present. And although the miners disowned it when they heard about it, the TUC went ahead.

On the morning of Wednesday, 12th May, they went to see the Prime Minister, Stanley Baldwin. He wouldn't talk to them at all unless they first unconditionally withdrew the strike notice. They did this in his presence but didn't press on to get a commitment on no victimization for strikers, or of the government's intention to implement the Samuel Report.

Baldwin had won outright. It's possible that he could have got the General Council to accept the Samuel Report beforehand. He chose to fight, and in the end didn't even have to accept the Report as a basis for

207

discussion. When the miners eventually returned, their conditions were even worse than those outlined by Samuel.

The day after the strike was called off, there were 100,000 more workers on strike than on any of the days of the General Strike itself. Some didn't believe it possible that it had been called off when things were going so well. Others already realized that they would now have to stay out to fight to maintain their old conditions of employment and wages. Employers set out on wage cuts and victimizations so violent that Baldwin had to intervene to obtain his object of 'getting the workers calm as soon as we can'.

From then until the end of November the miners held out, finally going in to work under terms worse than those posted at their pit heads on 30th April after seven months of struggle.

It is important to understand the relative autonomy of the Board of Guardians administering the Poor Law. (A broad outline of this has already been given.) The autonomy became quite critical during the lockout. As some Boards of Guardians were elected in areas with Labour majorities, they were often sympathetic to the miners. They tried to increase the amount of relief that was paid to dependants, thus enabling the miners to hold out longer.

The men themselves were ruled ineligible for relief in a Government circular sent in May to all Boards of Guardians. This stated that so long as they were able-bodied and work was available, no money should be paid. Although they were locked out of their pits, it was ruled that work was available for them. They would be entitled to relief only if they were considered no longer physically fit for work through starvation or destitution.

The government were very quick to tighten their central control on the administration of the Poor Law. They started to try enforcing the old regulation which demanded that men fit for work should live in the workhouse. Beyond this, Neville Chamberlain carried a Bill through Parliament entitled the Board of Guardians (Default) Act 1926 which enabled the government to replace Guardians with their own nominees. They did this on several occasions, most notoriously in Chester-le-Street, Durham at the end of August when the Board refused to cut the level of relief being paid to miners' dependants. A further sanction was that if a Board no longer had sufficient money from the rates to pay relief, the Ministry of Health had to give approval before it was permitted to borrow any. Of course, most Boards had to borrow money before the end of the lockout, and the Ministry used this as a means of enforcing cuts in the level of relief.

During the summer the Government introduced a bill increasing the miners' working day from seven to eight hours. This had been specifically rejected as a solution in the Samuel Report because it would lead to over-production and a further lowering of coal prices. The miners opposed it not only because it was asking them to work an extra hour for the same pay – and the last hour was always considered the most dangerous. They also realized that it would lead to higher unemployment and a greater pool of reserve labour for the owners to soak up only in times of boom.

The Eight Hour Bill clearly aligned the government with the mine-owners in the eyes of the miners, as the owners had demanded it. But generally the government was not active in forcing a settlement. After July, the owners' terms became increasingly difficult – eventually there was even refusal to meet the Miners' Federation, as they were only pre-pared to negotiate district settlements. After three months – the time the 1921 lockout had lasted – they expected that the miners' collapse was imminent. The government made one or two attempts to get the miners and owners to meet, but after the summer they, like the owners, seem to have just waited for the miners to give in. Before departing on his four-week summer holiday in France, Stanley Baldwin said of the lockout: 'Leave it alone – we are all so tired.' The result of the lessons the govern-ment learnt from the dispute were not presented until the next year in the form of the Trade Disputes and Trade Union Act. This forbade sym-pathy strikes and gave employers the opportunity to sue unions for dam-ages caused through disputes. It was not repealed until the 1945 Labour government took power.

2 The Beginning: April 1921–3rd May 1926

THE MINER FROM RAVENHEAD, BORN 1904

They had to keep the miners down to keep all the rest down. The miners were the first rank. All industry was run on coal and they needed it as cheaply as they could get it – that's why they needed to keep the miners' pay low.

THE COMMUNIST FROM THATTO HEATH, BORN 1902

The biggest thing that happened to me at that time was in April 1921 – the Black Friday affair – with the failure of the Triple Alliance of miners, railwaymen and transport workers to come out in support of the miners. I remember us all waiting in the Sefton Arms. We were waiting for news, because as far as we knew the strike was still on for the next day. One of our members was a tram conductor. At ten o'clock, he came to us with a telegram from union headquarters telling us to continue work the next day. That was a terrible shock. I thought till then that the leaders of the Labour Party were honest men – people like Jimmy Thomas, Ramsay MacDonald, Arthur Henderson and many others. I thought they might make mistakes but they were honest. That incident changed me; I decided they weren't honest men, they were rascals after their own careers.

The fellow who was MP for St Helens – James Sexton – was the man who seconded the motion calling off the strike. The Trades & Labour Council called a special meeting in 1922. It was the first time they could get him to attend a meeting to explain why he had been in favour of calling off the strike. He was in a bit of a quandary as a lot of the trade unionists in the area were miners – about 10,000 of them altogether. Anyway, a resolution was drawn up condemning Sexton's action in calling off the Triple Alliance strike. It was carried with only two votes against.

Even after 1921, I still agreed that there were people in the Labour Party who were socialists, and there still are – the Tribune group of MPs, a lot of them are. But I was much more certain of myself.

When the General Strike occurred, it was really a follow-on of 1921. That had failed as a result of the Triple Alliance's failure. The workers suffered – there were a lot of wage reductions. By the beginning of 1922, the workers had lost over six million pounds in wages. This had sunk in a bit among a lot of them.

THE MINER FROM SUTTON, BORN 1890

1921 was a relatively short strike but it was very viciously fought. We didn't get much out of it. This led to the continued trouble in the mining industry until ruthless action was taken against the miners in 1926. We couldn't see it coming as a General Strike, but we could see something coming because of the attack upon our standards – not merely of wages, but of conditions. In spite of the Samuel Commission findings, the Baldwin Government took action of a character which of course was unacceptable to the miners, but roused the indignation, the ire, of the Trades Union Movement. The miners didn't go on strike, they were locked out.

MINER FROM THATTO HEATH, A MEMBER OF THE COMMUNIST PARTY, BORN 1898

You could practically tell it was coming on. They were trying to make extra production. There are so many different ways of putting the pressure on. They'd fine you for putting even the smallest amount of dirt in the coal. They let you come up, and then they'd stop your lamp. You can't go down without it – you're no good without your lamp. That was done to them that weren't producing as it was thought they should. Another way of getting at you was making you work four days so that you had no dole for the rest of the week. The only reparation you had was to pack it in.

DELEGATE TO THE LANCASHIRE & CHESHIRE MINERS' FEDERATION

The miners' union couldn't see what it could do in the year before the strike, by itself, because it was not completely foreseen that the whole pressure of the state would be brought to bear. Before the lockout started, the mood of the men was the same right throughout the length and breadth of the country, they were determined to resist this onslaught upon their then miserable, low standard of life. Well, of course, the miners were determined to fight, but they felt that if the whole trade union movement supported them, at least there would be some amelioration of the conditions that were laid down. The miners were dependent on full support, particularly from the bigger unions.

THE MINER FROM SUTTON, BORN 1890

In preparation for the 1926 stoppage, the Federation prepared documents and speakers' notes – and there was a handbook on the Samuel Commission. The Tories held meetings and imported an audience. One was held in the Church of England School, Sutton, now demolished. Members of the Labour Party ward committee attended – a KC named Atkinson was the principal speaker, with other Tory bigshots. We asked awkward questions of Mr Atkinson and of course he was very decent about them all because he found he had people against him asking awkward questions he couldn't answer – the whole report was against the Tory government. So it was our meeting. There were two coachloads of Tories, mainly women, but we had too much support and the Bold branch of miners took over that meeting. In the middle of town it would have been even better.

THE COMMUNIST FROM THATTO HEATH, BORN 1902, WHO WAS VICE-CHAIRMAN
OF THE COUNCIL OF ACTION

In the Trades and Labour Council we'd already made plans for a Council of Action in the event of a General Strike. This was mainly due to prodding from the five Communists and five other left-wingers on the council. During the nine months, the Communist Party paper had come out with a headline each week – so many weeks to go before the end of the subsidy. We'd taken this in and got moving in the Trades and Labour Council. We had to do it as the council only met once a month. We got delegates from all the trade union branches affected by the lockout and strike itself: all the miners, railwaymen, transport workers, engineers and glassmakers, even though the engineers and glassmakers weren't called out till the second week of the strike.

21st April 1926

REPORT TO LANCASHIRE & CHESHIRE MINERS' FEDERATION ABOUT THE LAST
NATIONAL CONFERENCE OF THE UNION IN LONDON

The recommendations of the Executive [accepted by the conference] were:

(a) That no assent be given to any proposal for increasing the length of the working day.

(b) That the principle of a National Wage Agreement with a National Minimum percentage be firmly adhered to.

(c) That inasmuch as wages are already too low, we cannot assent to any proposal for reducing wages.

[At this conference, the Lancashire delegation moved that the Miners' Federation should support the call for 'a wage equal to the cost of living', but this received no backing.]

Sunday, 2nd May

COUNCILLOR BOSCOW, CHAIRMAN OF THE TRADES & LABOUR COUNCIL AT A MEETING ON BRIDGE STREET LAND, ST HELENS, ATTENDED BY 3,000 PEOPLE

I trust that if the call is given to you by your leaders, if it has to be given, it will be loyally obeyed by all in your effort to stand by the miners in their dispute. The matter is now out of the hands of the Miners' Federation and in the hands of the Trades Union Congress. That being so, the local organization will be the St Helens Trades & Labour Council from which you'll take your orders and instructions. As president of the Council I sincerely trust that every man working in St Helens who is called upon to down tools to stand by the miners will respond to the call.

COUNCILLOR CHAMBERLAIN OF WARRINGTON (SAME MEETING)

The labour forces will guarantee the health and food services of the country and provide the workers to do the work, but if the OMS [Organization for the Maintenance of Supplies] attempt to interfere from a blackleg point of view, the whole of the service will cease as far as the workers are concerned. Let there be no violence, no disorder. Fold your arms and do nothing, but what you are told by those who will accept responsibility.

JOE TINKER, MP FOR LEIGH (SAME MEETING)

I can see before me the greatest struggle in recent times. Make no mistake about that. We are opposed to the capitalist class who have made up their minds that this shall be the testing time as to whether the workers shall have their rights or not. This is what we have got to face and the only way we can get success is by solid backing by the whole trade union move-

213

ment. The miner cannot win alone. We've come to you for support and I know we shall get it when you know how we are placed.

The commission was set up by the government. The miners had no choice in the picking of the men. Therefore the miners have got to take whatever the commission agreed to give them. The findings have been issued, and I'm bound to admit that there are many good points, but the miners put forward as the only really successful means of dealing with the coal industry that it should be nationalized. That has been swept out of the way.

The Commission admitted that the mines have been badly handled, that reorganization should take place, and that during the reorganization period both employers and workers ought to make sacrifices.

It's on that point that the struggle is now taking place. The employers argue that the whole of the sacrifice should be borne by the workers. In Lancashire, which is typical of the other districts, the first offer is that we should accept 25% over the 1921 basic, or a 21% reduction of our present standard of life. That was rejected by the miners and the government got the coal-owners to make another offer – and this is the final offer, which to my mind is worse than the first one, namely they should accept the 1921 standard and also one hour a day longer. The coal-owners are spoiling for a fight. They want a fight because they can see this: if the miners are allowed to go on in a constitutional manner, the mines will pass out of the coal-owners' hands, as sure as there is the light of day in this market place, and the owners want to reach such a position that if they can smash the miners it will put back the whole of the movement 20 or 30 years.

If it comes, and I do not see much chance of its not, it will be the most terrible fight in British history. Everything will be done to get the workers against each other during the coming weeks. That is the time when we want to stand solidly in this struggle.

I want to say a word now of a man who had been much maligned by many of our people. I speak now of Jimmy Thomas [President of the railwaymen's union]. Let us be candid, friends, over this. Jimmy Thomas on this occasion has thrown the whole of his weight with the workers. Well, let us give credit when the man does right. If we had many more Jimmy Thomases there would be no more trouble with trade union workers! If we win, it will not merely be a victory for the miners, but for the whole of the working-class movement.

214

Monday, 3rd May

We have been meeting downstairs. First of all, the firemen have sent no representative, but the Enginemen and Boilermen, Tradesmen and AEU have sent representatives. The AEU and the Tradesmen have entirely agreed with us, but the Enginemen and Boilermen want permission to issue their own permits, to as many men as they consider are required to work for safety purposes. We pointed out to them that there will be committees and that representatives of firemen and their unions will be on that body, and that committee will be the one to decide how many permits will be issued and to whom. We stick to that. They were told we should go on with these arrangements and no one would be allowed to work except with a permit from this committee. They nearly came to, but Mr Forshaw says he cannot do any other as he has instructions from headquarters.

3 The General Strike: 4th–12th May 1926

THE COMMUNIST FROM THATTO HEATH, BORN 1902
The miners came up on the Friday, the General Strike was called on Saturday and the other workers came out on Tuesday.

THE MINER FROM SUTTON, DELEGATE TO THE COUNCIL OF ACTION
The Council of Action was set up by the Trades & Labour Council in St Helens. It was set up early and they did some good work. The Executive Committee was in continuous session.

The Council undertook the conducting of the supporting part of the General Strike. It was left to the local branches to picket transport and so on. Without a shadow of a doubt, staggering support was given. The Council of Action weren't in control of the town by any means – there were lots of things that were dealt with by the local branches of the other unions. There was very little disturbance with the normal communal life of the town, and this applied in other places. There was no interference – we never felt the effect of organized blacklegging, particularly on the lines it was done in the larger towns.

The TUC had nothing to do with the setting up of this committee. The Trades Council had to take over at local level the running of the General Strike. It was no surprise how quickly it was done. It was evident the temper was shown in the local Trades Councils. After all, the Government had been preparing for the confrontation since the Samuel Committee was set up.

THE COMMUNIST FROM THATTO HEATH, BORN 1902
In the General Strike, we had a meeting every day of the Council of Action. We met in the Railway Institute in Salisbury Road. The chairman was Councillor Boscow; the secretary Dicky Waring – his assistant was Percy Lowe, a left-winger. I was elected vice-chairman and had to take the meetings when Boscow wasn't there.

Anyone who wanted to move anything had to have a permit from the Council of Action or else. An hour each day was spent on deciding whether to issue permits. 'Permit' was printed on Trades & Labour Council notepaper with a pen. They didn't grant permits to everybody only where food was concerned. Arrangements were made with the Co-op Society before the strike began. The Co-op Society warehouses were to be used to store foodstuffs coming into town. If foodstuffs became scarce, it was important for us to have control of the food for the town.

There was a commissioner appointed by the Government who was to take control out of the Town Council's hands. The difficulty in St Helens was that they had a Labour majority. The Town Clerk was supposed to be the official to work under the commissioner. He was in a bit of a fix as he'd have to work under the Labour majority again when the strike was over. The best thing for him to do was sit quietly and do nothing, and that's what he did.

The question of controlling food supplies never really arose. The Council of Action was in control of the town. There was never any open challenge to anyone in authority. There was no support of the OMS. I never heard of anyone who was even in it. During the General Strike, there was no question – we were going to win. We were that solid.

DAUGHTER OF THE SECRETARY OF THE COUNCIL OF ACTION
I can remember the General Strike as a child. We used to have an enormous square table in the front room. I've seen coppers piled up that high. They had meetings and collections, which is where the money came from. They counted it there and took it to a branch of the Co-op Bank. It was to give them something to live off. There was one butcher in the town who gave away 20 joints of meat. My father had to look after them; it was left to my mother to allocate them. People came in in all sorts of conditions – people who hadn't saved anything at all.

THE COMMUNIST FROM THATTO HEATH, BORN 1902
The miners had pickets; they were the largest body. It was only small numbers of them picketing until later on in the struggle. The TUC General Council called out the first wave – heavy industry, transport, dockers. They called out the building industry, subject to their building hospitals and houses. This left things in a bit of a muddle, but the workers sorted it out for themselves by stopping anyway. There was tremendous

enthusiasm among the general body of workers – a lot who weren't called out did come out.

ELECTRICIAN FROM WINDLE

I suppose there was quite a lot of make-do-and-mend during the strike – I can't remember now whether we got strike pay. As far as we were concerned, it was just a holiday – everyone laughing and joking. I thought it was just the ideal thing – I thought it showed something of strength.

Power stations were all split, belonging to private companies and local authorities. I think there was a lot of bigheadedness among the electrical tradesmen in those days. They didn't want to know the boilerhousemen who worked at the power stations. I'm not saying the boilerhousemen weren't skilled, but they weren't organized – I don't think they were in the union. That was a mistake. The power stations didn't close down.

RAILWAYMAN, SECRETARY TO THE SUTTON BRANCH OF THE NUR

Each branch organized itself. I organized it for the people in our branch, another man for No. 2 branch with the traffic men like guards, porters and plate layers. We met in St Helens to co-ordinate efforts. We only needed the pickets on the first day. Then it was a matter of just taking a walk round. Watchmen were on all day in case of fire. They used to walk round the works every hour. We got strike pay, as it was an official strike.

PROSECUTING BARRISTER IN SUBSEQUENT COURT CASE

On 8th May, a lorry was dispatched by the railway company, in the charge of three volunteers, to the company's General Stores at St Helens Junction to pick up a load of pillows and bedding to take back to Manchester. The lorry arrived at the station at 2.30, was admitted by a constable and loaded by a volunteer. The lorry passed out of the store and reached the outside gate in Pealake Lane which was found chained and padlocked. A large crowd gathered round and refused to open the gate for the lorry, which was taken back to its stores, and the police were advised by telephone. When they arrived, Inspector Owen asked two men who were on picket duty, 'What are you doing?' Sheridan said: 'We have instructions from our committee not to allow that lorry to come through loaded without a permit from the Council of Action.'

He asked Sheridan to open the gate and allow the lorry to come through without interference, but they refused to do so. Inspector Owen then asked if any of the Council were present and he was told someone had gone for them on a bicycle. Shortly afterwards, six arrived. All the members of the strike committee were in favour of there being no trouble and Inspector Owen tried to persuade them to allow the lorry to proceed. John Smith said, 'If it goes out, let it, but it goes under the responsibility of the police and the driver; we have no authority to give protection as that should be applied for to the Council of Action in St Helens.' The storekeeper pointed out that the lorry was only going from one department to another, but Joe Harrison said 'It is to help blacklegs who have been working.' None of these men attempted to exercise his authority with the strikers, so the lorry returned to the yard and was unloaded. It returned empty. The gate was unlocked amidst a lot of booing and shouting and the lorry was let out and escorted to the borough boundary by Sergeant Pratt.

TRAM MECHANIC IN THE T&GWU, BORN 1897

Everyone came out. We had pickets at the works, but I don't remember anyone trying to go in. We got about 17s 6d a week strike pay. If you wanted to know anything about what was going on you had to go to the meetings at the club. Going to the Council of Action was left to the local secretary and one or two others. They got all the gen from there and reported back to us. When it finished, we were glad to go back because we were getting very short of money.

THE COMMUNIST FROM THATTO HEATH, BORN 1902

When the tram men were enthusiastic, I was amazed. They were a set apart – what with the job having unsocial hours, it meant they couldn't join in a lot of activities. They had a social club of their own. They were generally a highly respectable body of men, who normally wouldn't have thought of parading the streets with a sandwich board and advertising on the handlebars of a push bike. Bill Terry wanted to teach me ju jitsu so I'd know how to break a blackleg's arm. It was true, later on, of the miners. There were tremendous fights.

We organized a great deal of picketing. It was left to each branch of each union to organize it for themselves. They took reports of what they were doing to the Council of Action. The tram men used to meet every day at about nine o'clock in the morning in a social club at the Sefton Arms on the corner of Cotham Street. They were far more active than I expected. Some of them went on pushbikes to picket the Crosville buses, which were still being run through Prescot and Rainhill by non-union crews. In three days, the tram men stopped them completely. They used to wait at the bus stops and chat to each driver and conductor as they came by. When they were told, 'We've nothing to do with the union, nobody has called us out,' the pickets replied: 'We do. If you come back tomorrow, you're liable to get your windows smashed.' By Thursday, there weren't any buses at all. Then the tramdrivers went out picketing all the transport that was moving, including horse-drawn vehicles.

ENGINEER AT PILKINGTONS, BORN 1891

Pilkingtons had started a pension scheme. I had 1s 2d supplementary, and Lord Pilkington took a shilling off every man entitled to supplementary who'd come out on strike. That shilling is off my pension to this day – it's cost me a shilling a week. We were only out a week. They had to manage the best they could. The foreman and the apprentices kept the plant going. It was only the engineers, the plumbers, the blacksmiths and all the tradesmen who came out – not the glassmakers.

MALE BRICKWORKER

The brickworks carried on through the General Strike. Mounted police brought up a steam motor and trailer. It had a notice painted in white on black saying 'Priority Goods'. The colliery men were there, but they weren't picketing like they do now.

THE MINER FROM SUTTON, BORN 1890

For general information, the press was running – there was the British Worker. But we got our opinion to some extent by speakers crossing from area to area. The principal source was by communication between the several districts. We had speakers from St Helens going to Liverpool and outlying areas as propagandists; and the same applied, we had them coming to St Helens from Liverpool, Wigan, Warrington, Manchester and so on. It was a very fine source of communication. The meetings were colossal – very, very large meetings – and generally speaking the greater number were open air – the halls weren't big enough to hold some of them.

THE COMMUNIST FROM THATTO HEATH, BORN 1902

During the strike, the BBC got on to tricks that they've become expert at since. They used to report so many returned to work at different

View of the town centre from Rutland Street, with the Beecham's factory clock tower far right, 1976.

Above: Blacklegs wait to do a milk round during the General Strike, May 1926; they are standing in the yard of Greenalls brewery. *Below:* Joe Tinker (centre), miners' agent for St Helens and MP for Leigh, handing in nomination papers for the General Election in 1935.

places to break the miners' morale. They said 400 had returned to work at Gallis Green colliery when it hadn't been used for years – all that existed was a tumbledown shaft and a ruin of an engine house.

We got information from word of mouth to a large extent. The Communist Party was issuing bulletins from Liverpool – there were four or five during the nine days. They had motor-cycle dispatch riders riding between various towns. Four or five men came to offer their services from the tram sheds, and they went to Preston, Leigh, Warrington, Liverpool, Manchester. They'd go to the headquarters of the strike movement taking news from St Helens and bringing back bulletins from where they'd been. Of course, they'd get talking with people there and they'd exchange information like that. People were used to word of mouth, wireless didn't count.

Sunday, 9th May

COUNCILLOR BOSCOW AT A MEETING IN THE HIPPODROME

So far as St Helens is concerned the lockout is progressing most satisfactorily. We have in St Helens a splendid organization, an organization I am proud to be at the head of. If it becomes necessary, the public office of St Helens will be utilized in the interests of those who find themselves in the unfortunate position of not having any work to go to. Put your pride in your pocket and make use of the machinery in regard to the feeding of children that has been provided for you.

The End of the Strike

THE COMMUNIST FROM THATTO HEATH, BORN 1902

When the strike was called off, the Transport Workers' Union headquarters sent out telegrams to every branch. The Council of Action met that morning and the NUR delegation came to the council saying that the strike was being called off. We called them liars. We got posters stuck up all over the town saying 'Take no notice of the rumours. The Council of Action will tell you what is happening.' When I came back at two o'clock, I saw the branch secretary of the transport workers, who was quite left-wing, and he told me we'd had a telegram from Bevin saying the General Strike had been settled. The tram manager wanted to get the trams started right away, but we decided to wait till the next day to see what the situation was. We didn't know anything about the terms – some of the fellows wanted to stay out, but it would have been unofficial and that meant something then. Anyway, we might have won and there wouldn't be any point in staying out then. I thought the telegrams could have been fakes. You didn't really know where you were; I went into a sort of daze. Anyway the Daily Herald came out, the day after we'd started work with the banner headlines: GREAT WORKERS' VICTORY. It wasn't till a few days later that we got to know what had really happened.

THE MINER FROM SUTTON, BORN 1890
When the Council of Action heard the strike was called off, they felt it was a question of betrayal by national leaders. Many felt the pressure being brought to bear on the leadership was beginning to have an effect. In our lifetime, and in our long experience of the trade unions and working-class movement, the betrayal of the mineworkers – and it wasn't by the rank and file – was probably the darkest period of our lives.

Sunday, 16th May

JACK HOUGHTON OF THE TEACHERS' UNION AT A MEETING OF MINERS
I never saw in all my life such a demoralized, hopeless and down-hearted crowd as the one of 4,000 working men in St Helens and district assembled on the Bridge Street land on Thursday morning after the strike was called off. The morale of the working class was broken at that moment. It was broken because the thing for which they had come out on strike as a mass, in their estimation, had not been accomplished. The spirit of the working-class movement is behind you in this fight. I've seen the children being fed and I'm hoping that as on the last occasion when a strike was on, the children would be healthier and more physically fit than when their fathers had been working and earning a miserable wage.

THE COMMUNIST FROM THATTO HEATH, BORN 1902
If, in the General Strike, the TUC general council had stayed loyal for seven, eight or nine of the days, instead of crawling off after about two to try to get a settlement, we would have won. If the strike had been won, the miners would have gone back on the same wages and conditions as under the subsidy. They've never had a seven-hour day since then. If they'd won, it would have prevented the employers from going ahead and attacking all the other sections of workers. They would have been up against a practically united working class, and out of it could have come all sorts of developments, even revolutionary developments.

Some people say the General Strike was a revolution. Well it wasn't. You know what conditions Lenin laid down for a revolutionary situation: that the government will have lost control of the country. That is one of them, and the government never lost control. It would have been important for the Council of Action if it had developed instead of ending after eight or nine days. The Council of Action would have developed. With the arrangement with the Co-op society to store food in their warehouses, it would have controlled practically the whole of the foodstuffs coming into St Helens and the foodstuffs would have been a main plank in our programme. There was talk of setting up a workers' defence force – but nine days was insufficient. That was to defend workers' pickets against the forces of the capitalists. They'd have fetched soldiers, but soldiers won't always obey the line of the officers. Once that had happened, the revolution was on.

THE BRANCH SECRETARY OF THE NUR AT SUTTON
[The two men on the picket for the NUR at the stores]: They were sacked afterwards. I was the branch secretary, and we had to fight to get them back. We saw the manager locally and he said it wasn't up to him. It was referred down to Euston and the union dealt with it nationally and eventually we got them reinstated.

THE COMMUNIST FROM THATTO HEATH, BORN 1902 WHO WORKED ON THE TRAMS
They victimized me the following June. After the General Strike was over, the manager of the tramways decided that exceptional circumstances existed and he was entitled to nullify the 48-hour week. He'd put it in abeyance. Somewhere about May, the union branch asked for the week to be reinstated. He refused. The branch decided to put a ban on overtime and rest-day working.

I was one of the first to come on rest-day working. They didn't say anything then. A week later, I was called into the manager's office. I was dismissed. I went down to the tram sheds – a lot of the tram men wanted to go on strike. I argued against it, mistakenly believing in the union. Being a communist, I thought they could make something out of it if the men came out unofficially. I told them to take official action.

In July a deputation went to the tram committee, but a union fellow from Manchester didn't turn up, so they refused to receive the deputation. The following month was the holiday month – August. Eventually he came in November, and I went with him. At the committee he got up and said: 'I think there have been mistakes on both sides. We think it should be settled by the reinstatement of this conductor.' Then he sat down and whispered to me, 'Have you got anything to say?' Well, I hadn't been expecting to have to make the case myself so I stood up and made a case off the cuff. One of the rules in the national agreement was that work on a rest day was voluntary – and it was on a rest day I'd refused to work. Afterwards I got a letter and they backed the manager up.

4 The Continuing Lockout: May–July

Wednesday, 19th May

JOE TINKER AT A MEETING OF MINERS

I realize we have never been up against a sterner struggle in all our existence. Knowing all the sufferings that will follow in the coming weeks, I have no hesitation in saying to my people that if you are to give way now there would not be a man amongst you worth calling a man.

My appeal to you is this. Though the struggle may be a long one, we have got to realize in recognition to our own manhood, in recognition of the men gone before and with thought of those to come after us – your children – that the time has now come when you have got to make a stand. This fight has got to continue as long as human endurance will allow. It is only when you are driven back by starvation that we can accept the conditions of the mine-owners. All that is wanted is the great mass to be led the proper way, and there is no government, no body of mine-owners that can stand in your path.

THE MINER FROM THATTO HEATH, BORN 1898

Just after the General Strike, we were meeting the office clerks at Sutton Heath and Lea Green because they had them scabbing down below and we disagreed – they weren't down at any other time. There was a right scuffle, fighting. The clerks were taking lumps of coal home in paper. We took these lumps of coal and police sergeant Valentine ploughed into our lot with a horse. The same policeman vanished from the force that September, but he took the Clog and Stocking Fund with him.

We organized pickets. You'd only get about 20 – half of them were lookers on. We couldn't picket 24 hours a day – we didn't have enough people. The union leaders didn't organize pickets. They detested us; never mind making pickets. They weren't interested. All they wanted was food for the kiddies, they'd never been taught to organize.

225

The trade union funds obviously wouldn't last. The Federation pawned the offices at Bolton. They took out a mortgage which had to be redeemed afterwards. It was looked upon as the thing to do. It was done in the first week.

The Miners' Central Committee felt that they would like to tour the surrounding area to collect money and they had selected, for one weekend, Liverpool as the basis of this experiment of street collecting. They took a pony and a pit tub, on which they put special wheels, into the city and commenced to collect in the streets from the passers by. It was well received, but, although the police did not object to this, they saw to it that the people in charge kept on the move.

DEPUTY AT CLOCK FACE, BORN 1886

In 1926, I was assistant under manager at Clock Face. One night somebody came and told me the miners were waiting for me. They had been told I wasn't in the Under Managers' Union, so I should be out on strike. My wife was crying, she didn't want me to go. I said 'I'm going to work.' Anyway, I met a thousand men at Colliery Lane. They were all packed in the lane to stop me going to work. As I went towards the men, the secretary, Billy Cross, comes towards me. 'Oh,' he says, 'it's come to our ears you're not in the Under Managers' Union.'

'That's easily proved,' I said. 'Let your secretary meet my secretary.'

As they stood there, Al Martin said to them: 'This chap says the right thing. Our secretary should meet his secretary and we'll see.'

But another chap called out: 'He's not going to work while my kids and wife are starving.'

Al Martin said: 'Shut your trap or I'll do it for you. Make way, open up a gangway for him and let him go to work.'

I went through and went to work. It was only keeping the pumps going. Do you know we had 400 gallons a minute coming in down there? We had to keep the pumps going or else the pit would have been flooded. Clock Face would have been finished if we hadn't kept them going. Anyway, Billy Cross and Al Martin went to see Bill Ash, the Under Managers' Union secretary. He showed them the book, and my name was in it. A chap, name of Twist, was the manager. He was standing by his window when I met the crowd. He said, when he saw me, 'George, I wouldn't have faced that crowd for all the tea in China.'

I said, 'Oh you don't know them – they're just a lot of daft buggers.' My wage was £4 10s a week. To my surprise when the strike started and we were doing the pumps, my wage was £13 10s for the first week. There were clerks from Wigan who came to help us out.

The Fight for Relief

THE RELIEVING OFFICER, BORN 1900

When the strike pay ran out, all you could apply for was relief. It wasn't much, but it was all the town could afford. They learnt to get by in the most amazing fashion. Parish relief was paid out for miners' families in the strike. We had different centres set up. The Parish Church, Park Road – we had four or five centres. There was a scale laid down. I knew of families with eight or nine children who'd get 16s in vouchers and the same in cash – the vouchers were made out to Lennons or the Co-op. It gave a list of things that could be supplied. Single men weren't given assistance – they had to just scramble. I couldn't do anything about it. I had the power to do something in an emergency, but I couldn't give single men money. It was a bit stiff, just because a fellow wasn't married. (During the last strike at Pilkingtons in 1970 I don't think single people were given a grant.) If a single man couldn't get lodgings, he just had to sleep out. Some of them used to come and say: 'I'm going to get married on Saturday.' I had to give them something for their wives. I suppose quite a lot of chaps must have got married like that. You'd find a tremendous lot of humour although they were grim days.

THE MINER FROM NEWTON ROAD, BORN 1900

Me and my wife used to go down to the workhouse. They gave me 8s to keep us on. They used to think they were giving you the town. They wanted me to sign a paper to give it back when the stoppage was over. I said, 'You will, bloody hell, you didn't give it to me in the first place.'

MEMBER OF THE MINERS' CENTRAL COMMITTEE

One pleasant feature of all this was that particular year was one of extremely good weather throughout the lockout, so people could spend their time outside. There was nothing new about the question of the shortage of food, etc.; we were used to it. We put up with it and we put up with the very meagre financial support that was given to the families through the Poor Law.

There was a big demonstration over the amount of money paid. The St Helens Miners' Central Committee organized it to visit the offices of the Poor Law Institution at Whiston. The miners met at their several

227

districts and marched to the Town Centre. There were about 15,000 on the march. The officials of the Miners' Central Committee headed the demonstration accompanied by brass bands. With the officers were prominent citizens and members of the St Helens Trades & Labour Council and the St Helens Town Council. As the procession wended its way through the eastern end of the town, it was augmented by many people desiring to join in – and you could see groups of them coming down the side streets as we went. Many miners' wives attended and many sympathizers as well.

Thursday 17th June
THE MARCH AS REPORTED IN THE ST HELENS NEWSPAPER

The object of the demonstration was to ask for relief for single and married miners. Only the dependants of married miners are given relief while single miners get nothing.

In the streets adjacent to Bridge Street men were massed in their thousands from not only the centre of the town, but from Sutton, Parr, Clock Face, Sutton Manor and other districts. They were marshalled, and led by the British Legion Band, the imposing procession started on its five-mile trek to Whiston.

The Parr contingent were easily distinguished by the walking sticks which they carried and swung gaily and with which they assisted Shanks's pony. They carried their hats in their hands and in their pockets instead of wearing them on their heads.

Dense crowds lined Liverpool Road and Borough Road and the procession of necessity crawled very slowly amidst cheering and friendly advice from thousands of women lining the streets. Plain-clothes policemen could be seen moving amongst the crowd, but there was never the slightest trace of rowdyism or trouble.

Half-way up Liverpool Road, a body of miners' wives in remarkably high spirits joined in the procession and took a prominent part in the van ... At Thatto Heath Park another contingent of miners had assembled waiting to take their place. They joined the procession to the strains of the Westfield Methodist Band. Tram cars were used as grandstands by hundreds of cheering women who were thus making the journey to Whiston. A jazz band from Sutton Manor in particular appeared to appeal.

On reaching Rainhill the procession was joined by a contingent of unemployed from Widnes bearing a slate inscribed: 'We have no dole',

228

The demonstration demanding Poor Law Relief for the locked out miners (see p. 228) in June 1926. *Above:* Sutton Manor Miners' jazz band on the march. *Below:* Some of the 15,000 demonstrators on their way to Whiston Workhouse.

CLOCK FACE SOUP KITCHEN MAIDS

Above: Men preparing food for the soup kitchen at Clock Face during the miners' lockout in September 1926. *Below:* Women picking coal from the surface during the lockout.

and 'We want the right to live'. The vanguard moved to the Institution gates and marched down the road to the football ground.

About this time the deputation drove up in a motor car which was allowed to drive into the grounds.

After about an hour's deliberation the deputation was recalled and the chairman said that the Guardians, while prepared to adequately relieve the destitute within the limit of the law, regretted they could not relieve the able-bodied men married or single, but that the Board had decided to ask the ministry to allow them to relieve single men by a loan of ten shillings a week. In regard to families the Board had decided to raise the scale from 9s to 11s in the case of married women and from 3s 6d to 4s for the first two children and 2s 6d a week for each child afterwards, without any maximum. A third of the amount granted should be paid in money and not in food vouchers.

Sunday, 20th June

JOE LEAHY (PRESIDENT OF THE MINERS' CENTRAL COMMITTEE) AT A MEETING
I don't want any difference of opinion with regard to relief to develop – it's not a question of single versus married. Many men look at it from the wrong angle – the monetary point of view. The right angle is this – the Board of Guardians are not free agents. They are bound down by wrong laws, some hundreds of years old, some of more recent years, brought into being by the present capitalist governments. The Board of Guardians can only move in a prescribed circle under the coercive control of the Ministry of Health, and the present Ministry of Health would stop our breath, never mind our relief, if they could, with a view to defeating us and beating us back to the mines.

With regard to relief for single men: I told many single men not to rush and sign on but to wait and in conversation with Mr Mann (the clerk to the Guardians) we find that the Ministry has sent an inspector there on Friday evening . . . and told them emphatically it was illegal.

It was decided yesterday morning at the Miners' Central Committee that we should not let the matter rest there.

Soup-Kitchens

THE MEMBER OF THE MINERS' CENTRAL COMMITTEE

A feature of the lockout, particularly in the St Helens area, was the institution of several soup-kitchens. Sutton in particular had an extremely good and well patronized soup-kitchen. And I must say this, that the church organizations, particularly the Quakers, paid visits and gave practical assistance, as did local shopkeepers in several areas. This was not a case of credit; this was the local shopkeepers giving food for the soup-kitchens. They were done from either the clubs, particularly the Labour clubs, or the public houses where there were outhouses suitable for this kind of thing, and these were extremely well received by the people.

THE MINER FROM PARR, BORN 1893

From the first day, I remember, the St Helens Council decided to advise everybody to send their children to school for food. We were providing meals here in Parr two a day all through it for children in the schools and that was one good help. If they lived in Lancashire County, they didn't get it.

THE SECONDARY SCHOOL HEADMASTER

We set a kitchen in the big warehouse opposite the school. We built a cookhouse and served meals there. There was a means test – it wasn't just free for everyone; you had to prove you needed it before you got free meals. In fact there weren't that many miners' children in our parish, but most children got the meals. There was breakfast and dinner. Some of them weren't any worse fed than usual, but it's surprising how much they wouldn't eat. They were so used to going out to the chip shop, that fish and chips was about all they'd eat. When stews used to be served up, they'd pick out all the bits of meat and leave them on the side of their plates to be sent back to the kitchen. The teachers tried to coax them; I think we educated some of them. We just ordered the food and the local authority paid for it. They were all right at breakfast, with bread and jam and milk – we always had a lot of milk. It was the meat they didn't like.

JOE TINKER AT A MEETING

The teachers are just a little bit disappointed on one point. At the weekends, many of the children don't go to school for their meals and, knowing the state of the home, they think the children should take full advantage of the benefits and rights offered to them by the Town Council. Remember this struggle is not over yet and every meal that the child can get out of the school leaves another slice of bread for the other people.

Coal Picking
MINER FROM DERBYSHIRE HILL, BORN 1893

There was one place – Glade Hill – that was the name. There was crop coal, and access to it was really easy. Most of the shafts weren't more than seven or eight feet down. It was like a gold rush – stake your claim and that was your patch. We weren't digging coal for domestic use. One of the best customers was Rawcrofts, nugget manufacturers. Most of the fuel wasn't class stuff. If you didn't sell it when it was dug and the sun got on it, it used to go a rusty colour. It got the name of Dublin dust. When we went out on strike, most of the men took their tools home with them. The manufacturers were jumping at the coal and paying good money for it.

MINER FROM SUTTON, BORN 1900

During the lockout, they had police from Liverpool and St Helens guarding the stuff at Clock Face colliery. I went to Clock Face for coal once or twice. One time I was carrying some back with my brother-in-law when a bobby from St Helens and one from Liverpool saw us. We dropped the coal and they chased us. I got away, but they caught him. The policeman from St Helens asked him: 'Who was that with you?' He said 'I don't know.' The policeman said 'I do, it was your brother-in-law.' But they didn't fine us; they just took the coal down to the station and burnt it.

It helped to keep us going. It was only waste coal with a lot of dirt in it, stuff that the colliery didn't want, but it was still the property of the mine-owners. We were satisfied to get enough for ourselves, but some people sold it to families round about. It wouldn't take long to fill a bag if they let you take it, but you had to watch out all the time. I've seen a few scuffles there – men throwing bits of slack at the police. The men used to torment the police on the main road while one or two went round the back getting the coal.

MINER FROM NEWTON ROAD, BORN *c*. 1900.

I used to go picking coal – I turned out every day – and sold some. We got a couple of pounds with that. They let you pick it – you weren't supposed to get it all the same. We'd just got married and she wanted to come picking with me, but I wouldn't let her because they used such bad language. You know those two-hundredweight sugar bags? We were down a big hole one day and when we came up she'd got a bag full of bits as little as a thimble. I looked at my cousin and said 'Are you carrying this?' He said he wouldn't. I put the bag on my back and I sank up to my calves in the tip. At night time, we used to go ratting in a woodyard – we caught plenty.

THE SELF-EMPLOYED COALMAN

When the strike was on, I used to take coal into Liverpool. I saw a man there and said 'If I sold it you, I'd offer you a fair price. I'll come up here with two loads a day.' I promised him a regular supply. I did one load and Bloomer did one load for me. The colliery was between Carringtons and Shaws at Peasley Cross. I paid men to get it. They were digging from the surface. Sometimes they'd go a good way down – there was plenty of coal there. The rook [slack heap] had plenty of coal mixed with the dirt. Colliers used to get it, and when they'd got a bag or two they used to sell it to me for $8\frac{1}{2}$d a hundredweight. They weren't bothered; they were glad to get it for me. I never took less than a hundredweight. I never told nobody what was paid me. I made a profit, that's all.

Sunday, 13th June

JOE HUGHES OF THE MINERS' CENTRAL COMMITTEE AT A MEETING AT THE
      HORSE SHOE INN, PARR

Personally I draw no salary whatever. I'm a worker at the coal face locked out like everybody else. Mr Tinker now only draws his parliamentary salary and receives no salary as miners' agent. Neither does Mr Cook draw any salary as secretary of the Miners' Federation. McDonald, Cook, Tinker and the rest of the leaders know the spirit and the feeling of the miners in this dispute. They have got to tell you to fight to the last gasp. If any one of these men, even Cook or Herbert Smith, were to go back on their words, the miners would say to them: 'Get out and make room for better men.'

Friday, 25th June
ALDERMAN DICK WARING, LABOUR PARTY AGENT
May I make an urgent appeal to all those who are in a position to do so to support the Miners' Relief Fund? I'm sorry to say that some of the big tradesmen and men who in some cases are receiving a big income in vouchers from the Guardians and in orders from the Education Committee have not yet responded to the appeal for the Miners' Distress Fund. Perhaps they have not yet realized the great need. I must however thank the St Helens Co-operative Society for their donation of £200.

Sunday, 27th June
JOE TINKER AT A MEETING BY THE TRAM TERMINUS DERBYSHIRE HILL
Lord Birkenhead has told us we are worse than the Germans and ought to be starved back to work, that we have no right to have assistance from the Poor Law or anywhere else. He thinks we all ought to be treated like the Germans when taken prisoner. That is the psychology of the employing class. If this fight goes on as it will, they will attempt to stop payment from the Poor Law Guardians. That would be their last attempt to try to get the miners back.

Mr Baldwin said some time ago that he was prepared to accept the commission's findings and put them into practice if the miners and coalowners would agree. We were satisfied with that. The commission has laid down firmly that there's no solution in the increased working day. It would only result in competing nations increasing their working day also, and the miners of this country would be just as they were before. Now we have Mr Baldwin introducing a short bill in Parliament stating that the miners' hours can be lengthened which means in effect that the seven-hours act is a dead letter.

THE MEMBER OF THE MINERS' CENTRAL COMMITTEE
Cook [General Secretary of the Miners' Federation of Great Britain] came up twice during the lockout. He attended one meeting which was held on the grounds behind the St Helens hospital, and I would say this was the biggest industrial and political meeting of its kind ever held in St Helens. He was a great public speaker without a trace of doubt. But there were other good local speakers as well. There was a man in the crowd that day who shouldered his way to the front. He just sent up a

233

piece of paper to the platform saying that he was Page Arnott, and they called him up on to the wagons. Without a doubt, Cook had a personal effect on keeping the strike solid. He also relayed information from other districts.

Sunday, 4th July

COOK'S VISIT REPORTED IN THE ST HELENS NEWSPAPER

The biggest meeting ever held in St Helens took place on Sunday morning last week when fully twenty-five thousand people welcomed the Miners' Federation Secretary, Mr A. J. Cook, to St Helens. At the close of the meeting, after voting solidly as one man to go on with the strike, the crowd broke into enthusiastic cheering which could be heard at Thatto Heath, over two miles away. The scene was a most remarkable one. In the valley between St Helens and Victors Works the crowd was on the YMCA rugby football ground. The lorries were drawn up near the works and in front there sat the audience in a solid semi-circle. Behind them stood rows and rows of men and women. In the ordinary course of open air meetings, half the audience hear nothing. In this case, however, the east wind carried the speakers' voices to the crowd, and people sitting beneath the hospital wall were able to hear every word.

A. J. COOK (FROM HIS SPEECH)

I've not come today to back up Lancashire. I've come so I might get a little enthusiasm renewed in myself. Your enthusiasm and encouragement help others to win through. The battle's being transferred from London to the pits. The others have failed to beat your leaders. The whole issue is now in the hands of the miners. It's said the men aren't behind their leaders. The testing time will be in the next two weeks. The fate of the future is in your hands and we're going to test the industry of the Empire. Changes must come. The year 1926 stands as a great sign-post. What we want is human signposts pointing the way to the New Jerusalem. Three cheers for the miners, victory!

MINER FROM ASHTON'S GREEN

I remember A. J. Cook speaking behind the hospital. They reckon he was the best man we had. I reckon he was the best man we ever had for the miners.

234

5 The Crisis: July–October

THE DEPUTY BORN 1890
In the big strike, the management allowed us deputies to work three days a week. One half worked the first three days and the other half the other three days. We were just doing maintenance; we hadn't to handle any coal. It was an agreement between the miners' union and the deputies' union to do the safety work. A road's timbered, and as the weight comes on, the bars break; they have to have new bars to replace them. Then, it only needed a flick of your finger to put me in poverty. I had eight to keep.

Sunday, 25th July

WOMAN AT A MEETING IN PARR
The women demand that the safety men be withdrawn from the pits. There is a lot of scabbing going on at Ashton's Green Colliery. There are five boxes of coal lying under Ashton's Green screens and it is our duty to look after the matter if the union officials don't.

THE CHAIRMAN, COUNCILLOR WOODWARD (SAME MEETING)
It is quite evident that the women are taking a keen interest in the struggle. As an official, I will tell you the position of the officials. Last Monday, we received a deputation from a joint meeting of the pit committees of the Miners' Federation and the Winders' Association. Their agreement states that when all the coal has gone from the pithead – the fuel used for the boilers to get up steam for raising and lowering the cage for the safety men – the winders in the mine could bring up the coal about the pit bottom for that purpose only. Directly it was not used for safety purposes, the winders would withdraw from the pits. The deputation said that the coal-owners would probably get non-union men to wind this coal if the union men were prevented from winding it. Hard things were said

across the table and they came to the very strong decision that the Ashton's Green Branch of the Miners' Federation would not stand for anyone to wind coal for any purpose whatever. The resolution was carried by a big majority. The Ashton's Green Miners' Committee have done their part. It is no fault of the branch committee – someone else is to blame.

MINER FROM DERBYSHIRE HILL

Even Pilkingtons were feeling the pinch; they were on a three-day week. They imported coal from Germany. You know the railway line by Gerrard's Bridge? On the left-hand side, that's where they dumped a lot of it. There were traces of it for years. That coal was no good. A week after they tipped it, it went into dust. They claimed it was due to the transportation across the sea.

THE COBBLER

The only thing the shops benefited from was the issuing of chits for so much clothing. We were glad of these chits. It helped your business. The Town Hall gave cash for them. That was how we got paid for them. They gave every trader a bit. They were needed by all the one-man businesses – everybody ran up a debt.

JOE TINKER, AT A MEETING

Mr Baldwin is telling America that the children are getting three meals a day. As far as the facts are concerned, I don't think there are half a dozen places in the country besides St Helens giving three meals a day. Still, if communal feeding of the children is feeding the children better than they were fed before, then there was something radically wrong going on before. If the miners' families were better fed during a lockout, what sort of life were they getting when their men were working? Yet, though Mr Baldwin states miners' families are better off under lockout conditions, he is doing his utmost to get the miners to go back on worse conditions still.

PILKINGTON WORKER WHO WAS LAID OFF

The miners' strike affected us as we were just put out of work. The glass factory couldn't operate without coal. We just didn't get any money at all. We passed our time getting lifts on lorries for about six miles out of town. and then getting a lift back again. A lot of walking was done then. Me and a friend could walk seven or eight miles in the dark. We'd get to a pub and then we'd have to turn back again; we had no money to go inside. We just walked back and that was our entertainment.

MAN EMPLOYED AT GREENBANK BRICKWORKS
At the brickworks, we kept going through the strike by recycling cinder ash with slack. The slack came from different stock places and was brought on Fordham steam motors. Twelve miners came for jobs, but they found it beyond them. They called it a day. They claimed it didn't suit down the quarries. Of course it was wide-open spaces. They were getting too wet down there.

THE DOCTOR
We were very poor during the Miners' Lockout in 1926 and the year after. There were no payments. Money wasn't the be all and end all so long as you had enough to live on. I had no responsibilities – no family to pay for. You had to take the rough with the smooth. During the lockout you got tired, weary and broken down; the people with no guts – they were more ill. On the other hand, the miners were a very resilient, sturdy race with quite a lot of independence.

Tuesday, 10th August
JOE TINKER
When the lockout started, against the wishes of many colliery workers, the Federation decided to allow safety men to continue to work. I personally am in favour of that. We agreed to accept from employers lists of names of men who they desired to work. Local safety committees were formed and it was agreed that no non-union men would be allowed to work with union men. The firemen have not played the game with us. They desired to work the whole time through, but we managed to control it within certain bounds. What is happening now? Fourteen weeks have gone and many of the mine managers are beginning to back away from the arrangement. One point of that agreement is that no coal is to be wound. They are now trying to wind coal and they are getting – I am told – firemen to wind it. If this kind of thing goes on, we will withdraw every safety man at that particular colliery.

We had a meeting where this had happened. It was said at the colliery by some men in defence of what they had done, that they were not responsible for it. They said the roads had got to be cleared. If they thought it

237

legitimate work, all they needed to have done was consult the Safety Committee. We are satisfied to allow the winding of dirt. When we were assured it was to clear the roadway, we gave the permission and our men went and watched the dirt wound up. It shows we wanted to be fair.

DELEGATE TO THE LANCASHIRE & CHESHIRE MINERS' FEDERATION
The Lancashire & Cheshire Miners' Federation tried to meet right through the period. Of course, as the weeks and months went by there were murmurs of reaction taking place in several districts. But generally speaking the districts stuck together to the very last moment. There was bitterness because of attempts to get the men to withdraw their loyalty to the trade union movement. We saw this on a relatively small scale in St Helens – but what could the mineworkers do? At least the blacklegs were few enough to be individually isolated and known. There were one or two unpleasant scenes and incidents, which are always very regrettable with the meeting of blacklegs coming from the pits. Some of them were marched through the streets – escorted home, that kind of thing but generally the spirit was one of not accepting defeat – of being forced back.

WOMAN FROM CLOCK FACE
You know Great Orme's Head? My dad was platelaying there during the miners' strike. He used to go there and back to Wales every day to do it – to make a bit of money. You know Menai Bridge? There's a railway there. Mr Ashley was a contractor for laying these rails. It's a damn good way, and he had to get up at four o'clock and get back without anyone seeing. They'd have called it blacklegging because there was a strike on.

Blacklegs weren't in the union. They used to go from one town to another. Some of them used to stay in the pit yard in huts – they got two pints of beer and half an ounce of tobacco a day off the company. They were getting money in from the coal that was coming up.

Monday, 16th August
REPORT FROM THE ST HELENS NEWSPAPER
Suspicion has been rife that coal has been unlawfully raised at Sutton Manor for the last fortnight. The management said that in one of the seams the bottom coal had been drawn out before the strike and since that time a large quantity of coal which was on a seam slightly above the bottom coal had fallen so it was necessary to remove this. The colliery manager

238

decided to draw the boxes, which had been filled for some time, to the top and this being done openly on Monday when it aroused the neighbourhood. On Monday afternoon the local branch officials decided to fix pickets.

Tuesday, 17th August : Sutton Manor

REPORT FROM THE ST HELENS NEWSPAPER

The pickets kept watch during the night and on Tuesday morning a crowd in which there was a big sprinkling of women gathered round the pit and appealed to the men who were going on duty not to do so. This resulted in some of the men who had been working deciding not to go down the pit. Eight or twelve persisted, chiefly firemen who are in a different position with regard to their agreement.

DEPUTY FROM SUTTON MANOR

I went to Sutton Manor as a deputy. I was deputy up to 1926. There were three pits working, so the Under Manager came over one day and said: 'Some of you chaps will have to go on the dole.' And I was one of them. Eleven of the eldest got the sack. We didn't come out on strike, it was the management that stopped us, not the men. They said they were paying out too much. Up to then, we were working on odd jobs – maintenance. Then the men started drifting in – I got a note from the manager asking me to come in to get coal. I refused and I lost my job – it was about two months before the strike ended. I'd have gone back if it'd been my own job. But asking me to go back on the coal, I thought: 'No, I'm not causing any trouble.'

Wednesday, 18th August : Sutton Manor

PROSECUTING COUNSEL IN AN ENSUING TRIAL

At 7.30 a.m., two men – David Eden and J. Chisnell – were proceeding along Jubits Lane to Sutton Manor Colliery to work. Near the railway crossing were about a dozen men with sticks and pick shafts. The men were accosted by this crowd. William Henthorpe got Eden by the arm to pull him off his bicycle and William Ashall put a pick shaft into the spoke and this caused Eden to fall off. As they left the colliery, the hooting was reminiscent of a disallowed try by an unpopular referee at the rugby cup tie and could be heard half a mile away.

A crowd of about two hundred persons came from the direction of the Horse Shoe Way where there had been a meeting and stood outside Martha Platt's house. Someone shouted 'Let us put the windows in.' 'Snatch her out of the house.' 'Pull her out.' Mrs Platt went upstairs and saw Mrs Parr write something on a piece of paper and push it through the letter box. It bore the words: 'We as a body of men and women ask you to withdraw your husband out of the pit as a winder or there will be further trouble. Signed, Mrs Parr.' Mrs Platt also heard someone say 'Let's go to Ashton's Green with ropes and bring her husband home.'

MRS PARR

I was at the meeting at Derbyshire Hill and heard remarks like 'Let's go to Platt's first and we'll see what we can do.' Platt's a friend of mine or rather his mother has been a friend. I said: 'Give them a warning and give them a sporting chance.' Someone suggested breaking the windows, but I advised against this as it only causes trouble. 'I will write a letter and see if that will prevail on her husband not to go to work tomorrow.' Someone suggested that I should sign 'One of them' but I preferred to give my own name.

Thursday, 19th August

MR HILTON OF THE ENGINE WINDERS' EXECUTIVE AT A MEETING

I regret very deeply that the men have not acted as I consider they should have done. I have a list of the men who have not come out. I'll read the names. There is one I am particularly sorry to see. The man has been one of our officials and he is the last whose loyalty I would have expected to waver.

JOE TINKER

The memory of their conduct will live for years. I hope that when the present dispute is over they will be regarded as men apart. They will not be able to join in an argument over a glass of beer without the fear of someone demanding their rights to speak and recalling their present antics.

Sunday, 22nd August : Sutton Manor

JOE TINKER AT A MEETING

There's likely to be a struggle at Sutton Manor. The manager there has broken the agreement and has wound coal and asked for additional safety men. On Friday morning, it was decided that the safety committee should see him. We met him this morning and what I expected happened.

I put it to him: 'Are you wanting safety men?' But he refused to meet the question straight. I said 'We have come in answer to your letter. What do you want?' 'What do you want?' he said. That went on for the whole of the time and he would not give a straight answer. After a quarter of an hour, I told him that the interview was at an end and we have come to you with that.

His attitude this morning is one that is certainly not asking for safety men as far as we are concerned. We are not consenting to anyone working at Sutton Manor now. We have to carry out peaceful picketing. These pickets must only use their legitimate powers. If you can't approach I would advise you not to interfere. The police are too strong for you. What they are doing at this colliery is a sign of weakness of the other side.

LATER, TO THE HOUSE OF COMMONS

We went in orderly procession to Sutton Manor Colliery and on the way they were rushing police past us in wagonettes and charabancs. While the meeting was in progress the pulleys go round and some of the blacklegs show themselves right in the face of the crowd; a number of the crowd turned round ready to rush on to the premises. If that was not a direct incitement, then nothing could be. There were 3,000 men, a number of them on the point of starvation. That is the kind of incitement that leads people to rioting. Everything was prepared for it, and I'm told – I'm not going to say it's correct – the police were ready to rush in so that they could give us the lesson they thought we should have.

Tuesday, 24th August : Ashton's Green

REPORT FROM THE ST HELENS NEWSPAPER

The storm which had been brewing at Ashton's Green, Parr, came to a head on Tuesday afternoon when a crowd of miners and others numbering about 1,500 to 2,000 were charged by the police with drawn batons.

241

Ashton's Green Colliery belongs to Bromilow Foster and Company. It has been placed on the interdict by the safety committee. All safety men were ordered to leave the pit a week ago but a number of them had insisted on returning to work.

The police pursued the crowd back in an attempt to clear the main road. Eventually two mounted men and 24 foot policemen forced their way through for several hundred yards. Instead of falling away the crowd surged round in the rear and in a few minutes the police were surrounded. When a shower of stones began to fall the situation became serious. The small force looked like being overwhelmed and the order was given to charge. On one side of the road the crowd gave way, on the other they resisted fiercely and hard knocks were given and taken on both sides. After two or three minutes the crowd were driven into a side street and into fields and the road was cleared.

One of the policemen had his face gashed and most of them sustained bruises. A man named Newton was found suffering from severe concussion and head injuries.

MINER FROM ASHTON'S GREEN

We were truncheoned down by the police. There were Liverpool black-legs and our people blacklegging too. We used to go to the colliery and wait for them coming up. Then mounted police made a raid – they didn't half make a raid on us – they truncheoned us down. That was at Ashton's Green. They came from Wigan and Atherton and all around. We used to get together in gangs at the colliery head and stone the men who were blacklegging. It was like the charge of the Light Brigade when the police came down. We had to get away down the canals and ditches – they chased us across the fields. I finished up three miles away at the Finger Post to get away from it. We fought back and there were policemen hit on the head with stones. There was one lad seriously injured – he was trun-cheoned to the floor.

JAMES SEXTON, MP FOR ST HELENS, IN THE HOUSE OF COMMONS

A youth of 17 or 18 was sitting down reading the Evening Express. Two police officers passed him on horseback, then a solitary policeman came along and saw him. The evidence comes from three women who had no part in the dispute. One was hanging up her clothes and there were two or three others attracted by the noise; one carrying a baby who came to see what the disturbance was about. The boy ran into the backyard of an

242

ordinary miner's house. It is a place where you could scarcely swing a cat. The policeman got the boy into a cul-de-sac, threw the women away who were pressing him and batoned the boy unmercifully so that he was unconscious half a day. The constable, went out into the street and swung his baton and shouted: 'Come on you dirty bastard swine.'

A WOMAN FROM PARR
The women were all for the miners and this really shocked them – the young lad being beaten down in Tickle Street. The street – ooh, it was crowded and we heard it the other end. Myself, I try not to think back – you can't mend things by thinking back. I went out after it had happened and saw the lad – he was 14 or 15 and badly beaten. All that will be in the paper – there was a case over it; Dick Waring took it up. The women knew their men were in the right. They were all for them; they weren't going to see anything done to them, although in their own minds they must have wished they were going back – there were a lot with big families.

MINER FROM SOUTHPORT COLLIERY
I remember painting a blackleg's house in Newton Road. They'd wake up next morning with 'scab' all over their house. We got buckets of limewater and threw it all over the door too.

TWO SISTERS FROM PARR
There was a blackleg in Newton Road in the 1926 lockout and for years after that they walked down the middle of the road. Women never spoke a word to the wife. She was swanking to the miners' wives. She said 'Look, you could have this money if your husband worked.' One of them lifted her foot and kicked all the money out of her hand up in the air and she said, 'You can do what you want with it.'

REPORT FROM THE MANCHESTER GUARDIAN
The offenders – according to police – are mainly wild and irresponsible youths, many of whom do not live in the immediate neighbourhood.

House daubing is a grim form of humour and not exactly pleasant for the victims. It is being borne stoically and according to a police officer with whom I had some conversation is being treated as a kind of joke by some of the men upon whom it is visited. One safety man remarked to him: 'They couldn't have made my house look much worse than it is anyway.' Another expressed a wish that the demonstrators would paint his house all over 'because it might help keep the rain out'.

Of course, some of our picketing had to be done on the premises. They got these lads coming over in ones and twos – never more than three at a time – from Liverpool. They knew we were waiting for them at the pit entrances, so they tried to come over the fields to avoid us. I jumped straight out of a ditch in front of one of these men once and he bolted. To stop them, we had to try to be around the lamp room. Of course, that was trespassing on the company property and so we had the county constabulary to deal with as well. Some of us were caught – but we got off with a warning, in no uncertain terms mind you.

TRAM CONDUCTOR

I was working on the trams and I used to see a lot of it. There were a few blacklegs there. The police were mainly imported. The miners made a lot of attacks on police-supported blacklegs. It was then that PC Drysdale batoned that boy. They had fights every day at Fleet Lane. The miners were in the habit of congregating round this pub. If two or three joined in together to talk, a mounted policeman would charge them with his baton raised. They weren't within a mile of the colliery.

It was at Havanagh colliery they got some blacklegs working. Miners climbed up on to the stuff-rook above the entrance to the pit. The police tried to charge them off, but the miners pelted them with slack. There was no shortage of ammunition. The police made two or three attempts to get up from different sides, but the miners had men watching and they all congregated up there. When the blacklegs came up at the end of their shift out of the cage and saw the sky, they couldn't see the miners just above them and they got pelted. The miners held that stuff-rook till it was dark. They went back a second day at daylight and pelted the few blacklegs there were who came back to work. On the third day, the police must have got up in the dark, because when the miners arrived the police were already there. At one side of the rook there was a footpath and a canal that led on to Haydock. Fighting started on the path and two or three men were thrown into the canal. One or two men jumped in to avoid being batoned. A friend of mine got his arm broken by a policeman's baton. The trouble was the miners knew the area since they were schoolboys and the police didn't as they'd all been imported. It practically put a stop to blacklegging at Havanagh colliery.

They had these imported police in billets at Haydock. Richard Evans & Co. had some stables there, by where the industrial railway line crosses the road. The stables were at the side of the crossing. They hadn't been used for horses for a good year or two and they were made into billets for these imported policemen. Every time I went past in the tram I used to run up the tram steps so I could look over the wall. They were big fellows inside; some had bandaged heads, and some were walking with a stick. I was immensely cheered by the sight. It wasn't just our lads getting hit.

Getting By

MINER FROM ASHTON'S GREEN WHO WAS SINGLE

I was at Southport when the 1926 strike was on. It was the nicest summer we ever had – and it's a good job it was or we'd have died. Nobody had any money. Me and my father got half-a-crown a week each from the Church in Parr Road. My mother died when I was young; there was just me and him. We had no money at all. You couldn't go and ask for money – it had to be stole. My father went to jail for stealing potatoes. It was a case of having to do it. The police were in the farmer's fields. My father and another fellow got fighting with the police and that was how they came to be jailed. He was truncheoned down. While my father was four months in jail, I went to Liverpool with a wagon, and I got a shilling a day unloading cotton for a Bolton firm.

We slept out on the flags at night. I had one or two ferrets. Rats they got, and rabbits. You put nets over the rabbit holes and blocked some if you'd not got enough nets to cover all the holes. You put the ferrets in, keep quiet, and the rabbit bounces out. The farmers used to go bloody mad, especially on Lord Derby's estate. If you put a foot on there you'd get six months. There was only nobs who owned the land. There were notices up that said 'Trespassers will be prosecuted' and in the top right-hand corner 'or shot'. We used to go early in the morning – we used to get mushrooms; they are at their best then. If you didn't go early, somebody would be there before you. You'd got to get in before the farmer got up if you could – about four o'clock – get a few rabbits and that was it. That's when the pressure was really on, during the 1926 strike.

EMPLOYEE, LATER A DIRECTOR, OF THE CO-OP

At the time of the lockout in 1926, the Co-op lent the miners a hell of a lot of money and they never got it back. Of course, it was promised they would repay it, but they never did. It's a ticklish thing to deal with. The money was borrowed by the miners' union. Miners' families provided quite a big part of the membership, and there were one or two influential miners on the board, but we had to write the money off bit by bit. It didn't materially reduce dividends – other economies had to be made.

THE MINER FROM PARR, BORN 1893
There were all sorts of organizations running. There were more clubs in those days, and they set up self-help organizations. They used the old school down there. It was organized among the miners, those that could use their tools – especially those that could bring their own tools – and the leather and nails would be provided by the miners' relief fund. They'd repair their boots and so on.

PIT BROW LASS FROM LEA GREEN
I'd been working and came out at the 1926 strike. I'll be honest: I went to the pawnshop to get a bit of meat. I'll tell you, during the coal strike we used to go to the butchers to collect the meat and the grocers for vegetables. We used to make a washing boiler full of hot pot and they used to come for it with basins. It was all free. We did it nearly every week. We used to take it in turns. We peeled bags of potatoes – my husband helped me make it.

MINER'S WIFE FROM SUTTON
They didn't give us any strike money unless it was the odd half-a-crown now and then. I know we got food vouchers, that is all. We were really all in the same boat then – everyone was miners round Sutton. You could all console one another. It made a mess of the shops. Mr Bell, the grocer, hung himself. He had so much owing to him through the strike, he couldn't run his business any more. He was a good man; he gave out food on credit. We had a garden plot. They were more considerate one t'other then – they left the vegetables alone. Miners were soft on their money. If anyone was hard up, they wouldn't mind giving them a bit to help out. Shopkeepers said if the miners were doing well, they were doing well. If they got money they spent it; they didn't save.

Sunday, 28th August
GORDON MCDONALD (ON THE EXECUTIVE OF THE LANCASHIRE & CHESHIRE MINERS' FEDERATION) AT A MEETING
We are expected to agree to an eight-hour day, district settlements, and no concessions or subsidy from the other side or the Government. To

weaken our resolution the miners of the country are being told that Nottinghamshire is going back to work. We are told 5,000 men drew wages last week. We were not told that the number included all the safety men and that it was 5,000 out of 60,000. There are reasons why those who have gone back have given way. The withdrawal or cutting down of relief, the offering of specially advantageous terms on which to go back, and provocation from the police at Mansfield. The Midland miner is still as loyal as Sutton Manor, but the Midland miner has had temptations which we have not had. I don't care for the attitude of the Lancashire miner looking upon himself as a mighty being, and the other fellows in the other counties as weaklings. They are no weaklings but under great pressure and some have given way even as you might have done in the same circumstances. The world is astonished by the magnificent fight the miners have put up for 17 weeks in a battle line from Fife to Bristol. In a long line there is always a weak link and our opponents have probed every inch of the line trying to find that weak spot.

I am not going to blame the police force every time. I don't think the police force as a police force believe the miners ought to have lower wages. I don't think they are as antagonistic to us as some other people are. In a police force containing many thousands you will find dozens of brutes and cowards among them – in Sutton Manor, maybe, who will call Sutton women swine – but what I want to tell you is I am not here to label the police force blacklegs, and there is nothing on earth to be gained by the miners in taking a physical force fight with the police. Once force is used, the miner is beaten down to a frazzle. Stand steady, keep the peace and we shall pull through.

THE MINER FROM PARR, BORN 1893
No action was taken against people in arrears with their rent at the time of the lockout, to my knowledge. At that time I think there was a stand-still, pretty well. They'd realized the whole of this area of St Helens would be affected. The whole family in many cases worked in the mine; three of my family worked in the mine. So the families, in general, if they hadn't others working in other industries would be very hard hit.

THE MINER FROM ASHTON'S GREEN, BORN c. 1905
That went on for 26 weeks. We had a house in Newton Road which was privately owned – a fellow named Kitchener owned them. When we got back to work it had to be paid back – and the rent was 7s 6d per week.

247

First week in September: The Emergency Powers Debate in the House of Commons

JOYNSON-HICKS, HOME SECRETARY

The Hon. member for Leigh spoke in the thick of the district round St Helens where in the following few days disturbances broke out. This is what he said: 'If there is any real work to be done leave it to men like myself. You might do something and be taken while the authorities would be very much afraid of taking me, for instance, as a member of parliament.' The Hon. member for Leigh is to be allowed to say things which other men are not allowed to say that he may incite other men to intimidation and the law is not to interfere with him because he is a Member of Parliament. The law is not a respecter of persons.

MR TINKER

I want it to be known that what I said in my speeches was said calmly and deliberately and if it brings me within the law I am prepared to stand the racket. I would like to ask the Hon. Secretary when he got word of my so-called misdemeanours because on Monday, 23rd August, I was rung up by the Chief Constable of St Helens and told that there was rioting taking place, that he had addressed the crowd and that they had taken no notice and said they wanted Tinker. He asked would I go to them and speak to them. This was the man whose speeches have been inciting to a lot of trouble and yet the chief constable was prepared to go with the man and stand on the same platform. I refused and said why. Previously to that, some of our people had been batoned and I could not go on the same platform as the Chief Constable who I must hold responsible to some extent for that.

Tuesday, 7th September: New Terms

NOTICES PINNED AT THE PIT-HEAD

1. All workpeople who were in employment prior to the stoppage will be signed on as work becomes available for them.
2. The hours will be one hour per shift more than the hours in operation prior to the stoppage.
3. Up to 31st March 1927, wages in the grades hitherto regulated by percentages will be at the rates paid in April 1926, namely 46·66% upon the 1911 base rates.

4. The 13·1% hitherto paid to pieceworkers in respect of the reduction of hours will be withdrawn.

5. From April 1927

    (a) the additions on 1911 base rates will be according to the ascertained results of working in the months of December 1926 and January and February 1927.

    (b) the costs of production will be deducted from the proceeds and of the balance 87% will go to wages.

    (c) the minimum percentage below which wages cannot fall will be 32% on the 1911 rates, and the subsistance allowances paid under the 1921 agreement will be paid.

    (d) after March 1927 in no case will the wages of workmen 21 years of age or over be less than 7s per shift or that of adult female workers less than 4s 9d per shift.

6. In each month after April 1927, a similar ascertainment will be made in the working for three months. For example, the percentage for May 1927 will be fixed on the ascertained results for January, February and March.

7. If, in any month, the owners are called upon to make up any part of the minimum of 32% on the 1911 basis, they will be entitled to recoupment in future ascertainments.

8. The above terms will remain in operation until substituted either by an agreement or by notices posted at the colliery.

JOE TINKER

It comes to this – the pieceworker comes down from 3s 4d a ton to 2s 11d. When a quarter to two comes you will be entitled to work another hour in order to make up the loss caused by the reduction. We express ourselves pretty freely in the pit in language which is sometimes rather unparliamentary, and I can quite see a miner saying when he finds he has to work another hour to make up his wages: 'Chuck the bloody tools in the bag and we will finish.' That is what is called the psychological factor, and you will have to take that into consideration.

But that is not the worst of it all. The daywageman's rates will continue as stated the same as before until September. But if we go back we do not go back on those terms as a fixed rate. It is not a fixed rate at all. When September comes, the figures for July and August have got to govern September's wages, and we can fall then to 32% in place of 46·66% or go right back to the settlement of 1921.

Sunday, 12th September

JOE TINKER

With the exception of one delegate, the conference of Lancashire was unanimous that the terms offered by the owners should not be accepted.

Lancashire has always been in the forefront on the question of a national settlement. I want to explain why. Lancashire, North Wales, Durham and Bristol are among the poorer coalfields and with a district settlement they would be in a worse position. The market would be flooded with coal from better pits and it would mean that Lancashire wages would be forced down.

After 20 weeks' stoppage, the conditions offered are worse than before. So we must stand firm. The only question is – can we? That is a matter for you to answer.

Getting by (continued)

MINER FROM THE TOWN CENTRE

I was a very fortunate man because my wife had one or two friends. She used to work three or four days a week for friends of ours in the market. I was keeping pigeons then. I killed them and sold them to neighbours. Where I lived behind the Town Hall, there was only the odd miner.

MINER FROM DERBYSHIRE HILL

A character at the Finger Post toppled over a wagonload of spuds. It was Curly Dorkings, an Irish fellow – he was good looking with curly red hair. The spuds weren't in the road five minutes – the majority of the people were in the mining industry round there.

OFFICER OF HEALTH, REPORTING TO THE COUNCIL

Fifty people, men and women and children were on the Parr tip searching among the newly tipped refuse brought in from the ashpits throughout the town. As each cart arrived at the tip, it was immediately surrounded by the pickers, who scrambled among the refuse. The rags and jars were disposed of to various dealers and a man had formed an enclosure near the tip where he had accumulated big quantities of jars, lead, rags and scrap iron. There was a distinct danger to the health of the people who picked these things.

For a while, we used to go round selling wood – chopping trees down; Nuttalls, they had two trees lying in their yard and I said 'Can we have these trees?'

They said 'You'll have to see Mr Nuttall about them.' I went to see him at his house in Rainhill and he said 'You can have them, but you mustn't saw any others down. You can have the two on the floor.' We sawed them up. Then a friend who was down there with me sawed another one down, but we were never turned in.'

We went to a place in Brotherton Road. Arthur was well in with the farmer. He said: 'I can't let you have these trees. You'll have to go to the colliery owner.' I forget his name – he lived in Rainhill. I went to him. 'Has the farmer told you to come here?' he said. 'You can saw them down on condition you clear everything up.' We sawed about four down. We were going round selling wood.

We'd not been paying rent for a while and when the rent collector came round he says 'I'm not worried about anything.' So my wife told him: 'Don't come round till the strike's settled then.' He didn't care how long it lasted, we had to pay all the rent back.

I knew a man in our street, he was working on the new road to the station. He wasn't paying any rent. He was sloping at the shop – everything he used to get. I don't think he ever paid the rent up, or the shop. They let him have whisky, which was silly.

TWO SISTERS FROM PARR

Near us the road dropped right down into a little valley. The miners would wait for a food lorry to come. It would have to slow down to get up the hill. About four miners would get on and throw the food off. The others would be waiting to pick it up and put it in bags.

MAN FROM THATTO HEATH

In the strike, we went and flogged our war medals to a pawnbroker in Westfield Street. My brother-in-law said: 'Come on, Tom, we can get half-a-crown for these.' In the shop, there was a box as big as that radio-gram full of medals – the box was jammed full. They'd melt them down. That was the General Service Medal and the war medal that went then. We bought a few pints with the money. I don't believe in patriotism. There is no such thing as patriotism. These people invent it for unedu-cated people and they just suck it up like blotting paper.

DAUGHTER OF A PUBLICAN

We were at the Hen and Chickens during the lockout. We bought a box of margarine, and got Finch's bakery to get us some bread and all the customers we knew got a bit. I gave them half a pound of margarine as well. In fact, butter, tea, sugar and marge, anything they really needed. My dad did that and got pulled up at a meeting of the Licensed Victuallers' Association. When he went, this particular chap reported him for giving this stuff away and said that he was unfairly attracting trade. He turned round and belted him. He got expelled from the meeting and never went back. He didn't need to try and get trade – he had enough already. The fellow died a bit later on – you didn't know what he was worth – he scrimped and saved and kept his lights down. We could afford to do it – it was just being generous to people who couldn't afford it.

THE ST HELENS NEWSPAPER

A splendid hot-pot was provided at the Finger Post Hotel, Parr, by the proprietor and the business people of the district for out-of-work miners and their wives. Mr Crab of Park Street played several solos on his concertina and others present sang.

THE ST HELENS NEWSPAPER

It is a great coal mining centre employing 14,000 miners who have done no work since the strike in May began. As the coal yields about sixpence a ton to the local exchequer it will readily be seen what tremendous loss the town has sustained. On top of this, the Guardians have already shouldered a bill for extra Poor Law Relief of not less than £65,000.

Consequent on the rioting that took place in Parr and Ashton's Green, additional policemen were drafted into the town and later the miners will have their share of paying for their fun as the rates will have to shoulder the bill of about £400 a week to pay for the 50 or 60 policemen imported from Liverpool.

The Ministry of Health have sanctioned a further overdraft to the Guardians. They have urged upon the Board the importance of economy as the amount already spent represents an increased rate of 2s in the pound next year.

Sunday, 3rd October

Me and Mr McDonald are in a difficult position today. We are not to let our own ideas come into the matter. Twenty-two weeks have gone by but there has been no asking for a ballot. We have been prepared to let things go on. We think the time has come to take a ballot. I was at Atherton last week. I was met with this when I asked the men not to go back to work. Why can't we have a ballot? We want to see what the other parts of the country are thinking. If we can have a ballot throughout the country, then we will stand loyal to the mandate of the Federation.

6 Fighting the Return to Work

THE ST HELENS NEWSPAPER
Commencing on the 21st October, relief to miners' wives and children will be reduced by 10%. This being the decision arrived at a meeting of the Guardians on Monday afternoon. Mr Rimmer said the Ministry of Health were pressing for the relief to be drastically cut.

COUNCILLOR DODD IN THE COUNCIL DEBATE
The Government has not asked us to reduce and it is no use the Guardians blaming them. It looks like an attempt on the part of some who are supporting the owners to drive the men back to the pits on the cry of their hungry children. Some objection has been taken in the past to my remarks of Christianity on the Board and I repeat: it is anything but Christian to vote for a reduction. You are going to take the food out of the mouths of women and children in order that some people who pay rates may be relieved of a few shillings a year.

MINER FROM SUTTON
A number of people from round here went to the Midlands and Derbyshire when they started going back. The men played a prominent part afterwards in the Federation. They left the area and they damn well came back afterwards. But I'm not naming any names. It wasn't the rank and file who deserted the ranks; they were solid. There were breakaways where they just flitted away and there was very little action taken to stop them. But nowhere was more solid than St Helens. Where they went back to work, there was no organization to stop them – the general effort and impetus was slow. We all went back together at Bold. At some collieries, we picketed to the last damn moment. When did we lose hope? It wasn't a question of losing hope. The fact was we were battered and defeated. We only went back when the Federation determined it had reached a stage when we couldn't possibly win. It was organized here to the last moment.

254

We could collect money till the last moment, but even that was beginning to drop off. Everyone was on short shift.

The reason St Helens remained solid when other areas were going back was that it was a question of accepting leadership at local level. They did that here absolutely. The leaders were darn good socialists.

MINER FROM RAVENHEAD
In St Helens, there were collections for the miners at the gates of all the works – the miners weren't alone. In these mining villages they went working on a farm – that was their alternative, and if it was a seaside town, they'd go and wait for a boat to come in. That's why you get your Welsh miner more militant than any others. They remember the degradation – they'll never lose it, because they had nothing to fall back on.

Wednesday, 13th October
JOE TINKER AT A MEETING
I am going to give you some grim, hard facts. In many parts of Lancashire, the men have broken and accepted bribes. The same temptations will be put your way before very long. I understand at Sutton Manor they are offering £1 bribes, a load of coal and back rent knocked off. Employers have gone round and told men that unless they go back to work their places will be taken. That will succeed. Men from outside have come in. We have to persuade the men who have gone in to come out again and fight alongside us. St Helens will have to look to herself.

Rainford have broken away, and 60–70% have gone in because they were told unless they go in the colliery will be closed. I have been to Rainford and told them it would have been a godsend if the colliery had closed down many years ago. Every time I have met the management at Rainford, they have told me they are only kept going by the profits from Ashton's Green.

Why are the bribes being offered? They are cracking, the other side. They are not philanthropists. All the stocks of coal are exhausted and the supply of coal from abroad is being curtailed. Germany is the country which has been helping to supply this country with coal. France buys coal from us in ordinary times and is now trying to get it. The coal-owners and the Federation of British Industry are wondering what they will do to get a supply of coal. If we can only stand another few weeks, they will have to

come to their senses and give us decent wages. St Helens must stand
solid to the last man.

[At a Special Conference of the Lancashire & Cheshire Miners the
same day debating a resolution to continue to stand out for the Status
Quo (pay and conditions)].

MR GREENALL
It is not only a decision of the Miners' Federation of Great Britain but our
own men by individual ballot. By ten to one they turned the Government
proposals down in Lancashire. We fully realize the position in the country,
especially in some parts, but our hands are tied.

WORSLEY MESNES DELEGATE
The matter was referred to branches to decide either to accept or reject.
Nearly four thousand voted for the Government proposals, but today
nearly seventeen thousand have surrendered to the coal-owners' terms.

CHEAPSIDE DELEGATE
In the event of 55% of our members resuming work, what is our position
then?

MR GREENALL
Our position then is guided by the Miners' Federation of Great Britain.

BAMFURLONG DELEGATE
The Executive Committee have only met on about four occasions during
the dispute. My contention is this – that as far as the conducting of the
stoppage is concerned I am not placing the blame on the platform – we
have yet a lot to learn with regard to conducting a strike or lockout. When
I have gone in the various districts I have found there has been a lack of
central control. We have no machinery whatever set up to cope with any
incidents which may occur.

PARK LANE DELEGATE
We ought not to show a white flag yet, for that is what it means by some of
our friends saying there is no hope for us. We have got to decide today
between becoming slaves or rebels, and for my own part I am prepared
to become a rebel rather than a slave to the coal-owners.

WORSLEY MESNES DELEGATE

Last week we took a vote which showed a ten to one majority for fighting on. Now I think we can safely say that a great number of the men who voted for fighting on have succumbed to the coal-owners' blandishments. This resolution we are discussing says we should ask for the status quo, yet we have been willing to accept wages less than that.

SHERDLEY DELEGATE

I move that we reaffirm our former decision and that we stand out for a national agreement.

WORSLEY MESNES DELEGATE

I am instructed to move the rejection of these proposals, not because we do not agree with the resolution, but because we know as an absolute fact that it is an impossible resolution. Almost everybody in this room is instructed by the reports given.

JOE TINKER

Whilst I stated at Saturday's Conference that I was in favour of the resolution, in view of what has happened this morning, it does not alter my opinion on the proposals being the right thing but it certainly alters my outlook. I am of the opinion that we ought to reject these proposals, because I want us to have another National Conference as early as possible and find out what the Labour Party will do, and also get the opinion of the other districts. Are they strong enough to carry on along with Lancashire; is there any hope? Take Leigh: unless some hope is given, they will have broken this week and we cannot stop them. In view of the position, is it not better to keep the national body going, so that the whole position can be reviewed from time to time and give some hope to our members? Do not offer them a closed door or the best part of Lancashire will have gone by the end of the week. Yesterday even in St Helens which has been one of the strongest places, Mr Orchard sent for Ravenhead Branch and offered them terms. It was only when I put the position strongly that I prevented Ravenhead members from making a deal with Orchard. After what has happened this morning, I wonder whether I could have got them to do it now: that is the position, friends, and we have got to meet it that way. Some of you may say Tinker is retreating but I am not retreating.

VOTING

For the Resolution for the Status Quo   64

Against   54

Card Vote	All Lancashire	St Helens
For	693	107
Against	613	59

Sunday, 17th October

A. J. COOK DURING HIS SECOND VISIT TO ST HELENS, ON OPEN GROUND AT THE BACK OF THE HOSPITAL AT PEASLEY CROSS, TO 15,000 PEOPLE

If I find out tomorrow in the pits where I have addressed the men that they have gone back, then I am bound to lose my faith in the men I am fighting for. Just as your faith in us would be shaken if we were to betray you. But I know that here you are going to remain solid. It is from you that I got my faith so I can go on. It is not easy but hard fighting all the devils of hell. It is right against might but right will win the victory.

Wednesday, 20th October

REPORT TO THE EXECUTIVE OF THE LANCASHIRE AND CHESHIRE MINERS' FEDERATION

After the intensive propaganda campaign which has taken place in the country during the weekend, reports were given from the various districts and it was ascertained that the position was now very much more favourable. There were approximately 7,000 persons working.

Sunday, 24th October

JOE TINKER AT A PUBLIC MEETING

On the 13th there was a meeting of miners. On the following day, to my amazement, a paper of the high standing of the Manchester Guardian printed this story:

'There are two St Helens today. One came together at the Co-op hall. These are the die-hards who have been the backbone of the stand St Helens have made in support of the Federation.

'The other half stands apart and is beginning to refrain from attending these meetings. They are anxious to go back as fast as the pits will absorb

258

them. A very few were working a fortnight ago, but since then the dribble to the pits has been continuous and there are four or five times as many working now as there were then. The pits can't take them on fast enough. There are hundreds of names on the books of the collieries.'

Here are the facts. We have been defied at Ashton's Green for a long time. The firemen are getting coal with a few blacklegs but the whole of them belonging to us is not outside 50. At Sutton Manor not more than 70 have defied us. These are the worst. At Sherdley there is one, at Sutton Heath three, Collins Green four, Bold one. At Richard Evans, normally employing 5,000, there are 60 back. At Clock Face, four. The total is 1 per cent of the miners employed in St Helens.

Wednesday, 3rd November

[At a Special Conference of the Lancashire & Cheshire Miners' Federation a motion was passed by 645 votes to 644 to the effect that if the National Executive Committee reported the status quo conditions could not be secured, it be given the power to negotiate a settlement subject to a ballot of the rank and file.]

THE MINER FROM RAVENHEAD

[One of five thousand people in Britain to join the Communist Party during the lockout –the party started the year with one St Helens branch and ended the year with eight.]

I'll tell you how I was – it made me a revolutionary. When it started in 1926, I had about £17 or £18 saved up – I wasn't married. I gave my mother £1 a week till it had gone. When it had gone, we were only half-way through the strike. Then I had nothing. From there on, I started thinking – I'm worse than I was when I started. It made me think what was the cause of the lockout, with the result I remember asking Joe Tinker in a branch meeting at Ravenhead colliery: if we went from a seven-hour day to an eight-hour day to lower wages, and we outpriced other countries for coal and they did likewise to their miners, where would it all end? And Joe Tinker never answered me. So I started going into economics – I never knew what the word was before that – and I found out what caused it, and I was determined to remedy it. So I became a socialist.

The terms were so bad that we were resolved we'd go on as long as we could. At Ravenhead colliery, round the 28th week, they gave them £2 to sign on, and I didn't sign on. I didn't go. A lot of them were so glad to get the £2 signing-on fee that they went.

I was at the library, on the library steps – we used to call there to read the papers when we were out of work. One of the chaps had signed on – got the £2. We were against him for it but he'd bought cigarettes and he gave me one – it nearly knocked me out because I hadn't had any for so long.

When we went back, it was blooming degrading. That hour seemed like ten, and even less money.

St Helens was so strong because it was a Labour area – it was a Labour stronghold. You couldn't get a job anywhere else. If there had been other jobs but the coal industry, we'd have gone to them – we'd never have gone back to the pits.

It made more people bitter that strike. You'll never forget, you can't forget these things. Not till you die.

Monday, 15th November

[At a conference of the Lancashire & Cheshire Miners' Federation, with 15,500 out of 75,000 men back in Lancashire and 237,500 out of 780,000 back throughout the country.]

RAVENHEAD DELEGATE

With regard to the position of our branch, Pilkington Brothers have left the Coal Association and Mr Orchard is no longer a member of the Board. He has offered us an increase in wages of 4·5% to stand till December 1927, also a week's holiday with pay and a lot of other things besides. We have had a great task to keep our men back and have only 30 men back at work, out of which only three are colliers. What is going to be the position of our branch? We met Mr Orchard this morning and he asked what we intended to do; has he to wait on the doorstep until the Lancashire Owners have decided his terms, or are we going to accept his offer?

MR MCGURK

The Ravenhead Branch is expected to stick by this Federation's policy.

ACCRINGTON DELEGATE

The same as other branches.

MR MCGURK

This does not do any good, Mr Smith. Spare other people's feelings. Do not let your feelings run away with you.

Wednesday, *17th November*

[At another special conference of the Lancashire & Cheshire Miners' Federation, a motion was passed stating: 'This Conference does not accept the Government terms and the Lancashire delegates at the National Conference on Friday be instructed to vote against their acceptance.']

MR FLATLEY

We have to consider the position we find ourselves in. We have branches who have voted against these terms who have 75% of their men working.

MR MCGURK

Oh, no Mr Flatley!

JOE TINKER

We wanted to lead you in a certain direction, but now you have decided the other way, everyone on this platform will do all they can to carry out what you have decided. What we want you to do now is to do everything possible to keep your men solid. If men return to work, do not blame the platform and say it is because of them that they have returned to work. Help to take some of the responsibility which may come. There is too much saying, if an agent says a certain thing, he has influenced the men. We have not been able to influence the vote, have we?

[The national conference agreed to local negotiations. The coal-owners' terms were agreed in Lancashire on the 23rd November and confirmed by a conference two days later.]

7 Defeat

Sunday, 21st November

JOE TINKER (AT A MEETING)

We have lost men but this is not our fault. We have done all we could but there has been every fact against us. It would be utter foolishness to say to you now: 'Men, fight on. We can win.' Knowing we have no chance of winning, we ask you to accept the situation.

I went to Ravenhead branch of the Federation last week. I explained the Government terms. I advised the men to accept them, but not to return to work for a week. A vote was taken and the majority were in favour.

Voice: It's a lie, nothing of the kind.

Leahy: You will either give order or I will disperse the meeting.

Voice: And we members of the Federation want the truth.

Leahy: You'll get it at the end of the meeting. Ask your questions then.

Tinker: Now we are told the men have signed on. Not having the courage to face the decision themselves, they are saying Tinker advised them.

DELEGATE TO THE FEDERATION

There was a little victimization after the lockout. Below ground, there were little incidents of feeling between the mining officials and the men, but not to any marked extent. They were pinpricking incidents but nothing serious, and the peculiar thing about it – it soon wore off.

After 1926, there was no general victimization. Quite a number left the pits – they got jobs elsewhere. They were getting out of the industry. Some of these men who were blacklisted – it wasn't because of their activities. They were just named. One of the colliery owners had photographers out on the pickets. In 1926, all the delegates were reinstated – well, it wasn't a question of being reinstated – went back. We proved we were a threat. The same delegates attended the Bolton conference. There were very few new ones. The people who had served in the Miners' lock-out were the self-same people. There were a variety of ways of petty

262

victimization – people found themselves on a bad face, for example. It depended on the manager's attitude to the delegate or whoever he might be.

It took some time to build up the union afterwards – there were those who wouldn't pay. But there was a powerful majority who paid, after their first week's wages. There was a long queue in the colliery yards. In most places, there were lapses from the Trades Union. It took some reorganizing.

As a result of the lockout and the General Strike, people's politics changed. I'm certain about this. From that time onwards there was, without a doubt, a resurgence of support for both trade unionism and political action on behalf of the working class. The miners remained loyal to the Miners' Federation of Great Britain – it didn't affect their loyalty by any means. And it has remained so ever since.

MINER FROM PARR, BORN 1893
Mining collapsed after 1926. There was a surplus of everybody. I applied abroad and everywhere – if I could have got a job. I didn't rest. Every mine had its surplus of officials. In 1931, Ashton's Green closed here; it was only working half the time before. Collins Green closed about 1930, another on the outskirts here, Southport, closed, and Havanagh, all employing hundreds and hundreds of men. No industry was working; all industry had closed in the country, they weren't selling anything. They couldn't pay miners' wages, they had to partly use the welfare fund. And when the mines collapsed, the population of this town collapsed.

MINER FROM FLEET LANE
When Ashton's Green was going bankrupt, we got nowt. We had no wages for a fortnight, then we got some and then a fortnight after we had none again. They didn't explain – one Friday afternoon, we were told they had no wages. We got fed up so four of us said that we'd go to Australia – we went to Liverpool, for four days with red cheese and some bread and then we came back. The men who worked there and lived in Haydock took pit props from Southport colliery on their way to work. There was no timber there, the roof kept falling down and killing people.

THE TWO SISTERS FROM PARR
I always felt that women seemed to look down on miners somehow or other. Apart from being a dirty job, between the wars their wages went to

263

nothing. They didn't get any dole – the owners let them work four days and they were worse off than they would have been on the dole. They had quotas. If the pit got its quota up, they stopped and went on short time. They were always short of money; they must have been one of the lowest paid. I think it was because it was such a poor paid job they used to say: 'Oh, him, he only works down the pit.'

THE MINER FROM ASHTON'S GREEN

The miners were kept down by the high-class people. Lady Astor called us earthworms – they thought nothing of the miners. The miners were scum. When you came up the pit you used to see placards: 'Trespassers will be prosecuted or shot.' That's how the lords and ladies of this land were. They owned it all.

I found I had wood at both ends – I had a pair of clogs on for all those years and my head must have been made of wood to go down the mine.

When the collieries finished in 1931, this Ashton's Green colliery finished. We had nothing. There was no compensation – they left us all on the scrap heap. Four and two in the pound is what we got. We contacted Joe Tinker and he got it passed in Parliament – compulsory compensation. That was so others could get it. We didn't get it. I was crippled – take a look at that right foot – and I got five hundred four and tuppences. It was a private enterprise at that time – Bromilow Foster Brothers, and the firm went into liquidation. We were four miles underground; they said we worked under Warrington butter market, which is five miles. If you took raw bacon down there it was cooked by the time you got to the face – it was that hot. There were cockroaches a good foot long. They wouldn't spend any cash on it as it was going broke. You had to make do with any kind of timber, make do without any bloody rails for the boxes for a hundred yards from the face. The union wasn't as strong as a linseed poultice; the strike hadn't been successful. They left us on the scrap heap, the private enterprise mines. There were thousands of maimed and crippled men, some with two legs off and they only got a thousand four and tuppences.

That was the depression at that time, then. The queue for dole was twenty deep. Jobs were few and far between. I was out of work four or five years.

Index

269